6 MODERN MYTHS
ABOUT CHRISTIANITY & WESTERN CIVILIZATION

PHILIP J. SAMPSON

InterVarsity Press
Downers Grove, Illinois

InterVarsity Press
P.O. Box 1400, Downers Grove, IL 60515-1426
World Wide Web: www.ivpress.com
E-mail: mail@ivpress.com

Published in the United States of America by InterVarsity Press, Downers Grove, Illinois, with permission from Universities and College Christian Fellowship, Leicester, England. Originally published in England under the title Six Modern Myths Challenging Christian Faith.

InterVarsity Press® *is the book-publishing division of InterVarsity Christian Fellowship/USA*®*, a student movement active on campus at hundreds of universities, colleges and schools of nursing in the United States of America, and a member movement of the International Fellowship of Evangelical Students. For information about local and regional activities, write Public Relations Dept., InterVarsity Christian Fellowship/USA, 6400 Schroeder Rd., P.O. Box 7895, Madison, WI 53707-7895.*

Cover illustration: Roberta Polfus

ISBN 0-8308-2281-X

Printed in the United States of America ∞

Library of Congress Cataloging-in-Publication Data

Sampson, Philip.
  Six modern myths about Christianity & Western civilization / Philip J. Sampson.
    p. cm.
  Includes bibliographical references and index.
  ISBN 0-8308-2281-X (alk. paper)
    1. Civilization, Christian. 2. Civilization, Western. 3. Religion and science. I. Title.

  BR115.C5 S26 2001
  270—dc21

00-047172

24 23 22 21 20 19 18 17 16 15 14 13 12 11 10 9 8 7 6 5 4 3 2 1
21 20 19 18 17 16 15 14 13 12 11 10 09 08 07 06 05 04 03 02 01

Contents

INTRODUCTION
Stories & Myths

ALL SOCIETIES HAVE THEIR STORIES, AND EVERYONE HAS HEARD OF THE myths of ancient civilizations, with their gods and heroes. The animated Disney film about Hercules upset some modern-day Greek people because the legendary figure remains an important part of their national heritage. They perceived his Disneyfication as a slight. But in ancient Greece, Hercules was much more than national heritage. Heroes demonstrated to people how humans fit into the world and how to live a noble life. If Disney had made its film in classical times, it would have been in deep trouble.

Of course, the stories of ancient Greece were myths or legends and were not intended to be taken literally as history. They paint a picture of sharply etched contrasts, of heroes and villains, of the battle between good and evil, and of creation and destruction, and have the feel of a bygone age.[1]

Some theologians, especially in the nineteenth century, tried to read the Bible as if it were a myth. This failed because the Bible values historical narrative in a way that myth does not. Although the popular belief that the Bible is mythical still survives, few contemporary scholars would regard such a reading as plausible nowadays, preferring to use myth in more precise and limited ways.[2] In fact, we now know that the biblical narrative is quite unlike the structure of myths. Indeed, the Jews were probably the first to write historical narrative in the sense of a story moving steadily forward, with a beginning and an end. Certainly some of the Bible predates the histories of Herodotus, "the father of history." The Christian gospel, rooted in Judaism, is also a historical message. It is concerned with actual people and places. Jesus was a carpenter from Nazareth and Paul a tentmaker from Tarsus. New Testament authors emphasize the historical nature of the Gospel accounts, disparagingly contrasting them with "cleverly devised myths" (2 Pet 1:16).[3] In the words of theologian and historian Stephen Neill, "He who says 'Jesus' says also 'history.' "[4]

We sometimes suppose that it was our Enlightenment forebears who fought to free us from myth and superstition, and we forget that Western culture has been deeply influenced by this biblical vision. Our contemporary idea of history owes much to it. Indeed, we have become so accustomed to the idea of historical narrative that myth seems a thing of the past. Myths are seen as untrue, relics of premodern anxieties that science and progress have assuaged. The ancients may have relied on them, but we know better. However, some myths are still with us.

Just as the Bible cannot be regarded as mythical simply because it is an ancient text, so some modern stories of our place in the universe cannot be regarded as history simply because they are recent texts. Indeed, such stories may sometimes have more in common with ancient myths than with history. Of course, modern-day stories of who we are and how we fit into the universe are no longer told in the same way as the Greeks told theirs, but that does not mean that we have no such stories. The modern mind, no less than the ancient one, uses stories to reinforce its belief that we are more advanced and more "scientific" than other civilizations. But unlike the ancient Greeks, we clothe our modern myths in the garb of history or science.

Newton's Apple

At first sight this may seem a strange idea. Surely "science" is concerned with facts and logic, and can have nothing to do with stories and myths. So let me illustrate what I mean with an example that will be familiar to everyone.

As we know, Isaac Newton revolutionized science by his discovery of gravity. But if we were asked to explain this, most of us might be hard pressed to state Newton's law of universal gravitation even though we know that there is one. We rely on scientists whose training fits them to understand these things. We are not entirely ignorant of Newton's discovery, however, for everybody has heard the story of the great physicist sitting beneath his apple tree at Woolsthorpe Manor in Lincolnshire, England. It is said that while he was puzzling over the mystery of the moon's orbit an apple fell from a tree, some say on to his head, and Newton "discovered" gravity. If we visit Woolsthorpe today, we can picture the place where it all happened. Our "knowledge" is encapsulated in this story, and we trust in what the story signifies, even though we might not be familiar with the mathematics. The fact that the story was probably made up by Newton to satisfy someone's idle curiosity does not invalidate the truths of his *Principia Mathematica*, even though that book is mercifully free of falling fruit.

It is widely assumed that reason, science and history have replaced stories as the basis for our understanding of the world. But if we look at the way that our everyday knowledge of science circulates and is passed on from one generation to the next, we find stories, not mathematics. Most of us have met Newton as the man who had an apple fall on his head, but few go on to read the *Principia Mathematica* with its notable lack of vegetable references. If we have heard of black holes, those mysterious denizens of space, it is more likely that we learned about them by watching *Star Trek* than by reading the British physicist Stephen Hawking. We know that the earth revolves around the sun because we have heard the story of Galileo's clash with the Inquisition, not because we know Kepler's laws of planetary motion or understand the dynamics of Foucault's pendulum. Of course, if we study science at a university, we will learn the beautiful mathematical descriptions of gravitational theory and gain a deeper insight into it. Yet the lack of a physics degree does not prevent scientific discoveries from being part of everyone's picture of the modern world.

The story of Newton's apple encapsulates a difficult physical theory and helps us to pass on his great discovery in an easily understood way. Although this particular story is especially apt, any number of others could do the same. For example, it is said that late one morning Newton's housekeeper arrived to find him still in his nightclothes, sitting on the edge of his bed. The great man had been so deep in thought about the motion of the moon that he had forgotten to get dressed or have breakfast! Stories are part of our modern knowledge of the world, even of science. But they are not like ancient myths. If they were, no one would bother with them. They are told as if they were history, even if this turns out to be untrue.

Of course, the story of Newton and his apple is a harmless legend that is unlikely to cause much damage, even if it is apocryphal. However, it is more than just a convenient way to pass on difficult ideas about gravity. It also carries something more fundamental: a *myth* which, under cover of the story, perpetuates a romantic picture of the "scientific genius" as someone whose theories come in a flash of inspiration. A variation on the same theme lies behind the story of Newton lost in thought on the edge of his bed: the myth of the "absent-minded professor" who is so caught up in his theories (and it always seems to be "his" theories) that he has no time for the more mundane affairs of life. These myths are more significant than the stories that carry them, for they form our view of scientific discovery as a rather eccentric activity leading the lone genius away from everyday human interaction and life. They present science as a solitary activity, usually of rather emotionally uninvolved men, and downplay the cooperative effort of people working together to understand God's world. At best they give us a romantic picture of the lone pioneer, heroically blazing his own trail; at worst they present the image of the "geek" or the "nerd," alone in his laboratory or in front of his computer screen and isolated from human companionship and real life. "Nerds," incidentally, are almost always men.

Such myths are carried by the story, driving it forward and making use of the historical facts and the scientific evidence for their own purposes. Sometimes the myth distorts both the science and the history in order to make its point. For example, few historians suppose that Newton's idea came to him in a flash of inspiration when an apple hit him on the head. Indeed, Newton's own remark about having seen further than others because he stood on the "shoulders of giants" hints at the communal aspect of scientific activity. But the "flash of inspiration" picture is better suited to the romantic myth of the scientific genius, so it is this that the myth uses to construct its story. Such a myth of science may have very concrete consequences in either inspiring or discouraging budding young scientists. To some, the idea of science as indifferent to ordinary human life and human relationships may not seem so attractive and may help perpetuate the stereotype of science as a male preserve.

Science, then, is sustained and transmitted by stories as well as mathematics, and not all of them are as innocuous as they first appear. The same applies to history. Indeed, in recent years we have become accustomed to the idea that history is told by the victors and reflects the interests of the rich and powerful. Thus at school we learn about kings and queens, prime ministers and presidents. Recent scholars have shown that this traditional idea of history has neglected the concerns of ordinary people, while some feminist historians consider that women's lives have been so far excluded that a new discipline of "her-story" (rather than "his-story") is needed. These insights can easily become a suspicion that there is no *objective* history, just biased accounts reflecting sectional interests. We then ask not "Is it true?" but "What advantage do you gain from the way that you tell your version of history?" This suspicion about historical neutrality has found its way into popular consciousness, including films such as Oliver Stone's *JFK*, which brought conspiracy theories about the Kennedy assassination to a whole new audience. The adult cartoon show *The Simpsons* humorously exploited this trend in the episode dealing with "Whacking Day."

The Simpson family lives in the town of Springfield. Every year the good townsfolk celebrate Whacking Day, when the men hunt down the local snakes and beat them to death with large sticks. It is said that the history of Whacking Day goes back to the late eighteenth century when Jebediah Springfield, the town's founding father, hit a snake with his gun to drive it away. Lisa Simpson, the young daughter of the family, is a lively critic of cruelty and injustice of all kinds. She is suspicious of the "received version" of the Whacking Day story and discovers from her brother that, in reality, Whacking Day was invented in 1924 as an excuse to beat up the Irish. The story wore the garb of history, but behind it lay an attempt to justify ethnic violence; in more recent, tolerant times, its purpose shifts to the simple, homely pursuit of killing snakes.

The recognition that history may serve vested interests has led some to suspect that all narratives have a hidden agenda. Some historians argue that the increasing prevalence of such views makes relativism inescapable and "destroys the difference between fact and fiction."[5] But if Springfield's Whacking Day myth allowed the local community to express prejudice against an ethnic group, Lisa's discovery of this relied on an appeal to a history independent of sectional interests. The claim that we should treat all truth claims as relative is itself a (relative) truth claim and therefore contradicts itself. As the philosopher Roger Scruton wryly observes, "A writer who says that there are no truths, or that all truth is 'merely relative', is asking you not to believe him. So don't."[6]

Nowadays, then, a story has to be presented as history or as science in order to be taken seriously. This has not always been the case. Among the ancients, history was commonly regarded as inherently uncertain, involving local and particular events, the accidents and coincidences of everyday life. It was therefore unsuited to express eternal truths that are true everywhere and for all time. To express a truth in the language of history would have reduced its status, not increased it. Thus when Greek thought moved away from the mythic representation of universal values, it turned not to the uncertain tide of history but to an idea of reason as the bearer of truth. It is sometimes argued that the Bible is myth dressed up as history, but this naively assumes that just because the clothes of history automatically increase the status of a narrative in our modern world, the same was true of the ancient world. It need not have been so. The insistence that stories have to be *historical* in order to be taken seriously, while now a universal belief, has probably been a minority view throughout the ages. Where Bible texts claim to be history, it is because that is what they are, not because their authors had an eye to the beliefs of future ages. Without good evidence it would be extravagant to assume otherwise.

Stories, then, can form part of our account of modern scientific or historical knowledge (as with Newton and his apple), and they may serve sectional interests (as with Whacking Day). In doing so, they may distort and impoverish the history or science they use.

So far, we have looked at small-scale stories, little local affairs, misleading certainly but of little consequence. It is not always so. More widespread stories also exist that can influence the perception of a whole culture. For these big myths we have to look at what Douglas Adams calls "life, the universe and everything."

The Whole Story

In his book *The Pilgrim's Regress* C. S. Lewis has his Pilgrim meet nineteenth-century rationalism in the person of Mr. Enlightenment, who makes appeal to just such stories of science and history. Mr. Enlightenment offers his assistance to Pilgrim and advises him that God (in the person of the Landlord) does not exist. Those who believe that he does exist "have no knowledge of modern science and would believe anything they were told." "But how do you *know* there is no Landlord?" asks Pilgrim. "Christopher Columbus, Galileo, the earth is round, invention of printing, gunpowder," exclaims Mr. Enlightenment, adding that those who disbelieve "have not had the benefit of a scientific training. For example, now, I dare say it would be news to you that the earth was round."[7]

Mr. Enlightenment appeals to stories of science and history, clinching his argument with tales that we all learned at school: Christopher Columbus, who shows us the ignorance of the medieval church and who pioneered man's[8] voyages of discovery; Galileo, who epitomizes the human spirit's pursuit of truth in the face of the church's continuing bigotry and persecution; and discoveries such as printing and gunpowder, which illustrate the achievements of science and technology that make the modern world what it is. We might add Darwin, who showed us man's place in nature, or the Spanish Inquisition, which serves as a byword for the terror and oppression exercised by religion if it gets half a chance.

There are many such stories, and a selection of the most common ones forms the core of this book. The myths they carry are the modern mind's way of communicating its beliefs about the fundamental problems of origins and meaning that have puzzled philosophers and theologians for millennia. A myth, in my sense of the word, presents values and beliefs to us as though they were facts or history, and it uses stories to do so. Stories, then, are shaped by the myths that drive them, by the underlying worldview that organizes and justifies a multitude of particular narratives. A myth provides the framework into which other things are fitted and the light by which we see them. The story may be the medium, but the myth is the message. Once upon a time, it was heroes like Hercules who formed the raw material for myths. But nowadays no one would believe such a story, so science and history have replaced the Herculean tasks. Modern myths are characteristic of their time (today) and place (Western societies). We should not expect them to look like the myths of yesteryear.

A myth needs history and science in order to propagate itself. Newton's apple appeared as a historical fact but carried the romantic image of scientific discovery. History and science do not disappear, but they are distorted by the myth they serve. Modern myths are, as it were, messages woven out of history and science. But once historical events or scientific theories are incorporated into a myth, once the myth makes use of them, it feeds off them, and they become deformed and impoverished. Thus the story of Whacking Day distorted our understanding of the ethnic conflicts during the foundation of the community of Springfield. The legend of Newton's apple oversimplified the history of scientific discovery. To recover the historical richness, we must uncover the myth.[9]

The Big Stories of the Modern World

The stories we will be discussing concern the nature and meaning of life, the origins of humanity, and the nature of good and evil. These are subjects that were once the province of religion and philosophy but are now that of science and history. So it is no surprise that these stories often refer both to the religious explanations from the past and to the more recent scientific accounts, contrasting their respective claims to truth. Before looking in more detail at how such stories work, it might be helpful to have a couple of examples. We start with one mentioned by C. S. Lewis's Mr. Enlightenment: "the earth is round."

The flat earth. A common *grand story* contrasts the modern world with the superstition and bigotry that preceded it. The role of the bygone time is often played by the Dark Ages, with the church as the bastion of ignorance. The well-known medieval belief in a flat earth is one such story.

We all know the tale. In the Dark Ages people believed that the earth was flat and that sailors venturing too near the edge would fall off.[10] This belief was the official teaching of the church, and it put a brake on the voyages of discovery. The very term "Dark Ages" portrays a period of ignorance and decline. For Carl Sagan, "classical learning dwindled" with the birth of the church, and the "triumph of superstition" dominated the Middle Ages until the recovery of reason during the Renaissance.[11]

The story has a clear and simple plot line, which quickly found its way into the received wisdom. The villains are obvious: superstitious, ignorant and credulous priests—"flat-earthers" to a man. But like all good stories this one also needs a hero. Columbus is a popular choice, and he is presented as courageous, rational and moderate, standing alone against the might of the church and the Inquisition. For the purposes of the story Columbus has become an honorary member of the modern world, while all the ills of superstition and ignorance are concentrated in the church. The following version of the story comes from the 1887 book *Ten Great Events in History*:

> "But if the world is round," said Columbus, "it is not hell that lies beyond that stormy sea. Over there *must* lie the eastern strand of Asia." . . . In the hall of the convent there was assembled the imposing company—shaved monks in gowns . . . cardinals in scarlet robes. . . . "You think the earth is round. . . . Are you not aware that the holy fathers of the church have condemned this belief. . . . The Holy Scriptures too. . . . This theory of yours looks heretical." Columbus might well quake in his boots at the mention of heresy; for there was that new Inquisition just in fine running order, with its elaborate bone-breaking, flesh-pinching, thumb-screwing, hanging, burning, mangling system for heretics.[12]

Nearly a hundred years later student textbooks still tell the same story: "The Middle Ages were a dark period . . . [when ancient insights] were reshaped to conform to the teaching of the Church. The Earth became a flat disc with Jerusalem at its centre."[13]

It has been known for many years that this story is not true. All educated people of the time knew that the earth was round, and the confrontation between the church and Columbus reported above is fiction. The historian Jeffrey Russell has documented the story's growth in the nineteenth century and its popularization by John Draper and Andrew White, two authors we shall repeatedly meet.

Draper, in his book *History of the Conflict Between Religion and Science*, argues that the Roman Catholic Church of the Middle Ages was inherently opposed to scientific progress. "Intelligent sailors," astronomers and philosophers realized that the earth is round, but "as might be expected, [this] was received with disfavour by theologians." "Traditions and policy forbade [the Papal Government] to admit any other than the flat figure of the earth, as revealed in the Scriptures."[14] We see here that more characters have been added to the story. The church remains on the side of the "flat-earthers," but "intelligent sailors," astronomers and philosophers join Columbus on the side of reason and good sense.

Andrew White's book *A History of the Warfare of Science with Theology in Christendom* puts the more general case that theology, if it trespasses upon science, distorts it. Thus he asserted that the church fathers attempted to "crush" Aristotle's "ancient germ of scientific truth" of the round earth and claims that everyone is familiar with "the warfare of Columbus" with the church, which science ultimately won.[15]

Despite historians like Jeffrey Russell, the story persists, proving from "history" that religion is bigoted and opposed the truth of a round earth. In doing so it distorts both the history and the science of the period. The myth that drives this story is apparent from the titles of Draper's and White's books: the "warfare between religion and science."

The tale of the comet. The myth of the "warfare between religion and science" appears in many guises. A curious example concerns the "excommunication" of Halley's comet by Pope Callixtus III in 1456, a tale of the superstitions of a prescientific age that, as Carl Sagan tells us, "most astronomical writers relate."[16] He means, I think, most *older* astronomical authors. The majority of scholars today are aware of the tale's apocryphal nature, although it does persist in some popular science books. Thus Patrick Moore informs us that Callixtus III "excommunicated [Halley's comet] as an agent of the Devil."[17]

The story tells us that when Halley's comet appeared in 1456, Pope Callixtus III was alarmed at this portent in the skies. At a time of continuing conflict between Rome and the Turks, Callixtus naturally thought it "an evil omen somehow allied with the Turkish cause." Fortunately a remedy was at hand which was no less superstitious than his view of comets—its excommunication. And so, we are told, Pope Callixtus III is remembered by history for the insane act of excommunicating Halley's comet. Draper gives us a characteristically colorful rendition in which the unhappy comet is "exorcised" rather than the more customary excommunication:

> When Halley's comet came, in 1456, so tremendous was its apparition that it was necessary for the pope himself to interfere. He exorcised and expelled it from the skies. It slunk away into the abysses of space, terror-stricken by the maledictions of Callixtus III, and did not venture back for 75 years.[18]

We should remind ourselves that although Draper was a physiologist rather than a historian, his book was intended to be a serious work of scholarship; it enjoyed enormous influence at the time, was translated into eight languages and is still often cited.

The story of Callixtus III appears to have originated in an unreliable fifteenth-century *Lives of the Popes* by Platina. It was revived by the Enlightenment mathematician, the Marquis Pierre-Simon de Laplace, and has been uncritically repeated by astronomers until very recently. But the story does not end with mere ridicule of Callixtus III. It also has a hero: the same Enlightenment to which Laplace was committed turns out to be the New Dawn.

> The medieval treatises [on comets] are full of divination and portent, omen and blood, mysticism and superstition. . . . So, when the Renaissance and the Enlightenment finally came, a new breed of scholars arose who were predisposed to hold the Church responsible for superstition and ignorance—about comets and many other matters.[19]

We have passed from a local story about Halley's comet in 1456 to the open-mindedness of Enlightenment science and the ignorance of the church. Moreover, lest readers should think that this was a peculiarity of an especially superstitious period of Catholicism, the story is at pains to point out that it is equally true of all religions:

> [As for the] Protestant Reformation . . . The contending sects, divided on many theological issues, were in perfect harmony on the matter of comets [namely, that they are supernatural events given as signs].[20]

The received story envisages a simple correlation between the church and error, and between "scientists" and truth. The facts are rather different and much more complex.[21]

It is certainly true that many medieval authors regarded comets as an evil omen. For example, the Venerable Bede, writing in the eighth-century A.D., tells us that two comets appeared in A.D. 729, "striking terror into all who saw them . . . [and] seeming to portend awful calamity to east and west alike."[22] The source of this terror is, however, more uncertain. Beliefs about comets are probably linked to pagan astrological belief, generally with roots in the ancient Near East. They may also be connected to ancient Greek beliefs in the perfection and immutability of the heavens. Comets come and go; they indicate change in the changeless heavenly sphere, and if the heavens can change, what convulsions must be awaiting the earth. Whatever their origin, it does not seem to be either *religious* or specifically Christian. Astrology is not encouraged in the Bible, and those heavenly signs that do occur in Scripture, from a rainbow to the star of Bethlehem, do not usually portend evil. Rather the reverse.

Moreover, the emergence of a modern understanding of comets in the seventeenth century was not resisted by religious opinion. It was the Jesuit Horatio Grassi who advocated correctly that comets lie beyond the moon's orbit, while no less a person than Galileo rejected this in favor of the traditional Aristotelian account that comets are caused by an exhalation from the earth to the upper air. In 1692 Isaac Newton wrote to his friend Bentley, expressing his pleasure that his scientific discoveries would help intelligent laymen to understand more of the glory of God. Among other things, he refers to comets in the context of divine providence, with no mention of them as messengers of doom and no apparent sense of conflict between his discoveries and his belief in the deity. The fact is that the pioneers of seventeenth-century science simply did not think in terms of the modern division between science and religion. The modern myth of the "warfare between religion and science" has again tailored history to fit its needs.

The Warfare Between Religion and Science

The stories of the flat earth and of the excommunication of Halley's comet are presented as innocent historical accounts of the victory of science over superstition. In fact, they carry values and beliefs about the world and ourselves. They sustain myths, including those of a "warfare between religion and science," the myth of "progress" and that of "humanism."

The myth of a "warfare between religion and science" contrasts an earlier era of ignorance and intolerant superstition with today's world of science and enlightened toleration. It had its origin in Enlightenment anticlericalism, but it was systematically developed in the nineteenth century. The rationalist historian William Lecky pictured the rise of rationalism from the late eighteenth century as the triumph of civilization over barbarism. Dogma declined in direct proportion to the growth of science.[23] John Draper argued that religion, especially Roman Catholicism, destroyed ancient science, replacing it with superstition and precipitating the Dark Ages until reason broke free in the seventeenth century. However, it was historian and president of Cornell University Andrew White who put it most sharply. He believed that mutual damage was inevitable when religion dictates to science and gave many misleading examples that are still widely cited today. His book has been extremely influential; "the idea that science is a rational, truth-seeking discipline and theology is not" has become "a widespread cultural myth."[24]

It is important to realize that myths are not necessarily deliberately invented in the face of the known facts, nor need they arise from conspiracies designed to promote a particular point of view. Rather, myths find expression in the taken-for-granted vocabulary of a culture. They are cultural resources and carriers of meaning. On occasion, however, myths are deliberately fostered by groups of like-minded people to serve their own ends. The historian Colin Russell has argued that this is the case with the myth of a "warfare between science and religion." Russell believes that T. H. Huxley and his associates not only drew on this myth to increase their own status as scientists but were involved in something approaching a conspiracy to reinforce the myth in the public mind.[25] The role of individual ambition and of the prestige of social groups such as scientists is an important aspect of myth-making, and I will occasionally refer to it, but the focus of this book is more on the cultural aspects of myth and avoids notions of "conspiracy."

The myths of progress and humanism have their roots in the Renaissance and Enlightenment. They drive the familiar story that ignorance and fear dominated people's lives in the Dark Ages. Since the Enlightenment, it is said, we have broken the chains of superstition and religion and are now free to work together for the common good, to lift the burden of human misery through education and medical science. Man has come of age. Of course, religion continues to oppose this, as it is the business of the churches "to expound an unchanging truth, revealed once for all in utter perfection . . . [so] they become necessarily opponents of all intellectual and moral progress. [Thus] the church opposed Galileo and Darwin."[26] Authors such as Bob Goudswaard[27] have argued that this myth amounts to a faith with religious roots.

These myths establish a language that later storytellers can build on. For example, they define the connotations of key words, fixing them into new associations that perpetuate the myth. Thus in the above quotations about the flat earth and comets, we find *religion* associated with belief, omens, ignorance, superstition, heresy, excommunication, torture and blood. *Science,* on the other hand, is associated with enlightenment, scholarship, astronomy, intelligence, open-mindedness and observation. These very associations reinforce the myth that religion is credulous, ignorant and oppressive, while modern science seeks the truth by impartially weighing the evidence, promoting freedom and truth. Thus the word *Puritan* serves as a handy label for anything repressive, while the term *Enlightenment* unambiguously tells us how to regard the anticlericalism of the late eighteenth century. Once such a language is in use, there can be only one relationship between science and religion: warfare.

The historian Owen Chadwick calls the resultant images of science and religion "balloon duellists" in the "legend" of the warfare between them:

> Science and Religion were blown up into balloon duellists, science containing all knowledge, Religion containing no knowledge, and the two set side by side. . . . [It then] became possible to read back the antipathy [between science and religion] throughout history and see the ding-dong of duel through the centuries . . . [with] the Church putting the earth at the centre of the universe and Galileo proving it was not.[28]

Key words are also integrated into everyday language, squeezing out the language of religion. In 1977 a Church of England survey showed that young people have adopted the language of "science" without necessarily understanding what it refers to:

> In general . . . we find . . . an uncritical acceptance of a vocabulary of natural science which is . . . out of date . . . and is *capable of enshrining new myths within itself.* . . . Instead of religion our young people have a mild form of science fiction.[29]

The Persistence of Myth

All versions of the story of the "warfare between science and religion" agree that science has won the day, and human progress is the badge of its victory. Things are different, it is said, in those countries still dominated by fundamentalist religious beliefs, but in the modern world the "steeple's shadow," which once stretched over much of social life, has shrunk dramatically.[30] Society is now less religious, the church less influential and everyday life less dominated by belief and superstition. We no longer rely on religion but have other sources of reassurance and hope. Nowadays we do not turn to the gods to guarantee a good harvest but to the meteorological office, not to prayer for the success of an enterprise but to the stock market index. It is Galileo's discoveries that tell us our place in the heavens, not Zeus or Jehovah, and it is Darwin's theory of evolution, not Aphrodite, who explains to us our amorous nature. Thus the recognition that the earth is round, Columbus's voyages of discovery, the end of witch-hunting, Darwin's discovery of evolution—all these become metaphors for progress generally. The church may wage a rearguard action against progress, but it has had its day.

In view of this we would expect the role of religion in modern stories to fade over time. It is understandable that some eighteenth-century Enlightenment philosophers would be anticlerical and reject church doctrine; after all, the church wielded great power and actively opposed the Enlightenment program. Similarly, when the nineteenth-century biologist T. H. Huxley, known as "Darwin's Bulldog" for his aggressive support of evolution, founded the Sunday Lecture Society as an alternative to church worship, he was, among other things, attempting to poach the prestige of a church that still controlled entry to most universities and enjoyed great social status. In such circumstances opposition to religion is understandable. But by the early twentieth century the situation was different. Religion no longer had so privileged a status. Science had won its "war." And yet contemporary authors continue to contrast religion and science as if nothing had changed. Carl Sagan pictures science as a candle in the darkness of religious superstition, while Andrew Brown observes that for Richard Dawkins, "the world appears as bright islands of scientific enlightenment surrounded by a ravening darkness of ignorance and religion."[31]

Of course, stories have a certain momentum and continue even after they have been proved untrue. But there are deeper reasons for modern myths to persist that are related to their claims to truth.

Rational Foundations?

Many existing myths reflect a problem at the very heart of the modern worldview. The Enlightenment championed a particular kind of reason derived from Newton's insights into the physical world, and we are told, "The Enlightenment swept away the prejudice of the past and tried to establish, on a rational foundation, the study of humanity, society and nature."[32] However, this "rational foundation" has always been rather shaky; even in the eighteenth century there were doubts whether this kind of reason is adequate to the rich and complex nature of human life, and the Romantic movement rejected its cold heartlessness. Newtonian reason is quantitative and thrives on calculation; it cannot of its own motion enter the continuous calculus of qualities, feelings, values or experience. Thus at the very center of the Enlightenment worldview, a rift opened between blind mechanism and human freedom. But it is not just that logic is depersonalizing. Human reason itself turns out to be "merely an organ that has been developed by man's efforts to adapt himself to his environment."[33] And if reason has evolved in this blind displacement of one species by another, why should we place any trust in it? Darwin confessed "the horrid doubt . . . whether the convictions of man's mind, which has been developed from the mind of the lower animals, are of any value or at all trustworthy. Would any one trust in the convictions of a monkey's mind, if there are any convictions in such a mind?"[34] Presumably one such conviction is that of evolution, and so we come full circle. Newtonian reason is indeed a highway for our understanding of the physical aspect of creation. Yet, as modernity's Royal Road to all wisdom, it turns out to be a dead end. Rationalism, the very foundation of the Enlightenment, deconstructs itself.

As a result of its unstable foundations, modernity, the supposedly rational study of "humanity, society and nature," has found it easier to say what it *is not* than what it *is*. Specifically, it is *not* religion. But then the modern mind is involved in a dual task: it must wage war against religion, but it dare not defeat it. In fact, it needs actively to sustain and nurture an image of religion as a superstitious, prejudiced and ignorant opponent. For if science and reason were to defeat and banish religion, the modern mind would be forced to say what it *is*. As the philosopher Roger Scruton has observed, "A modernist needs to define himself *against* something, so that the very success of his enterprise threatens to undermine it."[35] The modern project needs religion, the old antagonist, as the image of what it *is not*, in order to put off the day when it has to say what it *is*. The stories of the "warfare between science and religion" admirably satisfy this dual task.

However, there is another, social, reason for the persistence of modern myths. Even as science triumphed, the hope that it would inevitably bring progress faded. An age that has seen more than eighty million people killed in wars, that has polluted its environment, that starves two thirds of its population in order to make the remainder obese and that is daily destroying numerous species of plants and animals seems less the embodiment of progress than it once did. But myths can bring reassurance in the face of such adversity, and the myth of the "warfare between science and religion" diverts attention from these failures of the modern hope, comforting us that it was even worse when the church burned witches and persecuted Galileo. Moreover, while the influence of institutional forms of religion may have waned, more informal varieties have prospered, so that religion's demise no longer seems as certain as twenty years ago. Add to this the resurgence of fundamentalisms worldwide, and we can see why the warfare myth is needed now more than ever to sustain modernity's rather embattled self-image.

Stories and Faith

Myths determine what is included and excluded from stories. They silence competing narratives and repress alternative worldviews. Indeed, the coherence of a story may be maintained as much by what is excluded as by what is told. The flat-earth story would lose its force if we were told that all educated people of the medieval period knew that the earth is round. The "warfare of science and religion" would seem less plausible if we knew that religious belief was intimately linked with the origins of modern science in the seventeenth century (see chapter one).

A good read: plot, characters, settings and props. Modern stories have some similarities with ancient myths. They both shun half tones and are repeated and transmitted from one generation to another. But there are also important differences. Ancient myths are not presented as history and are complex and varied. By comparison, modern stories tend to be much simpler and reduce the richness of history and science to a few general and repetitive plots with stereotyped characters. For example, a powerful church cruelly oppresses an intrepid hero, whether Columbus, Galileo or Darwin. The history is marshaled and organized to suit the underlying myth.

The stories that carry modern myths have, like all stories, a plot, some central characters, a setting to provide the context for the characters to interact, and some props to help the action along. The setting may vary: the Dark Ages, Galileo's Leaning Tower of Pisa, Darwin's Galapagos Islands. The props also change: a flat earth, Halley's comet, Darwin's finches, Galileo's telescope. But the plot and characters have an identifiable consistency.

The plot is intended to draw a sharp contrast between the Dark Ages and ourselves, between science and the church, between reason and superstition. It highlights practices and beliefs that seem alien and primitive to the modern mind: witches, earth-centered cosmology or the creation of the world in seven days. The plot must clearly identify the contending characters, the oppression and injustice they suffer, and point the finger at the guilty party. Naturalism, the belief that the supernatural is either nonexistent or powerless, is a plot feature common to all modern stories.

All good stories need a hero, whether it be Columbus, Galileo or Darwin, and with a hero comes a villain, whether the Inquisition, Pope Callixtus III, ignorant priests and bishops or just religion in general. As the villain, "Religion" appears not as the "power of God" but must play the role allotted to it by the myth.

Once drawn, the characters are set against one another: Columbus and the papal court, Galileo and the Inquisition, or Darwin and Bishop "Soapy Sam" Wilberforce. In order to maintain this opposition, the characters must be portrayed as one-dimensional, shorn of any compromising complexity. Thus, if it were known that the papal court was fully aware that the earth is round or that Galileo regarded himself as loyal to his church, the plot would become obscured beneath detail. Above all, the contending characters must be kept sharply separate. There must be no hint of Galileo's belief in God, of Newton's delight that his discoveries supported belief in "a deity," or that many of Darwin's most distinguished colleagues were Christians. The desire for simple, straightforward contrasts merges into stereotyping and misrepresentation. Such sharp contrasts ought to alert us to be cautious.

Stories as carriers of belief. Perhaps because its stories pose as history or science, the modern mind is blind to the extent to which its viewpoint is one of faith. Modern stories, driven by their underlying myths, are carriers of values and beliefs. Their commitment is to what is left of the Enlightenment project, with its trust in progress and the universal human spirit. They suppress, marginalize or disqualify Christian narratives in order to keep human beings at the center of things (the doctrine commonly called "humanism") and in order to present reality as malleable to our will.

I have already noted the roots of modern stories in the Enlightenment with its elevation of reason and man and its high ideals of equality, brotherhood and freedom. But the Enlightenment hope always rested more on faith than fact. The Reign of Terror put a brake on optimism, producing a conservative reaction against change in France and fear of radicalism in England. The modern hope revived in the mid-nineteenth century when many people again became optimistic about scientific progress leading to social reform. Writing at the turn of the twentieth century, H. G. Wells was fully aware that the industrial revolution, with its squalor and slums, had not fulfilled the hope of the eighteenth-century Enlightenment. Yet his faith was undaunted that science and the human spirit would prevail. In his novel *Men Like Gods*, he recapitulates and reinterprets the Enlightenment mind as he seeks a solution to the miseries and injustices of the nineteenth century in a utopian future.

> Utopia . . . a world fairly and righteously at peace, its resources husbanded and exploited for the common good, its every citizen freed not only from servitude but from ignorance, and its surplus energies directed steadfastly to the increase of knowledge and beauty. The attainment of that vision by more and more minds was a thing no longer to be prevented. Earth would tread the path Utopia had trod. She too would weave law, duty, and education into a larger sanity than man had ever known. Men also would presently laugh at the things they had feared, and brush aside the impostures [of religion] that had overawed them and [its] absurdities that had tormented and crippled their lives. And as this great revolution was achieved and earth wheeled into daylight, the burden of human miseries would lift, and courage oust sorrow from the hearts of men. . . . The sons of earth . . . purified from disease, sweet-minded and strong and beautiful, would go proudly about their conquered planet and lift their daring to the stars.[36]

Brian J. Walsh and J. Richard Middleton describe a faith commitment as the way we answer the four fundamental worldview questions: *Who am I? Where am I? What's wrong?* and *What is the remedy?*[37] Well's answers to these questions are clear.

Who are we? Children of the earth, sweet-minded, strong and beautiful.

Where are we? On an earth that is ours to conquer and whose resources are ours to exploit.

What's wrong? We are chained by ignorance and the impostures of religion that torment us and cripple our lives.

What is the remedy? Education to banish ignorance and superstition, and to free the human spirit to lift its daring to the stars.

The centrality of man is apparent, and Wells's agenda is comprehensive. The themes of harmony, progress and knowledge are united in the "daylight" of a new dawn, a modern Utopia. It is the irrational "absurdities" and "impostures" of religion and tradition that emerge as the villain of the piece. This was a common theme among humanists of the period. For example, Bertrand Russell regarded religion "as belonging to the infancy of human reason, and to a stage of development which we are now outgrowing."[38] The solution is reason and education, so that we may proudly occupy our "conquered planet" for the common good of all.

Affirming the Faith

The modern world's self-image is sustained by secular social institutions[39] that marginalize religion, but also by modern culture. We have seen that the modern mind, no less than the ancient one, uses stories to reinforce its belief that we are more advanced than other civilizations. The myths they carry communicate beliefs about the fundamental questions of existence. These stories have taken root because they reassure the modern mind about its own rationality and tolerance, qualities that the events of the last hundred years have cast into doubt. The myth of a "warfare between science and religion" persists long after it has been shown to be untrue because modernity needs an antagonist to divert attention from its internal contradictions and its external failures. An image of "religion" is constructed as the shadow of Enlightenment reason so that its supposed irrationality and intolerance reinforces the modern mind's trust in its own rationality and toleration. The stories of modernity constantly reinvent the image of the church, and of religion, in order to brush it aside.

Six Stories

This book takes a close look at six modern stories and investigates the tales they tell. As stories have their own color and rhythm, which are lost in paraphrases, I have tried to preserve their specific flavor by quoting the storytellers themselves whenever possible. The chapters form a sequence, with developing themes. But each is more or less self-contained and can be taken separately if the reader wishes.

We will see that these stories, despite their claim to be based in fact, are closer to myths than to history. My purpose is solely to show that modern stories, which have become modern-day "orthodoxies," are not transparent windows to history but richly textured accounts that support modern myths. The chapters are therefore not intended to be introductions to the subjects covered. The themes highlighted are dictated by the stories them-selves, and these are often highly selective versions of history. To present a full review of the events behind each story would be beyond the scope of this book, although the endnotes and bibliography will generally point the interested reader toward the relevant literature.

The modern world has two stories that have become widely influential in explaining to us our place in the physical and natural world. The story of Galileo tells us that God did not put us at the center of the universe, while that of Darwin puts us in our place in the animal world. Together they are often cited as ushering in the modern world and dispelling the myths of religion. It is with these two modern myths that we begin.

1

GALILEO
A Story of a Hero of Science

T HE FIRST OF THE TWO STORIES THAT TELL US WHO WE ARE AND HOW we fit into the modern world is that of Galileo. This story explains to us our place in the physical universe—that we occupy a small planet circling an average sun of one galaxy among many.

As any encyclopedia will tell us, Nicolaus Copernicus founded modern astronomy when he showed that the earth revolves around the sun. Columbus's voyage to the New World was hardly more epoch-making than this "revolution" in the heavens. But whereas the church sponsored the conquest of the New World in order to "search for gold and . . . convert the local people to Christianity,"[1] it tried to frustrate the advance of science. Let Bertrand Russell take up the story.

The modern period began, claims Russell, with the Renaissance, which started to free men's minds from superstition and religion, and established reason as the foundation for science. This new freedom, however, was opposed root and branch by the church, culminating in the clash between religion and science symbolized by Galileo.

> Galileo, as everyone knows, was condemned by the Inquisition. . . . He recanted, and promised never again to maintain that the earth rotates or revolves. The Inquisition was successful at putting an end to science in Italy, which did not revive there for centuries, but it failed to prevent men of science from adopting the heliocentric theory, and did considerable damage to the Church by its stupidity. Fortunately there were Protestant countries, where the clergy, however anxious to do harm to science, were unable to gain control of the State.[2]

This is presented as a transparent window on to history, but it is actually a richly textured narrative that puts character and plot into the foreground and pushes into the background features such as the role of the Puritans in the development of seventeenth-century science.

Writing in a similar vein, George Bernard Shaw remarked that scientific education teaches us that "Galileo was a martyr, and his persecutors incorrigible ignoramuses."[3] Ultimately reason prevailed over religion and reached its fulfillment in the eighteenth-century Enlightenment. The story, we are told, has a happy ending.

This familiar tale seems to have first gained widespread currency through the influential mid-eighteenth-century *Encyclopédie* of the French Enlightenment. Many contributors to *L'Encyclopédie* took a rationalist approach to religion, which they considered to be the invention of crafty priests who exploited the ignorant and superstitious masses. For them, Galileo's was the fate of anyone who opposes religious bigotry. In the nineteenth century the rationalist historian William Lecky developed this story further:

> It is, indeed, marvellous that science should ever have revived amid the fearful obstacles theologians cast in her way. . . . The constant exaltation of blind faith, the countless miracles, the childish legends, all produced a condition of besotted ignorance, of grovelling and trembling credulity that can scarcely be paralleled except among the most degraded barbarians.[4]

If the story predates Russell, it does not stop with his generation. The popular science writer Patrick Moore tells us:

> The Roman Catholic Church attacked Galileo because the [heliocentric] theory was not reconcilable with certain passages of the Bible. As a consequence, poor Galileo spent most of his life in open conflict with the Church.[5]

"Religion as the entrenched political power" is often contrasted with the liberating force of science:

> Science and religion have clashed frequently throughout history, most often with religion as the entrenched political power and with decidedly detrimental effects on the health of the scientist—as Galileo could confirm.[6]

As the eminent scientist Carl Sagan writes:

> Many felt that Copernicus and Galileo were up to no good and erosive of the social order. Indeed, any challenge, from any source, to the literal truth of the Bible might have such consequences. We can readily see how science began to

make people nervous. Instead of criticising those who perpetuated the myths, public rancour was directed at those who discredited them.[7]

Biblical Christian belief is here identified with both myth and the conservation of an oppressive social order. Sagan believes that science unsettles prejudice and exposes myth, leading to true humanism and social progress. This is a common aspect of the Galileo story. In his play about the life of Galileo, the twentieth-century author Bertolt Brecht presented him as a martyr to humanism and reason. Brecht has Galileo say: "I believe in Humanity, which means to say I believe in human reason." Galileo's disciple in the drama anticipates the progress that the new science will bring, and enthuses to Galileo: "To me you're the man who's battling for freedom to teach what's new."[8]

The Galileo story is driven by the myth that there is an enduring opposition between religion and science. It tells of a modern world based on science and technological progress. By contrast, religion is based on faith rather than reason and leads to superstition rather than science, to authoritarian oppression rather than to democracy.

Galileo: The Received Version

Like any story, that of Galileo has a plot, characters, a setting and props. The plot is the war between religion and science, and it is presented to us not with facts but through the adventures of a charismatic individual. Armed only with a telescope and reason, plucky Galileo stood against the might of the church. He was tortured by the Inquisition, condemned as a heretic, and wasted away in a prison cell; Italian science floundered. The main drawback to this plot is that most of it is untrue.

As the philosopher Aristotle sagely observed, a drama must concern but one action of one man, entire and complete. We know the action. The man is, of course, Galileo. As Bertrand Russell says, "everyone knows" about Galileo. Scientist and hero, he invented the telescope, discovered how the earth moves around the sun, conducted his famous experiment on the (even then) Leaning Tower of Pisa and courageously added to his recantation of the earth's motion: *"Eppure si muove"* ("yet it does move"). As it happens, little of this is true either. However, where decisive scientific discoveries are lacking, the myth supplies them: the Leaning Tower and the telescope build up Galileo's character nicely.

To become a martyr to knowledge, our hero needs an antagonist, and this is provided by the church, sometimes appearing in the form of Pope Urban VIII, sometimes as Robert Cardinal Bellarmine, but most commonly as the Inquisition. It is powerful, bigoted and ignorant.

The story has two settings, corresponding to the two *dramatis personae*. Galileo occupies the wide, sunlit high ground of reason and observation, free from obscurantist dogma and superstition: the realm of knowledge and facts. The church, on the other hand, prefers to live in the cramped monastic cell of religious dogma and faith.

The props are simple. Galileo has his telescope; the church has its Bible. And so the stage is set.

The Wrong Man

There is a puzzle here, however. Why Galileo? At first blush, the prime candidate for the hero of the Copernican Revolution must surely be Nicolaus Copernicus. Yet most versions of the story turn not on the retiring Canon Copernicus but on the name of Galileo Galilei, a man born some twenty years after Copernicus died. For Copernicus could not carry the plot forward. He was, after all, a canon of the Church and enjoyed the support of the cardinal of Capua and Pope Paul III. His book *On the Revolutions of the Heavenly Spheres*, published in 1543, circulated at little or no cost for some seventy years. Galileo is therefore much more congenial to the storytellers, for even though he received Church pensions, he was at least condemned by the Holy Office in 1633 for teaching that the sun is the center of the universe and that the earth moves around it.

Every schoolchild learns that "the Bible said that everything moves around the earth but Galileo's observations showed that the earth moves around the sun."[9] This puts the issue very clearly, so let us look at what Galileo observed, how this "showed that the earth moves around the sun" and whether it did indeed conflict with what the Bible says. First, though, we need to know a little about the astronomy of the early seventeenth century, which relied heavily on the work of Aristotle, the Greek philosopher of the fourth century B.C.

Scholarly Circles

From the late Middle Ages the dominant model of the universe in western Europe was derived from Aristotle, who reasoned that the heavens, the perfect and immutable realm, would also be unchangeable in its physical qualities and motions.

Aristotle's physics is complex and differs greatly from what is now taught as science in our schools, but it would be a great mistake to suppose that it was therefore foolish or self-evidently wrong. I can give only the briefest outline here, but the reader must remember that the majority of early-seventeenth-century astronomers were Aristotelians for reasons defended in logic and observation.

Aristotle pictured the earth at the center of a universe of concentric spheres. The nearest sphere carries the moon; the furthest carries the stars; the planets circle around, each on its intermediate sphere. In this scheme the heavens above the sphere of the moon are sharply distinguished from the earth below. Above the moon, all is perfect and immutable; all movement there is circular, as this is the only motion that eternally returns unchanging to its beginning. Heavenly bodies are perfectly spherical, without spot or blemish. The earth, however, is made of mutable matter, and motion on earth is linear, lacking unchanging perfection.[10] Moreover, all matter falls downward, toward the center of the earth, which is also the center of the universe.

Ptolemy's universe. In the second century A.D., Ptolemy constructed an astronomical system based on Aristotle's ideas. He found that Aristotle's picture of the sun and stars revolving around the earth on their crystal spheres could be made to fit the known facts quite well, but there were serious problems with the planets, which appeared to wander about in the heavens rather than move in simple circles. In order to explain this, he proposed that the planets themselves moved in smaller circles, each attached to their respective sphere. This resulted in an inconveniently complex model, and from early times, astronomers debated whether these smaller circles were real or just included to "save the appearances"—that is, to fit in with observation. Ptolemy also considered alternative models, including the Pythagorean view that the earth rotates. However, he rejected this for a number of empirical reasons, including that there is no steady wind as one might expect if the earth turned nor do objects dropped from the top of a tower fall at a distance from its base.

By the early seventeenth century, numerous problems had accumulated with Ptolemy's Aristotelian cosmology. Not only was Aristotelian physics increasingly criticized, but improved observations led to greater and greater complexity in the model. To try to resolve these difficulties Copernicus adopted the ancient Pythagorean hypothesis that the sun, not the earth, is at the center of the universe. This was not altogether successful, and Copernicus's final model of the heavens was ultimately more complex than Ptolemy's. It did, however, allow Copernicus to fix the order of the planets, perhaps his greatest achievement. In other respects Copernicus remained faithful to Aristotle, retaining the circular orbits as well as most of the Ptolemaic devices.

Galileo was a firm disciple of Copernicus, both in placing the sun at the center of the universe and in his otherwise conservative picture of the universe.

The "center of the universe" or "third rock from the sun"? Before looking at "what Galileo observed," it is worth spending a little time on the misunderstandings that surround Aristotle's belief that the earth is at the center of the universe, a theme I will explore further in chapter three. Bertrand Russell tells us:

> In the medieval world, the earth was the centre of the heavens, and everything had a purpose concerned with man. [After Copernicus, man lived on] a minor planet of a not specially distinguished star; astronomical distances were so vast that the earth, in comparison, was a mere pin-point.[11]

This connection between the Copernican Revolution and man's significance in the universe in a broader sense is very common. It blithely identifies Copernicus's "discovery that our world is not the centre and axis of the material universe"[12] with man's subordination in the scheme of things. Many authors assume that pre-Copernican men, living in an earth-centered cosmos, tiny in comparison with the vastness revealed by modern science, had an exaggerated and arrogant sense of human importance. God, it is said, created the universe for man's use, and man is therefore at the center of creation. The Copernican Revolution, and subsequently the Enlightenment, is supposed to have disabused mankind of its arrogant beliefs, instilling an appropriate humility about our place in the world and undermining belief in God. The science writer James Newman tells this story especially clearly:

> It will never be known when man first became convinced that he was of cosmic importance, but the date this pretension was disposed of is pretty clear. The *De Revolutionibus Orbium Coelestium* of Nicolaus Copernicus was published in 1543. . . . Nestled in the mathematics . . . was a concept that put man in his place in the cosmos, as Darwin's concept was to put him in his place on

earth. . . . Looking backward in history, it is easy for us to see that a moving
earth and sun-centred universe gravely subverted Christian theology. If man's
abode was not at the centre of things, how could he be king?[13]

Although this is a common subplot of the Galileo story, it is mistaken. There
is indeed a connection between the earth's physical "position" in the universe and its status, but not the one often assumed.

Aristotle emphasized the corruption of the earth in comparison with
everything above the lunar sphere (remember the moon is the first of many
spheres revolving around the earth). Indeed, in Aristotelian thought the
earth was so far inferior to the heavens that the latter were believed to consist of a higher, finer substance—the fifth element, the quintessence. The
earth was at the center not because of its significance but because it is everywhere below the heavens. Thus the pre-Copernican cosmology that the
earth lies at the center of the universe is no compliment to earth's occu-
pants. The center is the lowest place in the universe, not the most important. The hierarchy of perfection stretches up beyond us in concentric
circles, rank upon rank. Thus the fourteenth-century Florentine poet Dante
Alighieri, in *The Divine Comedy*, locates the pit of hell centrally in the "great
fundaments of the universe, on which all weights downweigh."[14] The heavens, by contrast, were everywhere lifted up above the earth, incorruptible
and divine.

The Copernican system, far from demoting man, destroyed Aristotle's
vision of the earth as a kind of cosmic sink, and if it did anything, it elevated
humanity. In making the earth a planet, a heavenly body, Copernicus infi-
nitely ennobled its status. Galileo exploited this changed status of the earth
when he had his mouthpiece, Salviati, say: "We seek to ennoble and perfect
[the earth] when we strive to make it like the celestial bodies, and, as it were,
place it in heaven, from which your philosophers [namely, Aristotle] have
banished it."[15] As for size, it matters, but not as is often supposed. Ptolemy
knew that the earth was a mere pinpoint in comparison with the heavens.
Moreover, the pre-Copernican cosmos, while physically smaller than ours,
was of far greater range, for it included a hierarchy of changeless celestial
beings, each the superior of man in the scale of being. "Man, his pleasures or
his pains," did not, as Draper supposes, become of little consequence because
the universe appeared larger than it had before.[16] Size is not so easy to measure as many imagine. In fact, there is little evidence that any of this was an
issue for Galileo's contemporaries.[17] All educated people knew that creation

was made for God, not man. Merely changing the cosmological model didn't affect this. As we shall see in chapter three, the doctrine that the earth exists for man's use derives from Greek philosophy, not the Bible.

A modest humanism? The use of the "Copernican Revolution" as a metaphor for a modest and realistic humanism seems to have first gained ground during the Enlightenment of the eighteenth century. As James Newman suggested in the quotation above, the nineteenth century joined it to Darwin's evolutionary metaphor and "put man in his place on earth," just as astronomy had put him in his place in the heavens. Human beings share a common evolutionary tree with all other animals and have not been specially created in the image of God. While this "modest humanism" is the official line, another, different, story lies concealed within it. As we have seen, if overturning Aristotle's vision of the place of the earth is to have any metaphorical meaning at all, it elevates humanity to the status of heavenly creatures. In this sense the Enlightenment was indeed a Copernican Revolution. For it made man the source and origin, as well as the measure, of all things. It placed him at the center of creation in a far more radical sense than that wrongly ascribed to pre-Copernican astronomy and the church. Man became his own god, or at least his reason did. As Charles Darwin put it, man's *"god-like* intellect . . . has penetrated into the movements and constitution of the solar system."[18] Indeed, as the astronomer Sir Fred Hoyle has pointed out, Darwinism similarly elevates mankind, for the neo-Darwinist picture of evolution relies on the predilection, fueled by "anti-religion," to see everything as centered on the earth.[19] Darwin's theory of evolution placed man at the very apex of nature, where a less geocentric point of view would take into account the constant interaction between the earth and the universe as a whole.

We find this same elevated vision of "Man" and his intellect in Bertrand Russell in the early twentieth century. After observing the meaninglessness and purposelessness of a materialist vision, he surveys the heroic image of "Man" as he appears in humanism:

> Undismayed by the empire of chance, [Man determines] to preserve a mind free from the wanton tyranny that rules his outward life; proudly defiant of the irresistible forces that tolerate, for a moment, his knowledge and his condemnation, [he determines] to sustain alone, a weary but unyielding Atlas, the world that his own ideals have fashioned despite the trampling march of unconscious power.[20]

Under cover of the claim to dispose of man's pretensions, Russell smuggles in "Man," the new Atlas, no longer just the center of the world but now the very creator and sustainer of the cosmos. In Russell's purple passage it is not hard to identify this new Atlas as Russell himself, the philosopher preserving his free mind and his proud ideals.

The official story that the Copernican Revolution demoted man from the center of things and undermined Christian theology conceals a story of man elevated to be the very creator and sustainer of the world.

With this brief summary of Aristotelian physics and its implications in mind, let us return to "Galileo's observations."

A Victim of Spin?

The Galileo story tells us that he invented the telescope and was the first to turn it on the heavens. In fact, it was invented by the Dutch lens maker Johann Lippersheim in 1605. Nor was Galileo the first to look at the sky. That honor probably goes to Thomas Harriot in England, who observed the moon through a telescope in 1609. Other achievements sometimes attributed to Galileo are equally apocryphal. He is unlikely to have dropped different-sized cannon balls from the Leaning Tower of Pisa in order to compare their rate of descent. Nor did he discover the dynamics of the pendulum or invent the pendulum clock, as is often asserted.

It has been said of Galileo that his fame rests on discoveries he never made and feats he never performed. This is a pity, as his real achievements need no supplementing by what he did not do. They are, however, more technical and lack the immediate appeal of a telescope or the Leaning Tower. Galileo's discoveries resulted from long, laborious hours of studying the heavens and from simple, though ingenious, experiments.

Galileo's major contributions to astronomy were the observations made before 1613, namely, the existence of sunspots, the irregularity of the moon's surface, the phases of Venus and the moons of Jupiter. It is not obvious how this proves "that the earth moves around the sun," and for a very good reason: it doesn't. Nor could it. Neither Galileo nor anybody else in the seventeenth century supposed otherwise.

Galileo's observations were important for another related reason: they conflicted with Aristotelian reason, for they indicated a lack of perfection in the heavens—the sun had "spots" and the moon blemishes. Moreover, his observations of Venus and Jupiter implied that the earth is not the center of all astronomical motion (although they do not imply that the sun is). Both of these conclusions are fatal to Aristotelian reasoning and therefore to Ptolemy's cosmology.

Before publishing his conclusions in *Letters on Sunspots* in 1613, Galileo took the precaution of checking that the incorruptibility of the heavens was an Aristotelian belief and not a Church doctrine. Indeed, the Church largely accepted his conclusions, although the die-hard Aristotelians in the universities did not.

These findings were revolutionary enough, but they did not prove that the earth orbits the sun. The fact is that during Galileo's lifetime there was insufficient evidence to show that the earth revolves. This is now widely accepted by scholars, some even suggesting that the then-known facts weighed heavily against the Copernican theory.

> [In the sixteenth century] sensible men all over Europe, especially the most empirically minded, would have pronounced [Copernicus's theory] . . . the premature fruits of an uncontrolled imagination. . . . Contemporary empiricists, had they lived in the sixteenth century, would have been the first to scoff out of court the new [Copernican] philosophy of the universe.[21]

As the historian of science Thomas Kuhn puts it: "Available observational tests . . . provided no basis for a choice" between the Copernican and Ptolemaic theories.[22] So if Galileo's observations did not bear directly on whether the earth orbits the sun, why was he condemned in 1633?

Galileo and the Church

Galileo delayed publishing his Copernican opinions for many years. He was nearly fifty when he first did so and approaching seventy at the time of his trial. Copernicus, also, had been reticent to publish. This hesitation is often attributed to fear of "the punishments of the Church." We are told that when Copernicus did finally publish in 1543, his fears were realized as "the Inquisition condemned it as heretical."[23] The truth is more prosaic. Copernicus feared ridicule by his fellow astronomers. In the dedication of his book to Pope Paul III he wrote of his fear that he would be "hooted off the stage" and admitted that "the scorn which I had to fear on account of the newness and absurdity of my opinion almost drove me to abandon a work already undertaken."[24] His views were, indeed, rejected by the Aristotelian astronomers, but his book circulated for seventy years without condemnation by the Church. Galileo feared the same fate and was afraid of looking stupid.

As he wrote in a letter to his fellow astronomer Johannes Kepler on August 4, 1597, he was "frightened by the fate of Copernicus himself . . . who . . . is . . . to an infinite multitude . . . (for such is the number of fools) an object of ridicule and derision." The "fools" in question were not Inquisitors but his fellow astronomers, especially the Aristotelians in the universities.

From 1613, however, Galileo unambiguously asserted that the earth literally moves around the sun and popularized his views in snappy Italian rather than the arcane Latin of the universities. This put his work at the top of the seventeenth-century bestsellers list, but it did not endear him to his academic colleagues. Galileo was first and foremost opposing Aristotle, not the Bible, and for the majority of early-seventeenth-century astronomers, this put him on the fringes of "science"; his was not a cutting-edge theory but an ancient Pythagorean view that had been discredited by Aristotle.

On the other hand, Galileo's relations with the Church were cordial. The orthodox story tells us that his telescopic discoveries "gave unbounded alarm to the Church. By the low and ignorant ecclesiastics they were denounced as deceptions or frauds."[25] But this is not so. Far from being constantly harried by obscurantist priests, he was feted by cardinals, received by Pope Paul V and befriended by the future Pope Urban VIII who, in 1620, wrote an ode in his honor. The historian Georgio de Santillana observed in 1958 that "it has been known for a long time that a major part of the Church intellectuals were on the side of Galileo, while the clearest opposition to him came from secular circles."[26] Although scholars may long have known this, the orthodox story assumes the opposite. When it is said that Galileo became "too advanced for the church," the case is rather overstated.[27]

Robert Cardinal Bellarmine was appointed to examine Galileo's teaching. A distinguished scholar, he was far from ill-informed and was told that Galileo needed to produce more evidence to establish his case; this, as we have seen, was precisely what he could not do because at the time it did not exist. Galileo was not condemned, but the Church did take a harder look at Copernicus's book. It was suspended for four years in 1616 "pending correction" and reissued with several changes, largely to make it clear that the heliocentric model is only a hypothesis. Galileo was not mentioned. How, then, did things go so wrong for him?

Freedom of speech. The Church's response to Galileo is often put down to "a fear of discussion and debate,"[28] but that is not so. Alternative astronomical hypotheses were freely discussed, including Copernicus's astronomy, which, as Bellarmine remarked (in a letter to Paolo Foscarini, April 12, 1615), made "excellent good sense" as a hypothesis.

Galileo was not content with this. In order to show that the earth truly revolves, he advanced an ingenious but erroneous theory of the tides, and in order to defend the Copernican picture of heavenly spheres, he argued that comets were a form of optical illusion. These views put Galileo out on a limb.

He went further than this, however. He sought to reinterpret certain disputed biblical passages in the light of Copernican reasoning and in contradiction of earlier authorities. This was contrary to the Council of Trent's admonition (which had been intended for the Reformers) forbidding the interpretation of Scripture against the authority of tradition. But perhaps just as significantly, Galileo alienated his friend Pope Urban VIII.

The book that led to Galileo's trial was his 1632 treatise *Dialogue Concerning the Chief World Systems*. This took the form of a debate between protagonists, each representing a different view. The Aristotelian opponent of heliocentrism was called Simplicio, a name that is a play both on that of an early commentator on Aristotle and on the word meaning "simpleton." Simplicio's role in the dialogue is to be a kind of Aunt Sally to be knocked down by Galileo. At the very end of his book, Galileo puts into Simplicio's mouth a favorite argument of his friend Pope Urban VIII and then mocks it. In other words, he concluded his treatise by effectively calling the very Pope who had befriended him a simpleton for not agreeing with Galileo. This was not a wise move, and the rest is history. Galileo himself was convinced that the "major cause" of his troubles was the charge that he had made "fun of his Holiness" rather than the matter of the earth moving.[29]

The *Dialogue* was confiscated a few months after it was printed; Galileo, elderly and probably ill, was summoned to Rome. But the stories of dank prison cells and torture are modern embellishments for the sake of the plot. It is even misleading to say that he was "imprisoned for some months" and "treated with remorseless severity."[30] He was certainly detained and was forced to abjure heliocentricism, but, as befitted his status, he was given his own rooms and servants. Moreover, he did not die a broken, lonely man in exile. He returned to his own home with his pensions from the Church intact. He could not travel freely, but he continued to write and receive visitors. As the philosopher A. N. Whitehead put it: "Galileo suffered an honourable detention and a mild reproof, before dying peacefully in his bed."[31]

There is no doubt that the judgment against Galileo resulted in greater caution in the debate over Copernicus. However, it is a gross overstatement to say, as does Bertrand Russell, that it "was successful at putting an end to science in Italy, which did not revive there for centuries."[32] Italy continued, as it still does, to produce many eminent scholars. As we shall see, Russell's belief that science developed in Protestant countries only because the church there lacked the power to suppress it is equally erroneous.

Galileo was interrogated by the Holy Office in April 1633. Modern scholarship has long rejected the simplistic myth, which has grown since the Enlightenment, of "a clash between enlightened reason in the form of Galileo and oppressive reaction in the form of the Church."[33] Galileo scholar Maurice Finocchiaro takes it for granted that the events of 1633 involve complex intrigues of politics and patronage rather than "dogmatic reservations of the Church" about biblical teaching.[34] As the historian William Shea puts it: "Galileo's condemnation was the result of the complex interplay of untoward political circumstances, political ambitions, and wounded prides."[35] Indeed, Galileo's rhetoric, his position as a court favorite and even contemporary eucharistic disputes have all been considered factors in his downfall.[36] But the received version of the Galileo story focuses exclusively on the supposed conflict between Galileo's science and the teaching of the Bible, so we will turn to that next.

A question of authority. Aristotle—not the Bible—taught explicitly that "everything moves around the earth." The question, therefore, was whether a passage such as Psalm 19:4-5, "The sun . . . like a strong man runs its course with joy," was to be interpreted according to traditional Aristotelian reasoning (the sun moves) or Galileo's Copernican reasoning (the light of the sun "runs its course" from sun to earth but the sun itself is stationary). In either case the question concerned which authority to use in discerning the "underlying" meaning of the Bible. The Roman Catholic Church's position, stated by Bellarmine in 1615, followed the Council of Trent in upholding interpretation according to traditional (Aristotelian) authority until observational evidence was available requiring its revision. Galileo was condemned, not because the Bible conflicted with observation but because he differed with the church over what authority should be used to interpret it.[37]

This debate, based on authorities, differs from the Reformers' approach, which held that Scripture does not require the Church to interpret it. Interestingly, Galileo himself came close to this view in 1615 when he said in his letter to the Grand Duchess Christina that the Bible is written "in order to [accommodate itself] to the capacities of the common people, who are rude and unlearned."[38] He seems to mean that phrases such as "the sun rises" are commonly used, in Scripture as in contemporary speech, without implying a cosmological theory. In this he was perilously close to John Calvin, writing seventy-five years earlier, who believed that the Bible is accessible to all without need of arcane interpretation. Whether or not Galileo was aware of this, the point was not lost on the Roman Catholic Church.

Of course, Bertrand Russell would have rejected this comparison between Galileo and John Calvin. In his eyes the Reformed churches opposed Copernicus and Galileo even before the Roman Catholic Church did. This is in fact crucial to his argument, for, if Galileo's science contradicted the Bible, a renewed emphasis on Scripture should arouse even more dogmatic opposition. Thus he claims that

> Calvin . . . demolished Copernicus with the text: "the world also is stablished, that it cannot be moved" (Ps 93:1), and exclaimed: "Who will venture to place the authority of Copernicus above that of the Holy Spirit?" Protestant clergy were at least as bigoted as Catholic ecclesiastics . . . [but] had less power.[39]

Russell gives no reference for this well-known "quotation," but scholars such as the historian of science Thomas Kuhn do; they tell us that Calvin wrote it in his commentary on Genesis.[40] But this is not true. Calvin does not mention Copernicus at all in that book. Indeed, Edward Rosen[41] argues that Calvin had never even heard of Copernicus. The quotation appears to have been invented in the late nineteenth century in order to substantiate the myth of an enduring "warfare of science with theology," exemplified by Galileo.[42]

Faithful investigation. If, then, Galileo's condemnation concerned competing forms of reason together with their founding worldviews rather than any simple warfare between science and religion, what effect did it have when the Reformers placed the authority of the Bible above that of Aristotelian tradition?

In his discussion of the Genesis creation account, Calvin argues that "Moses . . . addresses himself to our senses" and accommodates to our everyday understanding of the world rather than giving an exact scientific description: "As it became a theologian, [Moses] had respect to us rather than to the stars." Echoing Galileo's remark that the Bible is written for the "rude and unlearned," Calvin remarks of the "waters above the heavens" (in Gen 1) that they are "such as rude and unlearned may perceive" so that we may all appreciate the "wonderful providence of God."[43] Some 150 years later Isaac Newton echoed this view when he wrote that Moses had "described realities in a language artificially adapted to ye sense of ye vulgar."[44]

Andrew White, a keen advocate of the received story of Galileo and the probable source of the misquotation of Calvin, claimed that this "accommodation theory" of Scripture is a late invention aimed at rationalizing a nonliteral reading of the Bible in the light of scientific discoveries. But this is not so. Calvin, Kepler and Galileo held such views, as did Newton. In fact, they have an ancient and continuous history. In the fourth century Augustine had remarked that the Holy Spirit had "willed to make [the disciples] Christians, not mathematicians." In the thirteenth, Aquinas argued that God spoke to men "in the way men could understand and were accustomed to," while in the mid-fourteenth century Nicholas Oresme noted that Scripture conforms "to the manner of common human speech." Galileo himself quoted Cardinal Baronius's maxim that the "Holy Ghost intended to teach us how to go to heaven, not how the heavens go."[45]

Calvin found support for neither Ptolemy nor Copernicus in Scripture because it was written according to common usage so that it is accessible to all.[46] But if Calvin resisted speculative interpretations, it would be a mistake to suppose that the Reformation's return to the Bible had no effect on the rise of science in the seventeenth century. As has been widely recognized, science in fact flourished in northern Protestant Europe, and Protestants were disproportionately represented in learned scientific societies. Russell accounts for this by the Protestant churches' comparative impotence to resist science, no matter how much they may have wished to do so, but there are few scholars today who would accept this. In fact, there is a strong school of thought that detects not warfare between science and religion but direct connections between them. Far from trying to resist science, the Reformation replaced Aristotelian and Neo-Platonic reasoning with insights from the Bible and thus provided the soil that enabled science to grow. Thus Calvin advocated "careful examination" to "investigate the motions of the heavenly bodies" and believed that this would give us "brighter views of [God's] glory" and providence. The same view was expressed thus by Newton, in a letter to his friend Bentley in 1692: "When I wrote my treatise about [physics], I had an eye upon such principles as might work with considering men for the belief of a Deity; and nothing can rejoice me more than to find it useful for that purpose."[47] That his intention met with some success is evident from his reception:

> [Newton's system incites us] the more profoundly to reverence and adore the great Maker and Lord of all. He must be blind who from the most wise and excellent contrivances of things cannot see the infinite Wisdom and Goodness of their Almighty Creator, and he must be mad and senseless who refuses to acknowledge them.[48]

Space prevents a detailed discussion of the relationship between religion and the rise of science,[49] but I will briefly mention four aspects: the de-deification of creation permitting experiment without impiety; the biblical task of dominion that facilitated the growth of technology; the recognition of reason as within creation and not over it; and trust in God's covenantal faithfulness that suggests that it is worthwhile seeking laws governing the world.

Science and Religion

1. *Nature created, not divine.* Disciples of the Greek philosopher Plato taught that there is no sharp distinction between nature and the divine, and this view gained a renewed influence from the fifteenth century. If nature is itself a divine organism or is occupied by divine "beings" such as the planets, any attempt to subdue or control nature, and especially the heavens, has overtones of impiety. Man would in any case need the help of other divinities, which can be achieved only by magic. Frequently nature was personified as a goddess. To uncover her secrets and penetrate her mysteries is permitted only to a suitor from the pantheon; a mortal could do so only by harnessing the powers of the heavens.

Views such as these militated against the development of natural science, favored superstition and magic, and seriously distorted the biblical command to have dominion over the earth. Dominion over a divinity is simply not possible. A person might achieve temporary and precarious control but only at the risk of impiety. By rejecting Greek tradition as authoritative, the Reformers broke with the Greek deification of nature and opened the way for free inquiry without suspicion of impiety or magic. Conceptions of the earth as a goddess, or of nature as feminine, were rejected as idolatry.

Of course, these two conceptions of the world, one Greek and the other biblical, coexisted in the seventeenth century. Greek ideas persisted in the image of nature, if not as a goddess, then at least as feminine. Comparisons of the scientist-nature relationship with that between a suitor and his mistress were common. Experiment and scientific inquiry demanded a "masculine philosophy," as Robert Boyle's publisher put it in his promotional material.[50] Far from the biblical understanding of dominion, this Greek conception entailed aggressive, even violent imagery of assault on Mistress Nature. As Thomas Sprat wrote in 1667:

> The Beautiful Bosom of Nature will be Expos'd to our view . . . we shall enter into its Garden, and taste of its Fruits, and satisfy our selves with its plenty.[51]

By the eighteenth century the language of the Enlightenment philosophers was "redolent with metaphors of battle and the physical act of penetration."[52] "The earth is the Lord's" becomes "the world is man's and she is ours to do with as we please." Domination replaced dominion.

By contrast, Calvin understood God as the Creator, entrusting his world to human beings, constantly taking an interest in it and sustaining it as a sign of his loving care. In complete dependence on the sovereign Lord, we join with all creation in rejoicing in God's gift and faithfulness. But these "feminine" qualities of love, care and gratitude were banished from the "masculine philosophy" of observation and experiment.

2. *Dominion not domination*. Human beings, however, are not only to learn about the inexhaustible wonders of creation and thus glorify God; we also have the mandate that, as the image of God, we should exercise dominion over creation. This is quite different from the precarious and brittle attempts to control nature characteristic of the Greek worldview. The development of technology received a religious sanction: human beings should exercise responsible dominion over the world in love and service of one another. This insight was a feature of the Reformation but was only partially realized. The seventeenth century saw a return to Greek forms of the domination of a feminized nature by a male science. But however short-lived, it did result in a new respect toward the natural world as God's creation to be valued and cared for. This is reflected, for example, in the Puritan-inspired legislation of the mid-seventeenth century, which sought to reduce animal cruelty, which I will discuss in more detail in chapter three.

3. *Reason set free*. It is often said that the Greek concept of "reason," sup-

posedly bequeathed to the seventeenth century by the Renaissance, was the central feature in the growth of science. This assumption is characteristic of the arrogance that has afflicted the West since the Enlightenment, and which postmodern thinkers reject. There was, in fact, no shortage of reason prior to the seventeenth century; nor was the medieval world irrational. In a sense, the problem was one of too much reason, rather than too little. Greek thought emphasized that the structure of the universe could be deduced. As we have seen, the supposedly circular orbits of the heavenly bodies are dictated by a reason to which physical reality must, of necessity, conform. This Greek overvaluation of reason in relation to observation had a straitjacketing effect on scientific inquiry. Greek thought, by placing reason on the throne, distorted rationality itself and represented a narrowing of truth to what could be deduced. In his treatise of 1632 Galileo's hero constantly offers *observations* in reply to Simplicio's Aristotelian *reasons*.

The Reformation gave reason its correct place in the world as dependent upon God rather than as a preexistent form that constrained God's creative activity. In doing so, it set reason free and encouraged scientists to look at what God had made in order to explore and discover his creation. Central to this new freedom was a conception of the world (including reason) as dependent on its sovereign Creator, who faithfully sustains it as a sign of his love. Calvin regarded creation as a "mirror in which we ought to behold God,"[53] and which should evoke our wonder and awe.[54] Indeed, in *The Starry Messenger*, Galileo described just this sense of "wondering delight" as he looked at the heavens through his telescope.[55]

4. *Covenant law.* By giving reason its place within creation, the Reformers also facilitated a vital distinction between rationality and law. It is now widely acknowledged that an understanding of the universe as coherent and governed by laws was a major factor in the growth of seventeenth-century science.[56] Without such an understanding there would simply not be any sense in seeking lawful regularities. The Reformers provided just such a framework by emphasizing the biblical doctrines of God's covenantal dealing with his creation, and his providential governance of the world as a sign of his loving care. Thus, although the order of the world cannot be deduced by an overarching reason, it is nevertheless open to discovery. This was widely recognized by the astronomers of the period. For example, Tycho Brahe spoke of "the wondrous and perpetual laws of the celestial motions, so diverse and yet so harmonious, [which] prove the existence of

God."[57] This reliance on God's providential ordering of the world characterized the flourishing of science and justified reasoning about the world based on observation. "The fact is that Newton was convinced from the beginning that the universe is an ordered cosmos because he knew as a Christian that God had created it."[58] By the eighteenth century these insights had been greatly watered down, and "scientific" reason became autonomous, once again distorting the richness of creation as a single form of reason returned to the throne.

For Newton, "experiment" discovered God's actions in the world. The historian of science Reijer Hooykaas has concluded that "most scientists of the 19th and 20th centuries . . . have been unconscious of the fact that the metaphysical foundations of their discipline stemmed, in spite of all secularisation, in great part from the biblical concept of God and creation."[59]

Progress and Atlas

The Galileo story was developed by French Enlightenment thinkers as part of their anticlerical program, but by the late nineteenth century it had created a language of warfare between science and religion. Science carries the shield of tolerance and enlightenment with which to defend democracy against the invasion of religious superstition. Religion, on the other hand, fights a rearguard battle, sniping irrationally at new discoveries and cruelly oppressing the scientists whenever it gets the opportunity. This language survives in, for example, Richard Dawkins's remark that "scientific beliefs are supported by evidence and they get results. Myths and faith are not and do not."[60]

By polarizing science and religion, the Galileo story hollows out its discussion of both. Religion is reduced to ignorance and dogma, while science is torn from its historical context. Meanwhile, the ideology of progress slips in unobserved, and man, ostensibly disabused of his pretensions by science, in fact becomes the very Atlas upholding the cosmos.

The naive optimism that "science gets results" overlooks the kind of results it gets and whether they have always been those intended. Despite its obvious achievements, science is widely perceived as having failed to live up to its promises and, in many areas, to have made matters worse. From the destruction of the ozone layer to the pollution of the Aral Sea, from radioactive contamination to the greenhouse effect, science is increasingly seen as part of the problem rather than the solution. Techniques once hailed as the "white heat of technology" are now as likely to be greeted with skepticism or even, as with some genetically modified organisms, rejected. Many now raise serious questions about the possibility of any science achieving a desired end without unintended consequences and risk, and other stories are emerging to challenge that of modernity. I will discuss this changing role of modern myths in the conclusion. In the next chapter we will look at the other big story of modernity: Darwin and evolution.

2

DARWIN
A Story of Origins

THE STORY OF CHARLES DARWIN AND HIS DISCOVERY OF EVOLUTION has become as much a part of our culture as was the narrative of Adam and Eve three hundred years ago. It is "common knowledge" that all living things have evolved over millions of years, and that when this was discovered by the man who published *The Origin of Species* in 1859, his generation experienced "the immense thrill of Enlightenment."[1] As a result, we now know that we are no more the summit of the animal kingdom than we are the center of the solar system, since we share a long, continuous history with all the other creatures on this planet.

This familiar story is endlessly repeated in books, on television and even in the Hollywood film *Inherit the Wind*. Together with the story of Galileo, that of Darwin has cultural force, and it marks the turning point in human affairs when science dispelled the superstitions of religion to usher in the modern world. It has become more than a scientific theory: "Evolutionary theory is now one of the main myths of our time. It has to bear the weight of most of our hopes and fears about what being human really means."[2] Mary Midgley has discussed this religious aspect and refers to evolutionism as the "creation-myth of our age." "By telling us our origins it shapes our views of what we are."[3]

The twentieth century tasted the fruit of this myth and found it bitter. Nevertheless, it remains influential, and many neo-Darwinists fervently believe it. Indeed for some, Darwinism excels over the achievements of the eighteenth-century Enlightenment. With breathtaking arrogance, Richard

Dawkins makes it the very index of our progress as a species: "If superior creatures from space ever visit the earth, the first question they will ask, in order to assess the level of our civilisation, is: 'Have they discovered evolution yet?' "[4] So much for Leonardo da Vinci, William Shakespeare and Isaac Newton, all of whom pre-dated Darwin.

So what is the received version of the orthodox story of Darwinism?

Darwin: The Received Version

The mechanism of evolution is well known: change takes place by means of random mutation and natural selection. It is, in fact, a very simple idea. A random variation arises in an organism. If it is advantageous to survival, it is more likely to be passed on to the next generation. Over time, by the accumulation of small changes, new species emerge. Life on earth has a naturalistic explanation.

In fact, it is so simple an idea that T. H. Huxley mused that it had been extremely stupid of him not to have thought of it himself. But if Huxley had not thought of it, many others had. Aristotle, for example, wrote in the fourth century B.C.:

> In cases where coincidence brought about such a combination as might have been arranged on purpose, the creatures . . . having been suitably formed by the operation of chance, survived; otherwise they perished and still perish.[5]

Yet if the thesis was ancient, it was also disreputable. Aristotle had considered evolutionary possibilities, only to reject them as implausible. In the mid-nineteenth century most naturalists had done the same.

The peppered moth. Since Darwin's day, his simple idea has become increasingly technical and complex.[6] Fortunately there is a graphic example of "evolution in the wild" that is easily explained and familiar to most schoolchildren: the peppered moth.

> [It] rests on tree trunks by day. Its dappled wings are camouflaged against lichens growing on the trunks, and this protects the moth from insect-eating birds. Pollution kills off lichens, and as industry grew, the tree trunks turned black with soot from factory smokestacks. Dark versions of the peppered moth arose by mutation and were better camouflaged than the original form. Gradually the dark forms became more and more common.[7]

Lighter forms returned in the 1970s, when pollution decreased and the lichens recovered.

The peppered moth provides "evidence of the most striking evolutionary change in nature ever to be witnessed by Man."[8] The "typical assumption from the 'classical' perspective" is that darker forms have arisen "from 'spontaneous mutations' " followed by natural selection.[9] However, it has long been known that no new mutation is, in fact, involved. The point is well made by Richard Dawkins:

> It is often wrongly thought that after the Industrial Revolution natural selection worked on a single brand-new mutation [of the peppered moth]. On the contrary, we can be sure that there have always been dark individuals—they just haven't lasted very long [because they showed up on light-coloured trees and were eaten by birds]. . . . When conditions changed after the Industrial Revolution, natural selection found a ready-made minority of dark genes in the gene pool to work upon.[10]

The peppered moth, argues Dawkins, therefore provides evidence for natural selection rather than evolution. Unfortunately, this is not true either. Recent research has shown that whatever the origin of the color changes, it is not due to natural selection of the better-camouflaged dark individuals on sooty trees. In fact, we now know that the peppered moth does not even rest on tree trunks at all, sooty or otherwise, and the textbook photographs showing them doing so have been staged for the benefit of the orthodox story, sometimes by simply gluing the moths in place.[11]

The simple, graphic and false image of the peppered moth is the "touchstone" example of evolution "in the wild," and it illustrates the orthodox story's distortions of science for its own ends.[12] It also introduces the backdrop for evolution's emergence as a "creation-myth": the growth of modern industrial society. The tale of the peppered moth is part of the great nineteenth-century saga of industry and exploitation, of progress and grime, of fortunes made, and of grinding poverty. It links evolution with both industrial achievement (represented by the factory smokestacks) and its environmental consequences (the soot-blackened trees). It gives us a striking image of both evolution and the modern industrial world, with its benefits and its pollution. It even hints that the story could have a happy ending as new forms of life emerge and science controls pollution. We will be looking further at this industrial backdrop for evolution, but first we must turn to Darwin's own version of the tale.

Images and metaphors. Darwin's writing is particularly rich in metaphor. "Natural selection" itself is introduced by analogy with "artificial selection" in the breeding of pigeons. The evolutionary interconnections between organisms are pictured as "the great Tree of Life, which fills with its dead and broken branches the crust of the earth [i.e., fossils], and covers the surface with its ever branching and beautiful ramifications." Similarly Darwin inferred *"from analogy* that probably all . . . organic beings have descended from some one primordial form, into which life was first breathed."[13] Presumably the latter phrase is also a figure of speech.

Metaphors of evolution such as the peppered moth still have a prominent place in telling the orthodox story. Moreover, evolution as metaphor, as Midgley points out, has proved to be a powerful "creation-myth" and encapsulates many of the themes of modernity. Some biologists argue that evolution is a scientific theory and should not be confused with these wider issues. Whether it should or not, it is. And it is this wider story, rather than evolution as a putative science,[14] which I shall be discussing.

A Ship, a Journey and Some Finches

The story usually starts with Darwin's journey aboard *The Beagle* and his visit to the Galapagos Islands. Darwin noticed that the finches on each island were adapted to the differing environments; some had long, thin beaks to extract grubs from trees, while the beaks of others were short and stout to crush nut shells. And so, the story goes, he realized that his observations betrayed a history. Millions of years ago, when the islands were formed by underwater volcanoes, a few finches were blown there from the South American mainland. These finches evolved separately on the relatively isolated islands, each adapting to the particular food supply available. Thus we see the variety of beaks, each for its specialized task.

On returning home Darwin took the evolutionary ideas then in circulation and adapted them to form a metaphor for biological change. However, the orthodox version of this story explains that, like Galileo, Darwin delayed publishing his discoveries for fear of religious opposition. It is said that many years later when he wrote *Origin of Species*, he was greeted with "dismay and outrage," with "violent and malicious criticism"[15] from the church. In this also, he experienced the fate of Galileo:

> Darwin's theory caused a violent controversy—every whit as violent . . . as that which had greeted Copernicus' theory that the earth moves round the sun. . . . Churchmen were strongly opposed to it, mainly because it was tacitly assumed that, according to Darwin, men were descended from apes. . . . In 1925 Thomas Scropes [sic] was brought to trial in the state of Tennessee for [teaching] Darwinism.[16]

According to Isaac Asimov, this "controversy" illustrates "the strength with which human beings can turn away from facts and cling to superstition."[17]

If churchmen opposed Darwin, however, the orthodox story tells us that scientists, who relied more on evidence than faith, supported him:

> People were indeed outraged. Darwin was denying the truth of the Bible! . . . Former colleagues . . . turned against him. . . . But others rapidly recognised the good science in Darwin's ideas, and the vast amount of evidence which supported them.[18]

The story is familiar. The scientists and facts are on one side, while the church and superstition are on the other. Scientists gave Darwin an enthusiastic reception; the church offered "violent and malicious criticism." It seems like a case of rounding up the usual suspects.

The Darwin story has many parallels with the story of Galileo. We again have a hero and a villain, and a plot that sets one against the other. The actors, of course, have changed; Darwin has replaced Copernicus as the author of a new revolution. And yet the parallels between them are striking. For example, just as the story of the Copernican Revolution has little to say about Copernicus, so that of evolution relies surprisingly little on Darwin at its moments of dramatic confrontation. For, like Copernicus, Darwin would do little to advance the plot. A gentle, retiring man, not given to public dispute, and a "muddled theist," he does not cut the figure needed.[19] Therefore, just as Galileo replaced Copernicus at the dramatic moments of the Copernican Revolution, so Darwin is replaced in England by his "bulldog," T. H. Huxley, a popularizer and public debater, and in the United States by the persecuted schoolteacher John Scopes and his eloquent defense attorney, Clarence Darrow.

The plots also have parallels. Science, of course, is opposed by religion. Just as Galileo's discoveries "put man in his place in the cosmos," so "Darwin's concept . . . put him in his place on earth."[20] Both subverted Christian theology by undermining the belief that the universe revolves around us. Galileo and Darwin have led us far from the idea of "the blessed children of God, at the centre of the universe, walking among creatures created for our benefit."[21] The cosmos is a bigger place than the church imagined and reserves no special place for humanity.

As we have seen, the idea that the Copernican Revolution demoted the earth is a misunderstanding of seventeenth-century thought. It is equally misleading to suppose that Darwinism demoted man on earth, for just as Galileo elevated the status of the earth to that of a heavenly body, so Darwinism placed man at the very peak of nature. For Darwin, evolution "ennobled" man, whose "corporeal and mental endowments will tend to progress towards perfection."[22] As the astronomer Sir Fred Hoyle has noted, the very idea of the evolution of life on earth presupposes that the earth is the center of things and neglects its interaction with the universe as a whole.[23]

A Mixed Reception

A legendary showdown. All good stories have a pivotal moment of drama. For the Galileo story, it is the trial. In the case of evolution, we have two: in Britain, it is the celebrated showdown between T. H. Huxley (for the Darwinians) and Bishop "Soapy Sam" Wilberforce (for the church); in the United States, it is another trial—that of the teacher John Scopes.

The tale is told that at a meeting in 1860 of the British Association for the Advancement of Science (BAAS) Bishop Wilberforce insulted T. H. Huxley by referring to his ancestors as apes. Huxley is said to have delivered a crushing reply that demolished his opponent.

> [The bitterness of controversy] between science and religion [was illustrated by Bishop Wilberforce's attempt to ridicule Darwin at the British Association meeting in June 1860]. The zealous bishop had not himself troubled to read Darwin's *Origin of Species*, but he had been coached in his part by Sir Richard Owen. [But Huxley made a crushing reply.] Thus, the bishop was put in his place . . . the final consensus of opinion was overwhelmingly on the side of science and the great conception of evolution. . . . However, Darwin was for a long time denounced from the pulpits of almost every church in the land and met with religious hostility to the end of his days.[24]

> Wilberforce was annihilated by Huxley and Hooker, and Darwin's views on evolution started their conquest of the world.[25]

These accounts give the impression that Wilberforce was an ill-informed cleric, ignorant of Darwin's work, who had come to a scientific meeting in order to ridicule Huxley. Perhaps a good theologian, but no scientist.

In fact, Wilberforce was the vice president of the BAAS. Moreover, he was no cloistered cleric, better read in Hebrew than algebra. He was conversant with current science, especially geology and ornithology, and had a first-class degree in mathematics. Far from being "ignorant," having not "troubled to read" Darwin, he had already prepared a review of *Origin of Species*, which Darwin later admitted (in a letter to J. D. Hooker, July 1860) "picks out with skill all the most conjectural parts, and brings forward well all the difficulties."[26] Nor do contemporary accounts of the meeting agree with the received version. In a letter to Huxley dated July 20, 1860, Darwin wrote that the Oxford meeting had done good by "showing the world that a few first-rate men are not afraid of expressing their opinion."[27] This rather shameless flattery of Huxley makes no claim that he carried the day. The historian John Lucas has reviewed the evidence and concluded that the encounter is "legendary."[28]

The Dayton "monkey trial." The dramatic moment of the Darwin story in England was the Oxford debate, but in the United States it was, as in the Galileo story, a trial. In 1925, John Scopes was prosecuted for teaching evolutionary ideas at Dayton High School in Tennessee. William Jennings Bryan prosecuted at the trial, and Clarence Darrow defended Scopes. The trial was widely reported at the time and was dramatized in a long-running Broadway play. The legend grew and reached its peak in 1960 with the release of the well-known film *Inherit the Wind*; it now epitomizes the popular American perception of "religion versus evolution."

According to the legend, John Scopes was an "innocent victim of a mob-enforced anti-evolution law," dragged from his classroom for teaching about Darwin. He was put in jail to await trial and faced a fine and imprisonment.[29] In the Broadway play the representative of the church, the Reverend Brown, prays a "frenzied prayer" that the innocent schoolteacher will "writhe in anguish and damnation" for all eternity. However, the main action is between the two lawyers, Bryan and Darrow. Bryan, prosecuting the poor schoolteacher, is portrayed as "a mindless, reactionary creature of the mob," a bigot who quotes the Bible and rejects all science as "Godless." He dogmatically asserts that "the Lord began the Creation on the 23rd of October in the year 4004 B.C. at—uh 9 a.m." Darrow mocks him by retorting, "That eastern standard time?"[30]

By contrast Darrow, defending Darwinian evolution, is portrayed as an incarnation of liberal moderation and good sense. In the play we hear him say, "All I want is to prevent the clock-stoppers from dumping a load of medieval nonsense into the United States Constitution." He is demonized by the Reverend Brown, who says of him, "God didn't make him. . . . He is a creature of the devil, perhaps even the devil himself!"[31]

The facts are rather different. It all started when the American Civil Liberties Union offered to support a volunteer willing to test the law against teaching evolution. In Dayton, the usual biology teacher was absent due to illness, and John Scopes, who normally taught math and football, volunteered. He was not dragged from his classroom by the town fathers, nor did he face jail.

Moreover, Bryan was not the illiberal bigot of legend. He certainly believed that Darwin's theory found little support in Scripture,[32] but the recent authoritative study of the trial by Edward Larson argues that it was "broad social concerns" which largely motivated Bryan "rather than the theological attempts to date creation."[33] These social concerns are rarely mentioned in the orthodox account.

Bryan was a convinced democrat favoring progressive federal taxation and female suffrage. He did not discount evolution in the nonhuman creation,[34] but he regarded it as a "merciless law" by which the strong "kill off the weak."[35] Prophetically as it turned out, he feared the consequences of social Darwinism. He argued against Darwin's conclusion that women are the evolutionary inferiors of men, and he rejected eugenic policies.[36] A leader of the Democratic Party and three times a presidential nominee, he served as secretary of state and tried to negotiate an international treaty to avoid war by requiring the arbitration of international disputes. It is scarcely surprising that so politically aware a man should be alert to the social implications of Darwin's views. What then were these "broad social concerns"?

The book from which Scopes taught was an approved school text called *A Civic Biology* by George Hunter. The story tells us that Scopes read his class chapter seventeen of Hunter's book, which is said to be about Darwin and the *Origin of Species*. However, chapter seventeen is actually titled "Heredity, Variation, Plant and Animal Breeding" and, as befits a book of civic biology, is mainly about practical applications to farming. Indeed, the modern reader is surprised at how little this book has to say about Darwin. It certainly regards him as a "great name in biology" and attributes to him the discovery of evolution, but it focuses most on Darwinism's social implications. In particular, chapter seventeen discusses the application to human society of "the laws of selection" and approves the eugenic policies and scientific racism common in the United States at the time.[37] Hunter believed that it would be criminal to hand down "handicaps" to the next generation and regarded families with a history of tuberculosis, epilepsy and feeble-mindedness as "parasitic on society." The remedy, according to Hunter, is to prevent breeding:

> If such people were lower animals, we would probably kill them off to prevent them from spreading. Humanity will not allow this, but we do have the remedy of separating the sexes in asylums or other places and in various ways preventing intermarriage and the possibilities of perpetuating such a low and degenerate race.[38]

In common with many at the time, Hunter believed that the most evolved of the "races of man" is that of "the civilized white inhabitants of Europe and America," which is "the highest type of all."[39] If, as the story claims, Scopes was teaching his school pupils from chapter seventeen of Hunter's book, we might have some sympathy with the people of Dayton for wanting to stop him. Indeed, in his prepared closing argument Bryan expressly denounced eugenic ideas. As Larson makes clear, he was not alone among Christians of the time in arguing against the growing eugenic movement.[40] Bryan did not, however, seek to make an example of Scopes. Far from ranting against the smallness of the fine, he opposed any fine at all. Once again we see that the orthodox story of Darwin has tailored history to suit itself.

A Storm of Religious Protest

So how was Darwin's theory received by his contemporaries, whether churchmen or scientists? The received version of the story has scientists and churchmen in bitter conflict. But many leading scientists were Christians, and many of the clergy were keen amateur naturalists. Given this overlapping of interests, it is not surprising to find that Darwin's reception among churchmen was mixed. We can identify four different types of response.

1. Many rejected Darwin's views outright and did so for reasons ranging from a perceived incompatibility with the early chapters of Genesis to the scientific weakness of his case. Bishop Wilberforce was among these for, as Darwin admits, good reasons. The leading theologian Charles Hodge also rejected Darwin's metaphor, but as we might anticipate, his objection was theologically based. He rejected Darwin's understanding of purpose, not evolution as such.

2. Many nineteenth-century Christians accepted evolution, but the "official" story reports that they were forced to abandon their faith as a result:

"when Darwin's theory of evolution was made known, honest-minded Christians saw themselves faced with a choice between intellectual integrity and religious belief."[41] Darwin, we are told, completed the devastation of religion that Galileo had started. "If the stars and tides moved without divine intervention, thinking people began to find it more difficult to hope for such intervention in their own affairs. But there was some consolation," for man is the summit of living beings and "must reflect God's intention." Darwin's theory devastated even this pious hope.[42]

This "crisis of faith" subplot lacks evidence, however. Many Christians accepted evolutionary views without feeling that they conflicted with their faith, including the Harvard professor Asa Gray, a Congregationalist, who corresponded with Darwin on theological issues, and the epitome of evangelical orthodoxy, B. B. Warfield, an evolutionist (though not a Darwinian) most of his life. Nothing suggests that either lacked "intellectual integrity." In fact, there is evidence that representatives of evangelical orthodoxy were associated with least resistance to Darwin, not most,[43] and that far from being opposed to the religious ideas of his time, Darwin's theory actually relied on them.[44] The historian Owen Chadwick observes: " *'Darwin has disproved the Bible'*—as a historical statement, nothing could be more legendary."[45]

3. Some Christians responded by synthesizing evolution and Christianity: Henry Drummond, Charles Kingsley, H. G. Baden-Powell and Rudyard Kipling all produced amalgams of Darwinism and religion, often with a strong national church flavor. Pierre Teilhard de Chardin, president of the Geological Society of France, carried his synthesis in a more mystical direction. Such amalgams have generally been rejected in recent decades as distortions of both biology and theology.

4. Finally, many churchmen simply suspended judgment, finding the evolutionary metaphor speculative and ill-supported by facts. The Baptist preacher Charles Spurgeon appears to have taken this view and was unwilling to comment without further evidence. Interestingly, this response was shared by many in the established sciences, whether Christians or not.

Evolution and Scientists

If Darwin's ideas had a mixed reception by the church, the orthodox story is clear that they were "received with enthusiasm by most of Darwin's [scientific] colleagues."[46] A parallel is often drawn with Galileo:

For many years, Darwin was reluctant to publish his ideas on evolution by natural selection. It meant that animals and plants evolved naturally. He now believed that God had not created them. . . . Like the Italian scientist Galileo two centuries before, Darwin knew that speaking out against the accepted teachings of the Bible was certain to offend and cause a storm of protest.[47]

There is, indeed, a parallel here. For, as with Galileo, Darwin was not propounding a new, cutting-edge thesis but one that was at least as old as Aristotle. He knew that "the mutability of species" had already been rejected by "all the most eminent living naturalists and geologists."[48]

I am a bold man to lay myself open to being thought a complete fool. . . . Pray do not think that I am so blind as not to see that there are numerous immense difficulties in my notions, but they appear to me less than on the common view.[49]

Like Galileo, Darwin lacked evidence. And like Galileo, he delayed making public his ideas for many years. But if, as the orthodox story suggests, the reason was fear, it was the fear of ridicule from his fellow scientists, not of the church. Darwin was especially sensitive about the fossil record, as it simply did not contain the many intermediate forms that his theory required. For this reason, chapter nine of the 1859 edition of *The Origin of Species* is titled "On the Imperfection of the Geological Record" and is concerned to explain why this is so. The orthodox story either glosses over this or tells how the situation was reversed a few years later with the discovery of *Archaeopteryx*, a fossil intermediate between bird and reptile. The distinguished palaeontologist Niles Eldredge is disparaging of this one example where there ought to be many, and he calls chapter nine of *The Origin of Species*

one long *ad hoc*, special pleading argument designed to rationalise, to flat-out explain away, the differences between what he saw as logical predictions derived from his theory and the facts of the fossil record.[50]

It is not difficult to see why Darwin might have been nervous about the reception of his book among his colleagues.

In Darwin's day "natural history" (now mainly called "biology") had a very different status from "natural philosophy" (now called "physics"). Natural history had traditionally been pursued by clergymen amateurs, but physics was an exact science, requiring a rigorous training. As a result, physicists held natural history in low regard, feeling that anyone can collect fossils, but it needs a certain intellectual discipline to grasp Newtonian cosmology.

Darwin's "bulldog," T. H. Huxley, was keen to change the low status of natural history among scientists, but he had some problems. He was unable to do much about its lack of an independent method or the paucity of systematic evidence. Yet he was determined to establish a theory and to professionalize his discipline by excluding the clergymen amateurs. He saw his opportunity in Darwin. Evolution by natural selection was the next best thing to a theory yet produced and could easily be given an anticlerical spin. Moreover, it promised the final victory of science over religion, the solution to the perennial question of origins, and the establishment of progress as a law of nature rather than a pious Enlightenment hope. If he played his cards right, he might be able both to achieve scientific status and to poach from the church some of the social prestige endowed by the discussion of eternal verities. Although he failed to persuade the established sciences of evolution's merits as a rigorous discipline, he did succeed in promoting the myth of a warfare between science and religion, which has deeply influenced the debate in England ever since.

A Wave of Scientific Enthusiasm

We can try to assess Darwin's reception among scientists in several ways. First, we might look at scientists themselves.

1. *Contemporary scientists.* Many contemporary reviewers attacked Darwin's scientific method as merely descriptive, not amounting to a theory. Consequently, it could have no explanatory power, and many leaders of nineteenth-century science remained skeptical about its scientific merits. Physicists, the most prestigious scientists of the day, were especially reserved, and most simply ignored it. Lord Kelvin made one of the first attempts to test evolutionary theory using the established methods of physical science to estimate the age of the earth. He calculated that it was much younger than Darwin's theory required. Darwin was deeply troubled by this verdict and, ignorant of physics himself, asked George's (his mathematician son) opinion. George Darwin confirmed that by the standards of the day Kelvin was correct.[51]

The response was scarcely more favorable from leading representatives of the less precise sciences. Darwin had few allies in embryology, anatomy or paleontology. Rudolph von Kölliker and Karl von Baer, two of the founders of modern embryology, rejected Darwinism as speculative. Richard Owen, the chief anatomist of his day, and Louis Agassiz, the foremost naturalist of nineteenth-century America, both rejected Darwin's views. Adam Sedgwick, a pioneer of modern geology, "laughed until his sides ached" when reading parts of *The Origin*.[52] Poor Darwin! His nightmare of being ridiculed by his colleagues had come true.

The evidence of contemporary reviews is that Darwin had, at best, a patchy reception among fellow naturalists, and the majority of English biologists rejected the adequacy of natural selection as a mechanism for change for many years.[53] Darwin was not oblivious to his lukewarm reception, and in subsequent publications he changed his position to take account of his critics. By 1871 George Mivart could write that Darwin's latest version of the theory was virtually "an abandonment of 'natural selection.' "[54]

It is often assumed that Darwin's acceptance among scientists, if not always "rapid," was at least progressive. This is not so. Interest in the Darwinian metaphor has waxed and waned, reaching a peak in the 1880s and then declining in the late nineteenth and early twentieth centuries. Many of the early Mendelian geneticists opposed Darwinian gradualism, and it was not until the 1930s that Ronald Fisher and J. B. S. Haldane showed mathematically how the difficulties might be overcome.[55] But even then its acceptance was not unequivocal. In 1940 the distinguished geneticist Richard Goldschmidt suggested that evolution occurs by sudden leaps, because he doubted the evidence for orthodox Darwinian gradualism. As late as 1948 we find Bertrand Russell arguing for a similar view of large-scale, sudden changes, citing the power of x-rays to alter genes.

In recent decades, criticism of neo-Darwinism has again grown. Distinguished paleontologists have concluded that Darwin's optimism about the fossil record was misplaced. Darwin believed that further research would eventually uncover the host of intermediate forms required by his gradualist theory, but he was wrong. As Niles Eldredge pointedly observes: "No wonder paleontologists shied away from evolution for so long. It never seems to happen."[56]

> [The] certainty so characteristic of evolutionary ranks since the late 1940s, the utter assurance . . . that we know precisely how [natural selection] works, has led palaeontologists to keep their own counsel. . . . We palaeontologists have said that the history of life [in the fossil record] supports [the story of gradual adaptive change] . . . all the while really knowing that it does not.[57]

To those of us brought up on the official line that paleontology provides "one of the most important" pieces of evidence for evolution,[58] it will come as news that paleontologists have ever had any doubts at all, let alone that they "shied away" from it.

As contemporary biochemistry provides ever-deeper insights into the sheer complexity of biological mechanisms, it also has uncovered unexpected difficulties for neo-Darwinian explanations. Michael Behe has argued that the difficulties become greater the more we understand at the molecular level and that "irreducibly complex" systems are inherently resistant to neo-Darwinian change.[59] Stuart Kauffman says bluntly that neo-Darwinism is "wrong."[60] The molecular biologist Michael Denton judges that it is without factual support:

> The overriding supremacy of the myth [that evolution is as certain as that the earth revolves around the sun] has created a widespread illusion that the theory of evolution was all but proved one hundred years ago and that all subsequent biological research . . . has provided ever-increasing evidence for Darwinian ideas. Nothing could be further from the truth. . . . His general theory, that all life on earth had originated and evolved . . . is still, as it was in Darwin's time, a highly speculative hypothesis entirely without direct factual support and very far from that self-evident axiom some of its more aggressive advocates would have us believe.[61]

Regardless of whether or not we agree with Denton, it is remarkable that a molecular biologist can write in this way about the major paradigm that is said to govern his discipline. No reputable physicist could write like this about any comparable nineteenth-century physical theory.

As in the nineteenth century, the most skeptical scientists are still mathematicians and physicists. The best-known representative of this camp is the mathematician and astronomer Sir Fred Hoyle, who has repeatedly argued that life could not have evolved within the current geological time scale, concluding that "the claim that Darwinian evolution alone could account for the vast elaboration of species . . . is not well founded." He calculates that the probability of biological systems evolving according to a neo-Darwinian model is "insensibly different from zero," making Darwinian evolution "an uneasy combination of dogma and wishful thinking."[62]

It is, perhaps, not surprising that representatives of the more exact and experimentally secure sciences are most skeptical about neo-Darwinian orthodoxy, for different standards of evidence apply in each discipline. Nevertheless, the continuing skepticism runs contrary to the orthodox story that Darwin's views have been rapidly and universally accepted among scientists.[63]

2. *Learned bodies.* A way to assess Darwin's impact on fellow scientists is through his reception at learned societies, and here we find that Darwin's views fell largely on deaf ears. By 1869 there had been relatively few publications about *Origin of Species*, and learned societies generally avoided discussing what they regarded as a speculative theory. In fact, the book was not reviewed at a single meeting of a major London society in the first ten years following its publication. The immediate and enthusiastic reception of the orthodox story did not exist.

3. *Scientific awards.* Darwin's reception can also be assessed by the scientific honors he was awarded. Here the picture changes, for Darwin was honored throughout Europe and was elected to many learned societies. But scholars have found that in nearly every case the citation giving the reason for Darwin's election made "some attempt . . . to dissociate Darwin from his theory of evolution, especially the doctrine of natural selection." "Darwin was being honored for his solid work on barnacles or earthworms, not his speculations on the origin of species."[64]

The above discussion aims only to show that the story of Darwinism's immediate and widespread acceptance among scientists cannot be sustained. Indeed, the most prestigious scientists were among the most resistant, for reasons ranging from doubts about its scientific merits to concern over its social consequences. Moreover, general evolutionary ideas were in circulation long before Darwin wrote; these ideas were gaining acceptance among a younger generation of naturalists as the nineteenth century progressed. Indeed, Darwin drew from precisely these ideas and gave them new meanings in the *Origin of Species*. But the orthodox story tells us not of the growing prominence of a variety of competing evolutionary narratives but that scientists "rapidly recognised the good science in Darwin's ideas"[65] and universally embraced evolution by natural selection. In this the orthodox story is mistaken. It is widely accepted among scholars that Darwin's views were, as the biologist Julian Huxley put it, "eclipsed" in the 1900s by other evolutionary notions.[66] In his recent impressive study *Darwinism's Struggle for Survival,* the philosopher Jean Gayon notes that "it was only in the 1920s that the hypothesis of natural selection, as formulated by Darwin, took on even a semblance of validity." He estimates that following the publication of the *Origin of Species* in 1859, "between seventy and eighty years were to pass before the principle [of natural selection] was established as both an empirical reality and a theoretical possibility."[67]

We have, then, a very mixed picture of Darwin's reception, with scientists and churchman on both sides of the debate.

A *"new deity"?* Before leaving this aspect of the Darwin story, it is worth noting that some among Darwin's staunchest supporters were far from being the materialistic rationalists they are sometimes painted. Even those who were not Christians used religious language to tell their story. For example, T. H. Huxley personalized "nature," referring to it as "fair, just and patient," "a strong angel who is playing for love."[68] If this language, like his preaching "lay sermons" of the "church scientific," was partly rhetoric to poach the clothes (and status) of the church, it nevertheless relies on a religious vocabulary for its force. Others of Darwin's circle had clear pantheist leanings. John Tyndall pictured nature as "the universal mother who brings forth all things as the fruit of her own womb," as it was "utterly unimaginable" that "any form of life whatever" could emerge within a purely material universe.[69] J. B. S. Haldane, whose work contributed to the revival of Darwin's fortunes in the twentieth century, shared Tyndall's rejection of an inert universe.[70] As late as 1953 Julian Huxley conceded that his beliefs are "something in the nature of a religion."[71] The distinguished biologist Lynn Margulis has rather scathingly referred to neo-Darwinism as "a minor twentieth century religious sect within the sprawling religious persuasion of Anglo-Saxon biology."[72] Stuart Kauffman observes that "natural selection" has become so central an explanatory force in neo-Darwinism that "we might as well capitalise [it] as though it were the new deity."[73]

The Evolution of Natural Selection

All attempts to answer [the question "What is man?"] before 1859 are worthless and . . . we will be better off if we ignore them completely. (G. G. Simpson)[74]

Despite scientific skepticism about evolution, Darwin was a well-known figure in the late nineteenth century, and his fullest coverage was in the popular press.[75] He was widely discussed among lay people and had an early influence on the social sciences—especially anthropology. For Darwin was widely seen as raising questions about the nature of "man," and to see why his answer proved so popular, we need to return to Darwin's evolutionary metaphor in its social context.[76]

Stories of change. Karl Marx was among the first to note that the evolutionary metaphor was a case of seeing in the natural world Darwin's own

English society "with its division of labour, competition . . . and Malthusian 'struggle for existence.' "[77] This struggle was painfully familiar in mid-nineteenth-century England with its expanding industries and overcrowded cities. Richard Lewontin observes that the survival of the fittest was part of Darwin's everyday life as he checked the progress of his stocks and shares over his breakfast tea.[78] But it is not only "the struggle for existence" that finds an echo in Darwin's English society. We also find parallels to his idea that one species *gradually and continuously* transforms into another. Eminent paleontologists argue that this too is a projection into biology from the social world, but this time a projection of "the order, harmony and continuity of European rulers" in a time of threatened social change.[79] The prized continuity of gradual political change becomes the prize "discovery" of gradualism and continuity in evolutionary change. What are we to make of these comparisons?

It is true that nineteenth-century England was ripe for a new story of change. The metaphor of evolution, which undermined the idea of stasis in nature, was very agreeable to the rising middle class, which was questioning fixity of social stations. Yet Darwin was popular not only among the new rich. Evolution was also well received by liberals and radicals because it offered a scientific foundation for ideas of progress and political change. As Richard Dawkins has noted, the evolutionary metaphor has "superabundant power to explain,"[80] and this great flexibility has enabled ingenious people to apply it in the most unlikely contexts.

There are, however, limits. Some social contexts proved uncongenial for its survival and accordingly less receptive to Darwin's ideas. For example, they found a much less fertile soil in nineteenth-century France, where change was still associated with the revolutionary Terror and more weight was placed on social "fixity" by ruling elites. Darwinism in France lagged behind its development in England, Germany and the United States.

If the rise of Darwin's metaphor has been associated with political trends, so has its decline. Writing in the 1940s, Bertrand Russell observed:

> Survival of the fittest is not nearly so popular among biologists as it was fifty years ago. Darwin's theory was an extension, to the whole of life, of laissez-faire economics; now that this kind of economics, and the associated kind of politics, are out of fashion, people prefer other ways of accounting for biological changes.[81]

Indeed, contemporary critics of neo-Darwinian "survival of the fittest," such as Gould, Margulis and Lewontin, are, like Russell, also critics of competition as the motor of society. The parallels between the evolutionary metaphor and its social context are striking. Simply to argue, however, that Darwin reproduced nineteenth-century capitalism does not explain why his metaphor was so successful. To see this, we must look more closely at its role in legitimating its social context and in charging everyday metaphors of survival and competition with fresh authority.[82]

A natural setting. If Darwin's metaphor was a reflection of late-nineteenth-century capitalism as Marx suggested, I want now to highlight the other side of the coin: that same capitalism recognized itself in Darwin's metaphor. Darwinian evolution was useful to certain social groups in their struggle for existence—useful in very concrete, practical ways. First, it promised a sure foundation for ideas of progress. As Spencer had foreseen, it was because of evolution that "progress is not an accident, but a necessity . . . civilisation . . . is part of nature."[83] But the ideology of Darwinism could also be used to justify dangerous work, low wages and the exploitation of other countries. It provided an argument against reformers, many of them Christians, who wanted a framework of law to protect weaker members of society such as children and the poor. It was all of this, and yet it could also claim the status of a science.

The language of Darwinism found its natural application in legitimating unrestrained capitalism and colonialism, because its language was drawn from capitalist competition and the social survival of the fittest. Social Darwinism, by reflecting back to society the very same ideology that the theory of evolution had drawn upon in the first place, justified that society. Darwin's language and that of capitalism were the same.[84]

So Darwin's metaphor was well adapted to the aggressive capitalist environment of the late nineteenth century, and the theory of natural selection was naturally selected by businessmen, colonialists and generals. The "meme"[85] of Darwinism replicated in the lay population, where it found its natural environment. Evolution evolved.

In recent decades, evolution has faced a change in the social conditions that bred it. Unregulated competition no longer seems so desirable as it once did, and the contemporary economy is more mixed and varied. The everyday competitive language of Victorian capitalism that favored the replication of the Darwinian meme has been replaced by images of symbiosis, cooperation and coevolution. The single metaphor of the "survival of the fittest" finds itself in a different, less supportive social environment.

In response to this changed social and intellectual climate, a kind of postmodern Darwinism is emerging that gives increasing weight to a variety of models. Gradualism is supplemented by stepwise change, random mutation by design, competition by cooperation and evolution on earth by cosmic interaction. The "any-color-you-like-so-long-as-it's-black" model of both car production and neo-Darwinism has been replaced by a smorgasbord of choices from which customized models can be constructed. Of course, such heterogeneous models cannot constitute a science in the traditional sense, but they do provide a broad range of metaphors and analogies that are in the spirit of *The Origin* and stimulate a variety of diverse research programs.

Evolution and Civilization

The orthodox story sees Darwinism as a mark of civilization, leading to the wide-open spaces of scientific knowledge in contrast to the narrow bigotry of religion. Evolution promises freedom and progress. In order to assess this claim, we have to try to assess the impact of the Darwinian metaphor on society. It is often hard to identify precise influences, and we must treat large claims with caution, but scholars have pinpointed three areas where the metaphors of "social Darwinism" gave the everyday language of competition new meanings. It would be misleading to think in terms of causation, but we can ask whether the Darwinian metaphor enriched or narrowed the debates.

1. *Capitalism and politics.* Social Darwinists advocated unregulated laissez-faire capitalism. To mitigate inequality or to regulate markets would be to reduce competition and flout a primal law of nature. A trade union that tried to stop one workman working faster than another was acting in opposition to natural selection. The rich are better adapted to survive than the poor and should not be prevented from thriving. Social planning and state intervention for the relief of poverty or the prevention of child labor may appear to be humanitarian, but in fact they inhibit progress and sap a society's vitality. Ruthless commercial competition was justified by the "law" of the survival of the fittest.

When Herbert Spencer, an English advocate of evolution, visited New York in 1882, he was welcomed by many representatives of big business, including Andrew Carnegie, whose *Gospel of Wealth* of 1890 insisted that competition and survival is the engine of progress. After reading Darwin and Spencer, Carnegie observed, "Not only had I got rid of theology and the supernatural, but I had found the truth of evolution. 'All is well since all grows better' became my motto, my source of comfort."[86] William Sumner, American economist and champion of laissez-faire, concurred, "Survival of the fittest . . . is the law of civilisation."[87] Views such as these became increasingly debated throughout Europe and the United States from the late nineteenth century. In Germany they were popularized by Ernst Haeckel:

> The theory of [natural selection] teaches us that in human life, exactly as in animal and plant life . . . only the small privileged minority can continue to exist and flourish; the great mass must starve and more or less prematurely perish in misery. . . . We may deeply mourn this tragic fact but we cannot deny or alter it.[88]

Darwinism was taken up by the ideologues of cultural supremacy and ultimately found its way into the official doctrine of the Third Reich. But evolutionary racism, the combination of social Darwinism with nationalism, was not invented by Nazism.

2. *Race, gender and colonialism.* The full title of Darwin's book was *On the Origin of Species by Means of Natural Selection, or The Preservation of Favoured Races in the Struggle for Life.* From shortly after its publication in 1859 the gloss of the alternative title was used to buttress the view that it is natural for "favoured races" to displace "savage," "lower" ones. This reasoning reinforced existing prejudices favoring imperialist expansion, particularly during the aggressive period leading up to World War I.[89] Thus Wallace quotes from the title of Darwin's book:

> It is the same great law of *"the preservation of favoured races in the struggle for life"*, which leads to the inevitable extinction of all those low and mentally undeveloped populations with which Europeans come in contact.[90]

T. H. Huxley reached the same conclusion from the "facts" of evolution:

> No rational man, cognisant of the facts, believes that the average negro is the equal, still less the superior, of the average white man . . . in a contest which is to be carried on by thoughts and not by bites.[91]

Just as evolution justified distinctions between the races, Huxley explains that it also accounts for men being better adapted to achieve success than women, so that they inevitably win in the struggle of life:

> [The] big chests, the massive brains, the vigorous muscles and stout frames, of the best men will carry the day, whenever it is worth their while to contest the

prizes of life with the best women.[92]

"Man," says Darwin bluntly, "is more powerful in body and mind than woman."[93]

Opponents of the nineteenth-century women's movement used Darwinian arguments to argue that the subordination of women has an evolutionary advantage. The historian Evelleen Richards argues that "Darwinism gave a naturalistic, scientific basis to the class and sexual divisions of Victorian society," although Darwin's own contribution to the debate was modest in comparison with that of his followers. For example, despite his personal generosity to women, Huxley engineered their expulsion from the Ethnographic Society and tried to prevent their admission to the Geological Society, believing that "five sixths of women will stop in the doll stage of evolution."[94]

3. *The eugenic society.* Social Darwinism influenced social policy and legislation. Its child is known as "eugenics"—the scientific, rational control of human breeding through Darwinian mechanisms of selection. C. S. Lewis remarks of similar ideas, "It was their own child coming back to them: grown up and unrecognisable, but their own."[95]

To begin with, social Darwinism advocated "open competition," so that the more gifted could be more successful, and, to use Darwin's own words, the "most able should not be prevented by laws or customs from succeeding best and rearing the largest numbers of offspring."[96] But by the turn of the twentieth century, more positive action was advocated. At first policies encouraged the eugenically fit to breed. Then, from the 1920s, policy shifted to preventing the unfit (the poor, unemployed, alcoholic, and so on) from reproducing, and by the 1930s sterilization was increasingly being advocated. The spirit of the times is summed up by the pioneer of modern neo-Darwinism, J. B. S. Haldane, in his 1932 essay "Inequality of Man":

> The only clear task of eugenics is to prevent the inevitably inefficient one per cent of the population from being born, and to encourage the breeding of persons of exceptional ability.[97]

The development of eugenics has often been identified with right-wing politics that culminated in Nazism. This is mistaken. By the beginning of the twentieth century we find eugenic views widely defended by the ablest advocates of the humanist movement. Sidney Webb, H. G. Wells, Bertrand Russell, John Maynard Keynes and George Bernard Shaw all supported eugenic policies based on their evolutionary, though not necessarily Darwinian, beliefs.[98] One of the earliest eugenics societies was founded in Britain in 1907, and from 1911 until 1928 Darwin's son Leonard was its president.

Many of the early eugenicists were deeply committed to the cause, believing that the very future of humanity lay with the scientific application of this principle of "survival of the fittest." Dr. Marie Stopes, pioneering advocate of "birth control," recommended the sterilization of unfit mothers and the free availability of contraception: "For want of contraceptive measures the low grade stocks are breeding in an ever increasing relation to the high grade stocks, to the continuing detriment of the race."[99] For Leonard Darwin, "eugenics gave life new meaning and purpose," while George Bernard Shaw called for a "eugenic religion," and Francis Galton suggested that it was a new gospel that had so "noble" an aim as to entail a "sense of a religious obligation."[100]

Early eugenic laws were enacted in Switzerland and Denmark in 1928-1929 and were viewed as progressive and scientific. Sweden followed in 1934, and fifteen thousand mental patients were sterilized there between 1934 and 1945. It has recently emerged that up to sixty thousand people may have been sterilized by the time the policy was abandoned in the 1970s.

However, it was the United States that led the way until the 1930s. Early laws were proposed in the first decade of the century, and by the late 1920s twenty-four states had passed involuntary sterilization laws (mainly affecting poor, black citizens or those with learning difficulties). Eugenics was influential in the drafting of immigration restrictions in 1921 and 1924, including the 1924 Johnson Act, which selectively restricted immigration and was used in the 1930s to turn back boats of refugees from Nazi Germany. Seventy thousand people were affected by 1945, despite Pope Pius XI's encyclical opposing eugenics and compulsory sterilization.

From this brief survey it is clear that sterilization policies pre-dated fascist Germany and were regarded as liberal, progressive and the embodiment of scientific hope. Indeed, the most comprehensive law ever framed, which passed in Germany on July 14, 1933, was based on the American model. When he praised "natural selection" as an iron law of nature, Adolf Hitler was echoing the evolutionary beliefs of his day, but he experienced none of the qualms felt by Darwin that such a doctrine is appalling:

> Only the born weakling can look upon this principle [of natural selection by the survival of the fittest in the struggle of life] as cruel, and if he does so it is merely because he is of a feebler nature and narrower mind. . . . [In order to

prevent the inferior individuals from outnumbering the superior] a corrective measure in favour of the better quality must intervene. Nature supplies this by establishing rigorous conditions of life, to which the weaker will have to submit and will thereby be numerically restricted.[101]

While the view that social Darwinism was "one of the most important formative causes for the rise of the Nazi movement" seems overstated, it undoubtedly played an important part in Nazi ideology.[102]

Darwin's Position

Neo-Darwinists today blame eugenics on "Spencer's perversion of Darwin" and try to insulate Darwin from the social consequences of his ideas.[103] Poor Herbert Spencer, who readily embraced Darwin's ideas, finds himself the pariah: "the loudest supporters of eugenics were unsavoury characters who wished to place it at the service of prejudice and racism."[104]

As we have seen, many vociferous supporters of eugenics were in fact well-known liberals and humanists, but there is some truth in the view that Darwin was repelled by the consequences of his ideas. We know that he was a gentle, retiring man who was deeply sensitive to suffering in both the human and the animal world. He was undoubtedly shocked by some of the applications of his evolutionary metaphor and would have been horrified by the influence it had in Europe in the 1930s.

However, the sharp separation between Darwinism and its social consequences is implausible.[105] As Darwin's biographers observe, social Darwinism was not extraneous to "pure Darwinism" but was "written into the equation [by Darwin] from the start."[106] Darwin himself was driven by the logic of his evolutionary thesis to foreshadow eugenic science:

With savages, the weak in body or mind are soon eliminated; and those that survive commonly exhibit a vigorous state of health. We civilised men, on the other hand, do our utmost to check the process of elimination; we build asylums for the imbecile, the maimed, and the sick; we initiate poor laws; and our medical men exert their utmost skill to save . . . life. . . . There is reason to believe that vaccination has preserved thousands, who from a weak constitution would formerly have succumbed to small-pox. Thus the weak members of civilised societies propagate their kind. No one who has attended to the breeding of domestic animals will doubt that this must be highly injurious to the race of man. . . . We must therefore bear the undeniably bad effects of the weak surviving and propagating their kind; but there appears to be at least one check in steady action, namely that the weaker and inferior members of society do not marry so freely as the sound; and this check might be indefinitely increased by the weak in body or mind refraining from marriage, though this is more to be hoped for than expected.[107]

This is not Spencer but Darwin, whose suggestions for the application of his evolutionary metaphor to social policy are entirely consistent with later eugenics.

Evolutionary Offspring

The "meme" for Darwin's metaphor emerged in mid-nineteenth-century Britain, where it replicated without check in the competitive capitalist environment. It always had most difficulty surviving in the more rational environment of the scientific community, where its fortunes have waxed and waned. Unsurprisingly, therefore, it was most popular not among scientists but among businessmen, colonialists and soldiers, who recognized themselves in it and used it to justify oppression, injustice and war. Its role in eugenics was championed by progressive humanists as the realization of the Enlightenment hope. For A. N. Whitehead,

> [the] watchwords of the nineteenth century [drawn from evolution] have been, struggle for existence, competition, class warfare, commercial antagonism between nations, military warfare. The struggle for existence has been construed into the gospel of hate.[108]

This judgment underrates the significance of political, social and economic factors, but it does indicate the prominence of evolutionary language in the early twentieth century and is certainly nearer the truth than the story that neo-Darwinians such as Dawkins like to tell.

During the last hundred years the story of Darwin has obscured the cultural impact of the evolutionary metaphor. From the peppered moth to the legend of Huxley and Wilberforce, the story has distorted both science and history in order to perpetuate itself. In the following chapters we will see further examples of factual distortions as modern myths make use of history and science in constructing their stories. Sometimes, as with Galileo, this does not much matter, as the impact of events of the seventeenth century have ceased to ring in our modern day. Sometimes, as with Darwin, the echoes still sound, as the recent revival of the debate about social Darwinism shows. Poor Darwin, the gentle naturalist of Down House! Who would have thought his metaphor would give birth to such monstrous developments?

3

THE ENVIRONMENT
A Story of Mastery

THE LAST TWO CHAPTERS DESCRIBED STORIES ABOUT HOW WE FIT INTO the world. The story of Galileo explains that the earth is not the center of the universe and that of Darwin tells us that the animal kingdom no more revolves around humans than the sun circles the earth. Together these stories are said to debunk our inflated view of ourselves and to clear the way for more rational and modest explanations. A third, related story tells us that, once we realize that we are not the center of the universe, we also become more compassionate people. Peter Singer explains why:

> It can no longer be maintained by anyone but a religious fanatic that man is the special darling of the whole universe, or that other animals were created to provide us with food, or that we have divine authority over them, and divine permission to kill them.[1]

According to this third story the Christian dogma that the world revolves around humankind is associated with the belief that nature was created for the sake of human beings, who are the rightful masters of the world. We can therefore use and exploit nonhuman nature as we wish, indifferent to the suffering and destruction we cause. I have argued that there is much in the Galileo and Darwin stories that is closer to myth than to history. The tale of the Christian exploitation of nature also has a mythical flavor.

White on "Green"
On December 26, 1966, the historian Lynn White addressed the American

Association for the Advancement of Science on "the historical roots of our ecologic crisis."[2] By 1970, and despite scholarly criticism, his article had become "almost a sacred text for modern ecologists."[3] The story he tells may be simply stated: the destructive effects of modern technology, "the population explosion, the carcinoma of planless urbanism, the new geological deposits of sewage and garbage" are "at least partly to be explained . . . as a realisation of the Christian dogma of man's transcendence of, and rightful mastery over, nature." "Christianity bears a huge burden of guilt" for the emergence of exploitative technologies, and White proposes a return to the theology of Francis of Assisi as the source of a new ethic. His article remains one of the most frequently cited documents in the "Green" debate and is commonly taken to prove that of all the world's religions, Christianity is the most hostile to environmental sensibilities and is responsible for the modern despoliation of the natural world. Thus a *Time* magazine story of 1989 argued that the Bible says we can use the world as we wish.[4] It is not surprising that many environmentalists, believing this, are hostile to biblical religion.

When Tony Sargent, then the minister of Worthing Tabernacle in England, spoke out against the exportation of live animals from a local port in 1996, a bemused BBC interviewer asked him, "Does the Bible actually say anything about animals and their rights?" It is a good question. Does it? According to Jonathon Porritt, many would say that it is worse than silent on the issue:

> In any objective analysis of the root causes of today's ecological crisis, there are many who still incline the opinion [sic] that the Christian Church has always been (and still is) part of the problem rather than part of the solution.[5]

Arnold Toynbee used the same argument in the early 1970s and reached an even more radical conclusion:

> A right religion is one that teaches respect for the dignity and sanctity of all nature. The wrong religion is one that licenses the indulgence of human greed at the expense of non-human nature. I conclude that the religion we need to embrace now is pantheism . . . and the religion we now need to discard is Judaic monotheism . . . [together with Christianity which believes] that mankind is morally entitled to exploit the rest of the universe for the indulgence of human greed.[6]

The Argument

White's story makes two central assertions about religion:

1. "Christianity is the most anthropocentric religion the world has seen"[7] because it teaches that man is made in God's image and is commanded to exploit his environment for his own ends. It is a "Christian axiom that nature has no reason for existence save to serve man."[8] Humans therefore have no duties toward it.

2. In contrast to this "mastery" over nature, pagan animism encouraged a more respectful approach; each tree was imbued with its spirit that needed to be placated before a man could chop it down. "To a Christian, a tree can be no more than a physical fact," whereas it is a sacred grove to a pagan.[9]

This story proved both timely and flexible. To the modern mind it offered a way to preserve trust in science by pinning the responsibility for disaster on unpurged vestiges of the old enemy—religion. To those whose faith in the Enlightenment hope was waning, it opened romantic possibilities for a New Age pagan revival to replace the usurper religion and restore oneness with nature. In either case, the origin of the problem is in Christianity.

What are we to make of this view of religion and history?

A Distorted Image

Study of the ecological beliefs of ancient civilizations has concluded that Israel and the early Christian church rejected anthropocentrism. The idea that nature's "reason for existence" is its "usefulness to mankind" comes from Aristotle, not the Bible: "Plants exist for [the sake of animals] and the other animals for the sake of man . . . nature has made all the animals for the sake of man."[10] This view was extended by Roman civilization, which "treated the natural environment as if it were one of their conquered provinces."[11] Cameron Wybrow has specifically investigated the origin of the anthropocentric concept of mastery and concludes that, while it is common in classical Greek and Roman literature, it is absent from the Bible.[12]

The church has sometimes taught doctrines of "mastery" and "anthropocentrism" when it has drunk most deeply of Hellenistic learning. For example, Aquinas cited Aristotle rather than the Bible to establish his still-influential doctrine that animals are for human use. But there has always been a more authentic biblical voice that has roundly rejected anthropocentrism, and the Reformation developed distinctive doctrines of dominion (rather than *domination*) and stewardship.[13]

It was the Enlightenment that lapsed back into a Greek idiom and transformed *dominion* into *domination* and *stewardship* into *anthropocentrism*. The modern story replaces "creation" with "our environment," and it is this that sets human beings at the center of the world. The biblical narrative tells of God's covenants with his creation and does not oppose human beings to their "environment." Its reference point is God, not man.

A Matter of Facts

The Bible teaches that all things were made not for human beings but by and for Jesus, the eternal Son of God (Col 1:16). Their value arises from God's delight in them, and their purpose is to worship God, fulfilling his command (Gen 1:31; Prov 8:30-31). All creation is involved in this, each creature—whether animal, tree or mountain—according to its ability. When White argues that "to a Christian, a tree can be no more than a physical fact," he is attributing to Christianity a characteristically modern division between material "facts" and spiritual "values" that is foreign to the Bible. To a Christian a tree is a part of creation whose end is to praise the God who made it. Thus the psalmist can write:

> Praise the LORD from the earth,
> you sea monsters and all deeps,
> fire and hail, snow and frost,
> stormy wind fulfilling his command!
> Mountains and all hills,
> fruit trees and all cedars!
> Wild animals and all cattle,
> creeping things and flying birds! . . .
> Praise the LORD. (Ps 148:7-10, 14)[14]

The biblical authors unreservedly declare both that trees and mountains are more than bare "facts," and that they are preserved in creaturely dependence upon their creator God. The psalmist makes no attempt to dilute his language, despite the risk that it might be confused with the pagan belief of the surrounding cultures: that trees, mountains and so on are each imbued with an animating spirit. Indeed, the apostle Paul goes even further by declaring that created things reveal to us the very Godhead. But the biblical language mocks pagan belief even as it refers to it; for the "spirits" of nature, far from being animating deities, themselves bow in worship and declare the glory of their Creator. It is Enlightenment modernity, not the Bible, which has disenchanted nature into "facts." To a Christian, creation is reenchanted even as it is de-deified. However, it is essential to distinguish carefully between this reenchantment and the worship of nature. It has nothing to do with Wicca, Gaia or creation spirituality; instead the psalmist exhorts creation to join him in praising its Lord. As we shall see, this exhortation is intimately connected with God's covenanting activity.

If White is in error in attributing Greek anthropocentric doctrines of mastery to Christianity, his historical assertion that modern environmental exploitation derives from such doctrines may have some validity. However, the connection is not straightforward. For example, it is certainly not the case that environmental exploitation is a particularly modern phenomenon or even that it is uniquely a feature of Western culture.

White himself notes that thirteenth-century Londoners complained of smog from the burning of sea coal; much earlier examples are common. Despite their presumably pagan beliefs about "sacred groves," Neolithic and Bronze Age people deforested much of northern England, and fire-drive hunting techniques had serious effects on the ecology of pre-Columbian North America. The anthropologist Marvin Harris explains the widespread cannibalism in pre-Columbian Mesoamerica as a dietary necessity arising from the hunting to extinction of all the animals.[15] Evidence has recently emerged that fifty thousand years ago early settlers in Australia used fire to clear land, significantly reducing plant cover in the interior and disrupting a sensitive ecosystem to produce the desert we see today. This is a dramatic change by any standard.[16] Moreover, the exploitation of creation does not require a Western doctrine of mastery, let alone an allegedly Christian one. For example, the deforestation of imperial China took place in a Buddhist religious context.

However, it is true that the modern form of exploitation is connected with the particular beliefs that the modern mind holds about creation. Plainly, an anthropocentric point of view, which follows Aristotle in regarding the world as ours to master for our own ends, is likely to be insensitive to environmental concerns. This is especially so if the domination of nature is linked to market control and is monopolized by Western corporations. Ironically, the resulting anthropocentric mastery of nature is more likely to be in the service of agribusiness than of humanity. Enlightenment anthropocentrism deconstructs itself.

As well as man-centered attitudes, we have inherited a second, conflicting motif from the Enlightenment: the belief that humanity is bound by mechanistic biological and social forces, and lacks free will. Indeed, some critics of White have argued that it is this belief that technology is autonomous and out of our human control that has contributed most to the ecological crisis—the very opposite of the mastery hypothesis. From this point of view, to blame Christianity, as White does, merely reinforces our sense of powerlessness and is a diversion from the real task of ensuring that institutions and individuals accept their responsibility.[17] As the twentieth century discovered in so many areas, unregulated Enlightenment rationality, whether it emphasizes human freedom or social determinism, leads to oppression. The way that we treat creation can lead to curse as well as blessing.

In this Enlightenment setting, where did environmental sensitivity come from? In common with many environmentalists, White assumes that it suddenly arose in the late twentieth century, like Venus bounding newborn from the waves. Yet environmentalism did not spring from the waves, nor even from the Enlightenment, but owes its insights to the very Christianity that White castigates.

If we leave aside his romanticized view of pagans and their sacred groves,[18] White's only concession to precursors of environmental concern is Francis of Assisi. Yet it is not true that Francis was a lone voice crying in a wilderness of anthropocentric, exploitative theology. Indeed, whereas environmental exploitation has occurred in many cultures, the contemporary environmental debate has emerged precisely within a Western culture influenced by the Judeo-Christian tradition.

Many patristic and medieval theologians taught that Christians have a duty of responsible stewardship toward creation,[19] and reference to any encyclopedia of saints indicates that many are credited with a special relationship with animals and nature that, whether apocryphal or not, indicates an abiding understanding of dominion alongside Greek themes of mastery. But the most consistent expositions of sensitivity toward creation resulted from the Reformation's return to Scripture.

The Bible and Creation

White rests his argument that Christianity promotes anthropocentric mastery on the doctrine that human beings, unique among creatures, are made in the image of God and are given dominion over the earth. White refers to this as "man's transcendence of, and rightful mastery over, nature."[20]

It is certainly true that the Bible gives human beings dominion to change the world and make history. This is clear in Genesis 1:26-29.[21] We cannot simply read this, however, as though it were part of the Enlightenment faith in man's rational conquest of the world. The notion that "man" is the transcendent master of nature is not part of the biblical narrative, nor is it what commentators sensitive to the Bible have taught.[22] Indeed, the biblical authors are at pains to emphasize that human beings are, like the rest of creation, dependent creatures, not transcendent masters. Genesis 1:24-31 unambiguously puts humans alongside other creatures rather than above them. Animals, including "creeping things," were made on the same day as humankind; the command to humans to "multiply and fill the earth" is paralleled by the command to fishes to "multiply and fill the waters," and by that to birds. Humans and animals equally were made from the earth, have the breath of life, and were given plants and fruit to eat rather than one another. We originally cooperated in partnership with the nonhuman world and exercised dominion within a creation unified in declaring the glory of God (Gen 1:30; 6:17; 7:22).[23] God created us in his image and made us stewards of the earth, dependent not autonomous, having dominion but not arbitrary power or mastership. Andrew Linzey dryly observes that "dominion, so often interpreted as justifying killing, actually precedes the command to be vegetarian. Herb eating dominion is hardly a licence for tyranny."[24]

White equates imaging God with being transcendent over nature, but Genesis 3 presents the human attempt to become transcendent as the very opposite of what it means to image God. It resulted in our expulsion from Eden and our estrangement from the world, including our fellow creatures. However, even after the Fall disrupted the creation partnership, a remnant of the original unity remained. Indeed, human beings are described as the terror of animals and begin to eat them only after sin resulted in a further catastrophic disruption of natural forces at the time of Noah. Even then, God preserved the underlying integrity of creation.

This vision is far removed from the Greek motif of nature as a goddess, secularized in the seventeenth century as "Dame Nature," who would be ravished for her secrets by the penetrating power of scientific reason:

> She [Nature] (as it is said of other mistresses) is also a mistress, that soonest yields to the forward, and the Bold. . . . The Beautiful Bosom of Nature will be Expos'd to our view . . . we shall enter into its Garden, and taste of its Fruits, and satisfy our selves with its plenty.[25]

Compare this with the book of Job's appeal to the voice of creation:

> But ask the animals, and they will teach you;
>   the birds of the air, and they will tell you;
> ask the plants of the earth, and they will teach you;
>   and the fish of the sea will declare to you.
> Who among all these does not know
>   that the hand of the LORD has done this?
> In his hand is the life of every living thing
>   and the breath of every human being. (Job 12:7-10)[26]

This is not the language of unmitigated mastery, and it is certainly not anthropocentric.

The biblical story of creation, fall and redemption includes the whole of creation, not just human beings. This is clearest in the history of the covenants that God makes with his cosmos.

Creation and Covenant History

All creation was affected by human rebellion against God (Gen 3:17-19), in particular the cooperation between humans and the world. The first covenant made in Eden had been one of works, but subsequent covenants were of grace and, like the first, were made between God and all of creation, not just humankind. Thus God tells Noah, "This is the sign of the covenant that I make between me and you and every living creature that is with you" (Gen 9:12). God remains faithful to his covenants and continues to care both for human beings and for animals.[27]

> Sing to the LORD with thanksgiving;
>   make melody to our God on the lyre.
> He covers the heavens with clouds,
>   prepares rain for the earth,
>   makes grass grow on the hills.
> He gives to the animals their food,
>   and to the young ravens when they cry. (Ps 147:7-9)[28]

God repeatedly affirms that the new covenant is with the whole creation, so that the original cooperative relationships within creation, both animate and inanimate, will be restored.

> At destruction and famine you shall laugh,
>   and shall not fear the wild animals of the earth.
> For you shall be in league with the stones of the field,
>   *and the wild animals shall be at peace with you*. (Job 5:22-23)[29]

The fact that God deals with his creation as a whole does not diminish human dominion or the responsibilities that go with it. Indeed, the unity of creation under human stewardship emphasizes the fact, rediscovered in recent years, that human activity affects the whole world. It was as a result of *human* sin that animals suffered in both Genesis 3 and at the time of Noah (Gen 6:5-8). Similarly, the dominion of humans is emphasized in the Noahic covenant, which restored the animals that were *"with" Noah*; creation groans because of its "eager longing for the revealing of the children of God" (Rom 8:19), not simply because it suffers. Human dominion remains and so does our responsibility for the Fall, through which we have involved all creation in suffering. The Puritans, who took these things seriously, deduced from this not that we can do as we wish with the world but that we must be merciful toward creation, especially those aspects, such as fierceness in animals, which result from the Fall. We must not exploit such disruption for our own enjoyment by, for example, setting animals to fight each other.

Human dominion to rule over the world involves not carte blanche but stewardship norms, including the preservation of the richness and diversity that God has created. Adam was commanded to "till [Eden] and keep it" in the sense of serving and preserving it (Gen 2:15). Noah is told to take animals into the ark "to keep their kind alive upon the face of all the earth" (Gen 7:1-4).[30] The "Bible is firmly for the preservation of the environment. Sensitivity and responsibility to the land and to its creatures are expected from a mature Hebrew society."[31]

The Mosaic covenant spells out how dominion was to be exercised. For example, it forbade the exploitation of natural resources to extinction (Deut 22:6-7) and, contrary to modern practice, not even warfare justified deforestation (Deut 20:19-20). Josephus, the first-century Jewish historian, argued that Moses taught compassion for animals with a presumption against cruelty:

> So thorough a lesson has he given us in gentleness and humanity that he does not overlook even the brute beasts, authorizing their use only in accordance with the Law, and forbidding all other employment of them. Creatures which take refuge in our houses like suppliants we are forbidden to kill. He would not suffer us to take the parent birds with the young, and bade us even in an enemy's country to spare and not to kill the beasts employed in labor. Thus, in every particular, he had an eye for mercy, using the laws I have mentioned to enforce the lesson.[32]

The righteous person exercises obedient dominion (Prov 12:10), a duty taken for granted when Balaam is rebuked for beating his ass (Num 22:28-30). Animals and the land are included in both the weekly and seventh year sabbath "that your ox and your ass may have rest, and the son of your bondmaid, and the alien, may be refreshed" (Ex 23:10-12 RSV; Lev 25:6-7; Deut 5:12-15; also Deut 22:10; 25:4).

Obedience to this vision of covenant stewardship would have immediate practical consequences. For example, the "set-aside" scheme of the European Union could embody a sabbath for the land. But without a biblical vision it is more likely to be related to overproduction caused by "agribusiness" farming methods.

These aspects of God's covenant are as binding as any other, and we will have to give an account to God for our dominion over the world. Moreover, if we neglect the demands of stewardship and break God's covenant, then despoliation and pollution will result:

> The earth lies polluted under its inhabitants;
>> for they have transgressed laws,
> violated the statutes,
>> broken the everlasting covenant.
> Therefore a curse devours the earth,
>> and its inhabitants suffer for their guilt. (Is 24:5-6)

A History of Concern

It might be argued that White is referring less to biblical teaching and more to the church's doctrine. It is certainly true that the institutional church has sometimes, perhaps often, abandoned its biblical inheritance.[33] If, however, we restrict consideration to the Reformation tradition, which has defined authentic Christianity in terms of adherence to the Bible rather than tradition, then a story emerges that is the very opposite of that told by White.

The biblical story demands responsibility in dominion, sharply distinguishing it from domination. Luther's return to the Scripture marked a recovery of this truth. Although still deeply influenced by the Greek tradition, Luther taught that our mistreatment of animals will have eternal significance for which we will have to give account, that humans have to care for and protect the nonhuman creation and that the arbitrary killing of animals (e.g., for sport) is not permitted, even of wild beasts.[34] But it was the Puritan movement of the seventeenth century that most clearly developed this understanding of stewardship and human accountability to God, and their influence progressively undermined anthropocentric practices.[35] Thus the Puritan John Ray rejected the Aristotelian view that the world was made only for man:

> It is a generally received opinion that all this visible world was created for Man; that Man is the end of the Creation, as if there were no other end of any creature, but some way or other to be serviceable to man. . . . But though this be vulgarly received, yet wise men nowadays think otherwise.[36]

In England and through figures such as Jonathan Edwards in the United States, a deep sensitivity toward creation emerged, which informed arguments opposing animal cruelty. Indeed, as the historian Keith Thomas has made clear, there is little historical development in the argument against animal cruelty from the "strong Protestants or Puritans of the Elizabethan and early Stuart period" to "the Evangelicals, Methodists, sentimentalists and humanitarians" of the eighteenth century. Rather than classical authors, "the Old Testament was the authority most frequently cited." "Clerics were often ahead of lay opinion and an essential role was played by Puritans, Dissenters, Quakers and Evangelicals."[37]

From the eighteenth century the biblical account that creation exists through and for God was less readily accepted as public truth. However, its inheritance entered the language of the Enlightenment with its contrasting Greek idiom and was transformed and selectively appropriated. For example, "dominion" was transformed into "domination"; "creation" or "world" became "our world," defined with respect to humanity, and later "our environment."

This transformation of biblical truth had two differing outcomes.

1. Some of the insights of the Reformation were preserved relatively unscathed, albeit in an increasingly Enlightenment setting; thus sensitivity toward animal suffering developed a momentum of its own in nineteenth-century England.

2. Other insights either disappeared or were transformed out of recognition. In particular, the biblical teaching that God continues to care and provide for his creation as a whole was increasingly eclipsed by a mechanistic conception of nature, casting ecological concern into the shade for nearly a century.

In the second half of this chapter I will look at each of these outcomes more closely.

Creature Comfort

The campaign against animal cruelty "grew out of the (minority) Christian tradition that man should take care of God's creation."[38] But a second tradition from ancient Greece interacted with it. Thomas Aquinas, quoting Aristotle rather than the Bible, argued that hunting animals is "just and natural," and interpreted dominion in the Greek idiom as "mastership," which consists in "making use" of animals "without hindrance."[39] Despite Aquinas's prestige, these Greek views did not entirely eclipse the more biblical tradition, and there are many medieval examples of sympathy for animals and their welfare. An early fifteenth-century commentary on the Ten Commandments explains that the sixth commandment (against murder) permits the slaughter of animals but emphasizes that they are not ours to do with as we please and that we will have to give an account to God:

> It is granted to man to slay beasts when it is profitable to him for meat or for clothing or to avoid vexation. . . . And so God granted to man for to slay beasts, fish and fowl, to his profit but not to slay them for cruelty nor for pleasure or sport. . . . And therefore men should have ruth [pity] on beasts and birds and not harm them without cause and take note that they are God's creatures. And therefore he that for cruelty and vanity . . . torments beasts or fowl more than is speedful to man's living, they sin . . . full grievously.[40]

Biblical motifs here leaven Aquinas's Greek teaching. From the sixteenth century the Reformation began to develop these biblical themes. Calvin's commentary on the Deuteronomic law against cruelty in farming (Deut 25:4) is characteristically clear:

> God has formed and created [the brute beasts]; and . . . vouchsafes to preserve them through his providence, and provides them of food, and (at a word) cares for them and . . . when he did put them in subjection to us, he did it with condition that we should handle them gently: that as we deal rightfully with men, so we should use the like duty even towards the brute beasts, which have no reason, nor understanding, nor cannot complain of the injuries which are done unto them. . . . God takes pity [on the ox] because he is his creature; and he will not have us to abuse the beasts beyond measure, but to nourish them and to have care of them. . . . [Through the law] God meant to persuade men unto gentleness and humanity. . . . Uprightness and equity ought to be ministered even unto the brute beasts.[41]

Calvin is quite explicit in saying that we have a "like duty" to "deal rightfully" with animals as we have to do so with human beings. This is a long way from Aristotle's line that "nature has made all the animals for the sake of men."

The Puritans in England, Scotland and North America inherited and developed these insights of the Reformation. We can identify three features of their opposition to animal cruelty.

1. *A duty commanded.* Creation is for God's pleasure, not human use. Human responsibility toward animals is governed by stewardship norms exemplified in the law. Thus Humphry Primatt argues that "mercy to brutes is a duty commanded, and that cruelty to them is a sin forbidden" by Holy Scripture,[42] and the Puritan leader John Flavel, speaking of a blackbird that he had helped, referred to "pity and succour being a due debt to the distressed [bird]."[43] Human beings will have to give an account to God of their treatment of animals. Primatt notes that God

> will undoubtedly require of man . . . a strict account of his conduct to every creature entrusted to his care, or coming in his way; and will avenge every instance of wanton cruelty and oppression, in the day in the which he will judge the world in righteousness.[44]

Calvin makes a characteristically penetrating observation in this connection:

> God will condemn us for cruel and unkind folk, if we pitie not the brute beasts. . . . A beast cannot speak to move us to pitie and compassion; and therefore we must go to him of our own good will, though we be not moved or requested thereunto.[45]

Calvin's argument is important because it denies that our duty toward animals relies solely on our individual abilities to sympathize with them. The duty is "objective," not sentimental.

2. *A mercy required.* The Puritans taught that we must be especially careful to be merciful toward animals, as the disrupted relationships within creation are the result of our own sin:

> The antipathy and cruelty which one beast shows to another is the fruit of our rebellion against God . . . and should rather move us to mourne than to rejoice.[46]

Many Puritan authors noted that this rebellion resulted in humans eating animals, often after inflicting hideous cruelty on them:

> The way in which we now use the creatures bears witness against sin. When we eat flesh we do so, for there was no such grant in the first blessing; since sin our appetite has been more carnivorous.[47]

This thinking led to attitudes now more often associated with vegetarianism. Phillip Stubbes argued that animals should be killed for food only in the fear of God, commenting: "I never read of any, in the volume of the sacred Scriptures, that was a good man and a hunter."[48] The devout eighteenth-century poet William Cowper protests in *The Task* against the cruelty to animals that flowed from the Fall, and he exhorts man, "Carnivorous, through sin, feed on the slain, but spare the living brute."[49]

3. *A sensibility acquired.* The Puritans were genuinely revolted by cruelty and have been widely misrepresented on this score, most notably by the nineteenth-century historian Lord Macaulay:

> [Puritan antipathy to bearbaiting] had nothing in common with the feeling which has, in our own times, induced the legislature to interfere for the purpose of protecting beasts against the wanton cruelty of men. The Puritan hated bear-baiting, not because it gave pain to the bear, but because it gave pleasure to the spectators. Indeed, he generally contrived to enjoy the double pleasure of tormenting both spectators and bear.[50]

This "jibe" is described as "wholly unfair" by historians of the period as diverse as Hill[51] and Gardiner.[52] More characteristic of Puritan sentiment is Stubbes's sixteenth-century condemnation of bear-baiting which, remarkably, he makes a test of genuine Christian confession:

> What Christian heart can take pleasure to see one poor beast to rent, tear and kill another, and all for his foolish pleasure? And although they be bloody beasts to mankind, and seek his destruction, yet we are not to abuse them, for his sake who made them, and whose creatures they are. For notwithstanding that they be evil to us, and thirst after our blood, yet they are good creatures in their own nature and kind, and made to set forth the glory and magnificence of the great God and for our use; and therefore for his sake not to be abused . . . we are not in any wise to spoil or hurt [animals]. Is he a Christian man, or rather a pseudo-Christian, that delights in blood?[53]

From the 1640s the English Puritans had some opportunity to legislate against cruelty. Bearbaiting had been attacked as "a full ugly sight" as early as 1550, and Parliament ordered its suppression in 1642. Cockfighting was attacked by Perkins among others and finally prohibited by Cromwell in 1654.[54] However, the momentum for reform was lost on the Restoration with the eclipse of direct Puritan influence and the shift of power to the nobility with their traditional sports.

Opposition to animal cruelty resumed with the Methodists and evangelicals of the eighteenth century, who inherited a "strong Protestant sentiment . . . opposed [to] cruelty" and were again able to bring their theology to bear upon public policy. Horace Walpole is said to have remarked in 1760 that a certain man was known to be "turning Methodist; for, in the middle of conversation, he rose, and opened the window to let out a moth."[55] William Wilberforce and Lord Shaftesbury, better known for their reform of industrial abuses and opposition to slavery, spoke against animal cruelty. During this period, concern for animal welfare entered the sensibilities of the educated middle classes, although the identification of cruelty in sport stopped at the lower-class entertainments of cockfighting and did not, as with the Puritans, extend to hunting and racing.

It is a mark of how we have squandered our Christian heritage that the BBC interviewer cited earlier in this chapter had to ask whether the Bible even refers to animal welfare. People were astonished when Sargent posted the text of Proverbs 12:10 on his church bulletin board to coincide with the cruel transport of live animals from the local port. It read: "A righteous man has regard for the life of his beast, but the compassion of the wicked is cruel." As the eighteenth-century Christian Humphry Primatt wrote: "If I know that a man is cruel to his beast, I ask no more questions about him. He may be a noble man, or a rich man . . . or a church man, or anything else, it matters not; this I know, on the sacred word of a wise king, that, being *cruel* to his beast, he is a *wicked* man."[56]

Enlightenment Neglect

During the eighteenth century these insights of the Reformation were increasingly expressed in the language of the Enlightenment, which splintered and transformed the biblical vision. The Enlightenment story has two incompatible motifs: anthropocentric human freedom and the deterministic mechanisms of science. As the insights inherited from the Reformation were expressed in this increasingly secular Enlightenment language, they were eclipsed as public truth and were split apart by the two conflicting motifs. Each motif produced a distinctive way of speaking about animals and has informed divergent streams of public policy.

The Enlightenment motif of anthropocentric human freedom sheered Puritan sensibilities from their justification in "how God intended men to behave towards the lower creatures"[57] and expressed them in the language of the humanitarians and sentimentalists of the eighteenth century. Calvin's emphasis that our responsibilities toward animals arise from the "objective" Word of God and not from our individual feelings was transformed into a subjective response relying on our ability to sympathize with animals. Inevitably, this distortion of the biblical vision has favored creatures that can engage our sympathies. Dolphins, whales and small furry creatures attract more concern than the less appealing sloth or vulture.

The second Enlightenment motif of mechanistic science reduced God's providential care for his world to a belief in human progress.[58] This motif had been anticipated by Descartes, for whom animals were merely complex mechanisms. He observes that animals excel humans in some abilities but despite this they have no soul:

> [Rather] it is nature that acts in them according to the dispositions of their organs; as one sees that a clock, which is made up of only wheels and springs, can count the hours and measure time more exactly than we can with all our art.[59]

In the eighteenth century this language acquired the grammar of materialism and was employed to advocate scientific inquiry into the mechanism of animal anatomy rather than sentimental concern over their sensibilities. We can owe no duties to machinery and have no responsibilities of stewardship toward a merely material world, nor duty of care over its creatures. Claude Bernard, a leading figure in nineteenth-century scientific medicine, regarded the resultant indifference to animal suffering as a scientific duty:

> The physiologist is not a layman, he is a scientist; he is a man gripped and absorbed by the scientific idea that he pursues: he no longer hears the cries of animals, he no longer sees the blood that flows, he sees only his idea, and perceives only organisms that conceal from him the problems he wants to solve.[60]

This hard-nosed Enlightenment approach toward animals had little time for the emotional appeals of sentimentalists who had divorced their horror at vivisection from any reasoned justification for its control. Bernard regarded it as a duty to which a scientist should aspire and appears oblivious of how dreadful such a vision is.

Thus the Enlightenment secularization of Reformation insights fractured them into sentimentalism on the one hand and dispassionate, scientific indifference on the other. The nineteenth century extended this divorce. On the one hand, reform continued, often at Christian initiative. But on the other, scientific cruelties also proceeded apace and were advocated by materialist heirs to Enlightenment reason, despite Christian opposition.

Since the mid-nineteenth century the inheritance of the Puritans has continued to find a place in modern sensibilities toward animals. But the Puritan foundation in the Bible that undergirded these beliefs has now largely gone as public truth. Moreover, the middle-class sentimentalism that carried welfare reform in the nineteenth century is also losing momentum. Fortunately for the cause of reform, the Enlightenment devaluation of animals is also waning, although it continues in a small way in phrases such as Richard Dawkins's reference to animals as "survival machines" for their genes.[61]

In place of the modern languages of sentimentalism or hard-nosed reason, new justifications for our behavior toward animals are entering the field. Increasingly this postmodern sensibility favors the equality of all species, including Homo sapiens, and the establishment of animal rights. Combined with a denial of materialism in the New Age and pagan movements, a variety of local initiatives have forged links between compassionate sensibilities and reasoned (though not rationalist) beliefs about the world. Many different languages are used to justify opposition to animal cruelty, which are quite distinct from the language of modernity—ranging from the pagan worship of nature to a belief in reincarnation. As the advertisement says: "When you come back as a whale, you'll be bloody glad you put Greenpeace in your will."

From Creation to Environment

Although the Christian concern for animals partially survived Enlightenment distortion to enter nineteenth-century middle-class sensibilities, biblical insight into God's providential care for his creation did not, and it was largely eclipsed from the late eighteenth century. It has come to light again only under the pressure of the environmental catastrophes of recent decades.

For the Puritans, God's care for his creation extended beyond individual animal welfare to what we would now call "the ecosystem." Our stewardship of creation means that it is not lawful to "destroy any one species of God's creatures, though it were but the species of Toads and Spiders (because this were a taking away one linke of God's chaine, one note of his harmony)."[62] Most English scientists and theologians of the eighteenth century believed that all created species had a part to play in creation as a whole. However, the increasing domination of public truth by Enlightenment thought during the nineteenth century promoted mechanistic rather than providential images.

At first these images of mechanism coexisted with the more biblical motifs of care and providence. Thus William Paley argued for the existence of God from a discussion of the balance within creation and the fitness of each creature for its natural setting. But his most striking image is that of creation as a watch, implying design—but also mechanism.[63] For Darwin, only the mechanism remained, and his evolutionary metaphor spoke of an autonomous natural world, each organism in competition with every other in a fight for life. The survival of the fittest replaced any sense of creation's dependence on God or his providential care.

Darwin's metaphor of antagonism and struggle obscured the environmental consequences of human exploitation of the natural world: "If nature's way is to be our guide, it is pointless to complain of mass extinctions or pollution."[64] The ecological disasters of our own time have prompted contemporary environmentalism to rediscover the neglected language of care and dependence that was once so common in Protestant theology.

The Recovery of the Language of Dependence

It is rarely recognized that contemporary ecological ideas have any connection with the belief that God covenants with his world, preserves it and cares for it. However, as the historian Keith Thomas has made clear, "The . . . idea of the balance of nature . . . had a theological basis before it gained a scientific one."[65] Contemporary biologists have rediscovered the symbiosis of environment and organism, and the ecology and Green movements have popularized it.

When we look around us, we find that survival by cooperation with others in a favorable environment is very common. Indeed, many species provide such an environment for one another to their mutual benefit. The ecosystem is now known to be self-sustaining and homeostatically self-regulating. For example, cleared forestland is colonized first by groundcover, which provides an environment for trees to reestablish themselves. However, some interactions, while mutually supporting, are finely balanced. Once disrupted, the consequences can be irreversible. Rain forests maintain the fragile soil, which in turn supports them; when the trees are cut down, the soil erodes.

These discoveries have been associated with a reaction to the neo-Darwinian orthodoxy that the mechanism for evolutionary change is the survival of the fittest and the emergence of the postmodern models discussed in the last chapter. A new language is being created, better suited to environmental concerns.

Richard Lewontin believes that neo-Darwinism owes more to its inheritance from nineteenth-century capitalism than to empirical science and regards the neo-Darwinian notion that organisms are passive objects acted on by the environment as an "impoverished and incorrect view."[66] Margulis calls neo-Darwinism a "quaint, but potentially dangerous aberration," whose exponents "wallow in their zoological, capitalistic, competitive, cost-benefit interpretation of Darwin."[67] She refers to Darwinian accounts of origins as "'just-so' stories that rationalise the existence of present-day life forms . . . by thinly veiled comparisons with the profit motive," and feels that a paradigm shift is necessary if biology is to have an adequate understanding of its subject matter.[68]

This new language speaks not only of competition between organisms but also of dependency, cooperation, unity and a world created by the living activities of the organisms within it. Organisms form an interacting community symbiotically cooperating, coevolving rather than struggling competitively against one another. Differences can be pooled and become the opportunity for sharing characteristics rather than for the competitive elimination of the weakest. Just as the individualism of laissez-faire capitalism has been rejected in favor of a more collective conception of society, so the unit of biological study has become the symbiotic system or community, not the individual organism. Rather than competing, organisms join forces to accomplish together what they could not achieve as individuals. The reciprocal actions between organisms and environments, not struggle, is the chief agent of change.[69]

This new language has stimulated innovative research and has brought novel phenomena to light. For example, Lynn Margulis has revolutionized the metaphors used to describe cellular evolution. She argues that the cell structure we see today is the result of the cooperation and symbiosis of more primitive organisms. Whether or not we agree with Margulis that this metaphor is to be taken literally, the new language has drawn attention to the cell as a community and has generated related research.[70]

Similarly, James Lovelock argues that the earth is a self-regulating mechanism, a unity, an organism. He points out that throughout geological time

the earth has maintained an environment suited to life despite a large variation of factors that could have destroyed it. For example, the heat received
from the sun has varied, and yet the earth has maintained a surface temper-
ature that life can tolerate. The salinity of the sea and the relative propor-
tions of gases in the atmosphere have been maintained between the narrow
limits favoring life. Mechanisms exist to redistribute trace elements essential for living organisms. These are not simply isolated observations but
suggest research programmers into novel areas, such as the relationship
between ocean organisms and the climate.[71]

This recovery of a language of dependence and balance is indebted to
pre-nineteenth-century theology, but it does not presage a return to the biblical vision. Rather, the biblical motifs are transformed in their postmodern
setting, sometimes out of all recognition. For example, the biblical understanding of the unity of creation takes on a distinctive autonomy and transcendence as it is read in the context of the Greek nature goddess Gaia
rather than God the Creator. Rupert Sheldrake[72] explicitly argues for the
restoration of the concept of nature as an organic, living entity, the mother
goddess of Greek religion. As a result, the biblical exercise of dominion is
weakened in favor of magical or esoteric control.

A Religious Issue

We started with White's broadside against Christianity as the fount of the
emerging ecological crisis. In one respect he was on target. He correctly
identified the crisis as a "religious problem" but located it in the wrong
place as a result of his oversimplified account of Christianity in the West.
The doctrine that "nature made the animals for man to do with as he
wishes" is Greek, not biblical, and was more prominent in the language of
the Enlightenment than in that of the Reformation. Similarly, the Renaissance of a Greek idiom in the sixteenth century set man firmly at the center
of things and pictured nature as a goddess. It was this Greek inheritance
that gave birth to the anthropocentric language of the eighteenth century.
The Enlightenment secularized the goddess into Dame Nature and set man
against her in images of penetrative violence. The biblical authors are precisely not man-centered but constantly point beyond the human to God, the
Creator and Sustainer of the cosmos. His providential care of nature and
our human responsibility to image God in this respect are the distinctive
biblical themes that the Puritans bequeathed to later generations.

Contemporary environmentalism draws both on modern anthropocentric language and on the postmodern languages of the Green movement. Thus the essentially Enlightenment argument that the ozone layer is useful to us provides a reason for doing something about its destruction. Postmodern paganism argues more directly that nature is sacred and deserves respect. The biblical teaching is that creation is dependent on its Creator and is good because of this continuing relationship with God. Rare species should be preserved as part of our dominion of creation neither because they may help us (although they may) nor because they are in themselves sacred (which they are not). In the practical task of befriending the earth, alliances are obviously possible, but both the modern and postmodern dialects represent a fractured and impoverished transformation of the biblical language. Alliances must therefore remain uncomfortable. We should learn the lesson of the past that once our attitude toward animals is divorced from the full biblical foundation, it survives, at best, as a vulnerable sensibility. At worst, it may be excluded altogether by rationalizations of human aggrandizement and domination over the creation.

4

THE MISSIONARIES
A Story of Oppression

STORIES OF THE CHURCH'S PERSECUTION OF GALILEO AND DARWIN stand for the supposed conflict between religion and science that is so entrenched in the modern mind. The tale of the Christian exploitation of nature further develops the theme of oppression. For the very image of bigotry, however, we must turn to the story of Christian mission. For many people, missionary exploits prove that the Christian claim to have a monopoly on the truth inevitably leads to the oppression of other people and their culture. Meanwhile, the modern mind, enlightened by reason and science, is portrayed as tolerant and humane.

Conquistador Cannon and Colonial Gunship

Stories are best told simply, and children's authors tell us the plot without mincing words. Missions, they say, are places where "representatives of one of the Christian religions live. They try to make the local people join their religion."[1] But things do not go well for the native converts:

> By a system known as encomienda, the [Spanish who had already taken the native's land] could acquire an Indian workforce in return for instructing them in the Christian faith. Such instruction was often little more than a ritual baptism, while the Indians were committed to a life of perpetual slavery.[2]

This portrayal is not restricted to children's books. The philosopher Bertrand Russell recounts the supposed missionary technique of the Spanish in his discussion of baptism: "The Spaniards in Mexico and Peru used to baptise Indian infants, and then immediately dash their brains out: by this means they secured that these infants went to Heaven." Absurdly he concludes, "No orthodox Christian can find any logical reason for condemning their action."[3]

The activities of missionaries are regularly linked with those of colonists and criminals, acquiring a guilt by association:

> The Europeans regarded the Aborigines as a heathen people who needed to be converted to Christianity, and put to work for the benefit of Europeans. . . . Aboriginal lands were confiscated, their children taken away and put in Christian mission stations, their water holes poisoned, and many of their people massacred.[4]

Norman Lewis tells a story of corruption, exploitation and forced conversion, and implicates missionaries in all the evils of Western colonialism. For example, he records appalling atrocities in modern Brazil, including mass murder. He then cites an "authoritative" newspaper report to show that:

> In reality, those in control [of the areas where the majority of the atrocities had occurred] are North American Missionaries . . . they disfigure the original Indian culture and enforce the acceptance of Protestantism. . . . It was missionary policy to ignore what was going on.[5]

Such portraits are unforgiving. Missionary influence is said to spread through fear or by gaining rice-bowl converts. Missionaries are accused of exploiting natives for commercial gain, colluding with expansionist colonialism and even committing "ethnocide." They are implicated in the theft of land, the forced removal of children from their parents, the destruction of habitats, torture, murder and the decline of whole populations into destitution, alcoholism and prostitution. Even when they provide disaster relief, they are guilty of "buying" converts.[6]

Philip Goldring refers to such stories as the "secular disparagement of mission," which has "gone to the extent of suggesting that missionaries threatened native culture more gravely than traders did."[7] The allegations made almost routinely against missionaries could scarcely be broader or more serious.

Vulnerable Native and Exploiting Priest

The characters and setting of the orthodox story are painted in sharply contrasting colors. Flint-faced Protestants and repressed nuns impose rigid, joyless and patriarchal rules, implementing "all the usual bans on pleasure."[8] Native people, on the other hand, are portrayed as vulnerable residents in an idyllic land, the victims of the full might of Western oppression incarnate in the person of "the missionary." They allow themselves to be tricked out of their land and readily give up their own beliefs out of fear or awe of white culture, or through the poverty that forces them into dependence on European wealth. There are no half tones.

The props of the orthodox story are simple: the land and the Bible. As Jomo Kenyatta famously said, "When the white man came we had the land and they had the Bible. They taught us to pray with our eyes closed and when we opened them, they had the land and we had the Bible."[9]

Of course, missionaries have not been entirely innocent. Given that they comprise a worldwide movement that spans almost two millennia, examples of collusion and oppression are inevitable. Indeed, we know from the Bible that the Council at Jerusalem ruled that Gentile converts had been unnecessarily burdened with the cultural customs of Judaism (Acts 15). The appraisal and reform of customs and traditions is healthy for a church that seeks the will of God. Criticism is not to be feared, but honest criticism must be fair.

The failure of those cited above to differentiate between mission and colonial or trading activity naturally results in the identification of mission with oppression. Yet it would be surprising if this easy equation of Christian mission with Western interests over a period of some five centuries does justice to the facts What of the power of those commercial enterprises that missionaries in fact opposed—from the conquistadors and their search for gold to the British South Africa Company? What of the Enlightenment visions of "civilization" and "progress" that inspired colonial activity from the eighteenth century and rejected faith in God for faith in reason? What of the evolutionary origins of eugenics that classified "natives" as a less evolved species? No doubt some missionaries were closely associated with imperialist expansion and shared the prevailing Enlightenment faith in progress or Darwinism, especially in the late nineteenth century. But is the identification of missions with oppression fair? If, in fact, scholars have known for many years that the story is a parody, why does it thrive?

This chapter is not intended to be a comprehensive look at the complex and diverse world of missions, nor is it an assessment of how far missionaries have been seduced by modern ideologies. Given the vast historical and cultural range of missionary endeavor, such an enterprise would fill many more pages than are available here. Rather, I will be concerned with the sweeping claims and misrepresentations that underlie the story. For these are not simply misleading stereotypes. They also suppress the story of native and missionary *resistance* to oppression, and the role of modern beliefs in the widespread destruction of communities and cultures that continues to this day.

Civilization, Enlightenment and Christianity

A fundamental error in the story of missionary oppression, the "everlasting story of the West against the Indians," is the identification of Western civilization with Christianity.

> Christian-cum-Western civilization [has] . . . exploited the Indian for centuries, and having taken a large part of his culture away from him without replacing it with anything at all of value, is still pursuing its work of pillage and destruction. And it always does it in the name of what it holds as its most sacred principles: democracy, progress . . . Christian charity, and the expansion of the reign of God in Indo-America.[10]

The belief that the gospel is inherently Western clearly cannot be supported. No biblical authors were from western Europe, and most biblical events took place in Asia and Africa. The culture assumed is pre-industrial, often nomadic. For two hundred years the strongest churches were in North Africa and what is now modern Turkey, and African theologians deeply influenced Christian doctrine.[11] Early missionary journeys were to, not from, Western Europe. Moreover, the centers of gravity of the church moved to Africa, Asia and Latin America some years ago, and some of these churches now send more missionaries to the West than they receive. The orthodox story's assumption that Christianity is a Western religion is certainly Eurocentric and possibly racist.

Moreover, the language of oppression owes little to Christianity. Advocates of national or colonial expansion often speak of native people as "barbarians" or "savages," the unproductive occupiers of land, holding up civilization and, since the eighteenth century, progress. But neither *civilization* nor *progress* is a scriptural term, nor are they mainstays of biblically sensitive commentary. Where then does this language come from?

The word *savage* has long been used of people who were believed to live in the primal forest by hunting, and *barbarian* derives from the ancient Greek disparagement of non-Hellenic languages. The French encyclopedists used the term *civilization* to denote the progress they believed reason and Enlightenment would bring. The "civilized man" was rational, progressive and secular, in contrast with the superstitions of less developed societies. From the late eighteenth century this sense of *civilized* had "behind it the general spirit of the Enlightenment, with its emphasis on secular and progressive human self-development."[12] The modern vocabulary of *savages* and *civilization* derives from this Enlightenment hubris rather than Christian beliefs. Indeed, *civilized* often refers to a modern world freed from religion and religious faith.

By the late nineteenth century, under the influence of evolutionary ideas, "savagery," "barbarism" and "civilization" were seen as a progressive sequence. "Barbarian societies" were capable of benefiting from Western attempts to civilize them, but evolutionary thinkers such as Darwin believed it more likely that "savage" people would become extinct rather than evolve. This language provided rationalizations for the aggressive colonialism of the late nineteenth century.

It is therefore naive to simply identify "civilization" with Christianity. Indeed, for some the Enlightenment vision of civilization and progress was opposed to Christianity. Bertrand Russell saw it as a Western duty to civilize "primitive" people, but for him Christianity was an obstacle, not an instrument of progress. Late Victorian moralists did combine Enlightenment ideas of civilization with a truncated understanding of the gospel—Charles Darwin supported missionary societies believing they would have a "civilizing" influence—but there is little to suggest that he had more than a vaguely deistic faith. Some colonists and traders exploited the social power of established churches for their own interests and grossly distorted the gospel of the cross. It is possible to find examples of missionaries who subscribed to this view, but most were more concerned with the light of the gospel than with the "benefits" of civilization, and this has produced conflicts with colonial or national interests. By identifying Christianity with Western civilization, the orthodox story has ignored these conflicts. It has also suppressed the role of modern ideology in oppressing native people.

Aristotle, Evolution and Slavery

Any distinction between "civilized" people and "savages" readily justifies exploitation. For example, the enslavement of native people during the early modern period was defended through the Aristotelian teaching that barbarians are inherently inferior to civilized people and suited by nature to slavery. But from the eighteenth century, Enlightenment concepts of civilization and progress began to replace the philosophy of ancient Greece, and by the nineteenth century the language of scientific classification was regularly employed to justify oppression. Attempts by anthropologists to discern innate deficiencies in supposedly separate species of humanity were particularly popular. The missionary Lancelot Threlkeld reported that the early-nineteenth-century colonists at Newcastle, New South Wales, regarded the Aborigines as "a species of the baboon, that they might be shot down with impunity." A French specialist in phrenology confirmed their "innate deficiency" by the scientific study of their heads. As Threlkeld caustically observed: "Perhaps the Aborigines think that there is an innate deficiency in the bulk of white men's skulls, which prevent their attainment of the native language."[13]

With the publication of *On the Origin of Species by Means of Natural Selection, or The Preservation of Favoured Races in the Struggle for Life*, defenders of Western civilization acquired a ready-made "scientific" language to express the belief that it is natural for the "favored" or "superior" races to displace "savage," "lower" ones. Evolutionary ideas of progress mixed with Greek ideas of the inherent superiority of civilized peoples and proved a powerful ideology for colonists and traders. Just as animals evolve, so do "the varieties of man . . . [with] the stronger always extirpating the weaker."[14] As Darwin observed, the "favoured races" replace the "lower" ones as European civilization expands:[15]

> Remember what risk the nations of Europe ran, not so many centuries ago, of being overwhelmed by the Turks, and how ridiculous such an idea now is! The more civilized so called Caucasian races have beaten the Turkish hollow in the struggle for existence. Looking to the world at no very distant date, what an endless number of the lower races will have been eliminated by the civilized races throughout the world.[16]

A Common Humanity

In contrast to the Greek belief in barbarian inferiority and the Enlightenment ridicule for the "uncivilized races," missionaries have long believed that native people are made in God's image and are of common descent with Europeans from our first parents, Adam and Eve. This belief in the radical equality of all human beings inspired the Dominican bishop Bartolomé de Las Casas in his opposition to slavery in the sixteenth century. It was this same belief that encouraged Dr. John Philip of the London Missionary Society to support native rights in South Africa in the early nineteenth century; the same belief that led Lancelot Threlkeld to demand equal protection under the law for the Awabakal people of Australia and also inspired John Eliot to persuade the Massachusetts courts to find in favor of native people against settler claims. Even so unsympathetic an author as David Stoll concedes that contemporary evangelical missions in Latin America "tended to treat native people with more respect than did national governments and fellow citizens."[17]

This biblical vision of humanness even enabled Bishop Las Casas radically to reverse the language used to describe native people. He transformed the implications of the term *barbarian* by claiming that all men, regardless of cultural origins, become barbarians when they commit "cruel inhuman, wild and merciless acts." He was thus able to indict the conquistadors as "barbarians" and regard the Indians as "civilized."[18]

During the late nineteenth century the Darwinian picture of humanness challenged the Christian vision. Richard Burton regarded the Christian willingness to treat black people as "men and brethren" as a dangerous error at odds with the evolutionary facts.[19] Darwin himself was more sympathetic toward missions. But he believed that aboriginal people inevitably become extinct and was surprised to hear of the success of the mission among the Tierra del Fuegans. Darwin knew Tierra del Fuego well, having visited it during his voyage on *The Beagle*, and according to Alan Moorehead, his first thought on catching sight of the native people had been that "they were much closer to wild animals than to civilised human beings."[20] He had therefore assumed that they would die out and that missionary activity would be pointless. Darwin wrote: "The success of the Tierra del Fuego Mission . . . is most wonderful, and shames me, as I always prophesied utter failure."[21]

Darwinism was particularly influential in the newer colonies at the turn of the twentieth century. In Australia the Aborigines were seen as an inferior race that was bound to become extinct under the evolutionary pressure of the new arrivals. The future of Australia lay with the superior white race, justifying the expropriation of Aboriginal land and the supposedly humane protection of Aborigines while they died out.[22] As Gill notes, it is difficult to overestimate the significance for a people despised as a subrace on the road to extinction when told that they are not only equal to whites, as all have been created by one God, but are preferentially loved by God in contrast to the persecuting whites.[23]

By identifying Christian missions with the Western ideology of cultural supremacy, the story of missionary oppression obscures the role of Enlightenment and evolutionary beliefs. By blaming the oppression and abuse of native people on Christians, it provides the modern mind with an alibi for its own complicity in oppression. Against this background we will look at some specific examples of the treatment of native peoples. I will focus first on the dispute between missionaries and slavers, and second on the conflicts between missionaries and colonists during periods of national expansion.

Slaves, Missionaries and Greek Humanism

Bertrand Russell's astonishing allegation that "the churches, as everyone knows, opposed the abolition of slavery as long as they dared"[24] is a frequent plot feature of the story of missionary oppression. It is a travesty of the truth, but this does not prevent its frequent repetition. The same story appeared in the book accompanying the BBC TV series on *The Missionaries:*

> With the invading armies came priests and friars whose presence justified the subjugation of the people and the use of whatever coercion was judged necessary to bring them to the faith. Under the guise of evangelism came harsh exploitation and eventually the enslavement of the Indians.[25]

The systematic enslavement of the New World did indeed begin in the late fifteenth century, and church opposition to it began soon after. In 1511 the Dominican Antonio de Montesinos preached a sermon against the sins of the white colonists of the Americas:

> Tell me, by what right and with what justice do you keep these poor Indians in such cruel and horrible servitude? By what authority have you made such detestable wars against these people who lived peacefully and gently on their own lands? Why do you keep them so oppressed and weary . . . you kill them with your desire to extract and acquire gold every day . . . Are these not men? Do they not have natural souls? Are you not obliged to love them as you love yourselves? Be certain that in such a state as this, you can no more be saved than the Moors or Turks.[26]

The colonists sought to have Montesinos punished, but his outrage was taken up by that unrelenting opponent of slavery Bishop Las Casas, and later in the century by Acosta, who rejected vehemently "any kind of force or violence in the preaching of the Christian faith to the Indians."[27]

In fact, slavery was justified not from the Bible but by the teaching of Aristotle, for whom a slave is a "live tool" and inherently inferior to a civilized person. Thus when Spain sought to clarify the rights of the crown over the peoples and land it had occupied, its case was championed by the humanist Juan Ginés de Sepúlveda, who argued that native Americans were Aristotle's "natural slaves," and could justly be treated as such by their conquerors. He was opposed by the theologians who rejected Aristotle's doctrines as incompatible with Christian teaching and asserted that the Spanish Crown had no rights in the Indies other than those of peaceful mission.

In Valladolid in 1550 and 1551, Sepúlveda and Las Casas debated slavery. For Las Casas:

> all the peoples of the earth are men. . . . All possess understanding and volition, being formed in the image and likeness of God. . . . Thus all mankind is one and all men are alike in what concerns their creation and natural things.[28]

For Sepúlveda, however, "natural slaves" benefit from government by others. Missionaries also opposed slavery in practice, often at personal cost.

> In Brazil Jesuits took courageous stands against the abuses of slave raids and evoked great wonderment from the natives as word sped through the jungles that among the Portuguese there were some who defended them.[29]

Christian insights have repeatedly been involved in the reform and abolition of slavery. Quaker and Puritan states were among the first in North America to reform slavery laws. William Wilberforce, of the evangelical Clapham sect, formed the Society for the Abolition of the Slave Trade in 1787 and cultivated links with missionaries. In fact, opposition to slavery has been a repeated feature of missionary activity.[30] Many nineteenth-century missionaries were appalled at the slave trade and did their best to try to change it. William Burns opposed the "coolie" trade in China and protested to British government representatives. If Livingstone is going to be slated for his paternalistic attitude to Africans and his failure to understand African cultures, we must also note his many attempts to discourage Arab slave traders. Missionaries in East Africa were horrified at the local slave trade and were at a loss as to what to do about it. Mere protests were ineffective, so they began buying slaves in order to free them. Large sums of money were provided for this by antislavery as well as missionary societies.

Cardinal Lavigerie, founder of the White Fathers in 1868 and militant opponent of the slave trade in Africa, was instrumental in convening the Brussels Conference for the Abolition of the Slave Trade in 1889. He set up villages for orphaned children and used the same strategy to free slaves as had his Protestant counterparts.[31]

Missionaries and Collusion

A subplot of the story of missionary oppression is the assumption that military, commercial and colonial interests go hand in hand with the aims of missionaries. Like much of the story, this suppresses the frequent conflict between missions and other interests.

National expansion and divided loyalties. From the priests said to have blessed conquistador cannon, to the Protestant missionaries who allegedly follow "orders from Washington," collusion between missions and national interests is taken for granted.[32]

It is true that from the sixteenth to the eighteenth century the European powers were relentless in their pursuit of territorial control. However, missionaries were in a more marginal position and owed their immediate loyalty to Rome or to a missionary society rather than to the emerging nation states. This became an increasing hindrance to territorial expansion. For example, the Portuguese authorities imprisoned the Jesuit missionary Padre Samuel Fritz and destroyed the missions he had established in Peru in the early eighteenth century in order to extend their territorial control and enslave the native people. In 1895 Chief Khama Boikano (together with Sebele and Bathoen) used the independent communication and organization of the London Missionary Society to prevent Cecil Rhodes from including Bechuanaland in the area of the British South Africa Company.

This conflict was not limited to a few isolated missionaries and sometimes extended over long periods. Where the independence of the missionaries could not be controlled, national governments expelled them to prevent their publicizing atrocities or intervening to help the native people.[33]

Missionary independence of national majority interest continued into the twentieth century. David Stoll, no friend of missions, notes that much of "the leadership of current native rights organisations in the Peruvian Amazon comes out of [the missionaries'] bilingual schools."[34]

Missionaries, traders and colonists. Charles Boxer sardonically observes that the behavior of "most European pioneers in the tropics was apt to be based on the theory that there were no Ten Commandments south of the equator."[35] The behavior of traders and colonists toward indigenous people reflects this and has varied from mutual coexistence to cruelty beyond belief. The orthodox story of missionary oppression emphasizes such abuse and identifies missionaries as hand in glove with the exploiters. The complex patterns of interaction between missionary, trading and native interests are suppressed.

In challenging the orthodox story's generalization that missionaries routinely colluded with injustice, I do not wish to fall into the opposite error: that no missionary or priest has ever colluded with colonial or trader oppression. It is clear that collusion did sometimes occur. Oppression is most readily documented after the initial missionary period, when the occupying power and the priesthood shared loyalties (national, economic and social status) and local interests (servants, cheap labor or food), or where priests relied more on Aristotle's *Politics* than on the apostle Paul's letter to Philemon. For example, the Instructions of the Archbishop of Lima in 1665 gave strict rules of conduct for visiting priests in their behavior toward the native people. This suggests that both collusion with the colonists and abuse of the natives was a risk, if not actually occurring, although it also establishes that attempts were made by the more independent authority of the archbishop to prevent it.

However, even clear cases of apparent collusion between missionary and trader can turn out to be more subtle than at first appears. Take, for example, the well-known quotation of David Livingstone from his address at the Senate House in Cambridge in 1857: "I go back to Africa to make an open path for commerce and Christianity; do you carry out the work which I have begun."[36]

This link between commerce and Christianity seems conclusive enough and is frequently cited in the orthodox story. However, the situation is more complex than at first appears. Missionaries in Africa were opposed to slavery from an early period, and they used a variety of means to oppose it, including buying slaves and establishing plantations for them to work on. From the mid-nineteenth century they hit upon a new scheme to undermine the slave trade: the provision of alternative, legitimate "commerce" to attract traders away from the profit to be made from human misery. Livingstone's enthusiastic support for commerce was, in significant part, motivated by his horror at the cruelties of the slave trade and his desire to do everything he could to stop it. Like the ultimately unhappy strategy of buying slaves and employing them on plantations, the missionary support for commerce led to alliances with traders who did not share the values of the gospel. But it is surely misleading to simply identify missions with commerce without further comment or to quote Livingstone as though he were an apostle of trade rather than a disciple of Jesus.

Missionary conflicts. In fact, conflict between missionary and trading or colonial interests was common. The independent lines of communication enjoyed by missionaries (and from the late eighteenth century, their links to antislavery and aboriginal protection societies) proved a constant irritant to the colonizers and to unregulated trading empires such as the East India Company, the British South Africa Company and the Peruvian Amazon Company. The missionaries insisted on treating native people as human beings who are entitled to the protection of the law, and this rubbed salt into the wound. It should come as no surprise, therefore, that colonists and traders often *opposed* missions.

The clash between missionaries and traders was not, of course, new. The idol makers in Ephesus were angry at their loss of trade when Christianity caught on, and the more oppressive the business interest, the stronger the opposition.

As at Ephesus conversion often results in changed behavior that can threaten some kinds of trade, whether of alcohol, idols or slaves. Las Casas tells of a group of native people who burned their idols on their conversion. When Spanish conquistadors arrived in their village, they expelled the missionaries and forced the recently converted native people to buy new idols from the Spanish and to worship them instead of God. He comments:

> [The Spanish] have done their level best to prevent missionaries from preaching, presumably because they felt that the spread of the Gospel would in some way stand between them and the gold and wealth they craved.[37]

Las Casas's reform of the encomienda system produced violent opposition from the colonists. Such conflict was not peculiar to Roman Catholic missions in the Americas. In 1676 Eliot protested at the unjust treatment of the Algonquin, and was himself abused and threatened by the settlers.

Moreover, traders and colonists resisted the evangelism of native people, seeing conversion as the first step to indigenous people gaining access to the resources of Western culture and hence to the power that colonists wished to keep to themselves. In North America, David Brainerd complained that the traders opposed missions, as they wished to keep the natives exactly as they were so that exploitation through drink sales and land theft could continue: "Some [white men] in all parts of the country where I have preached to [native people], have taken pains industriously to bind them down in pagan darkness." They told the natives that they were "happy," "good" and "safe" enough already and did not need to become Christians. Native people who wished to break free of the settlers' stranglehold and worship God were immediately persecuted by the white traders.[38]

Henry Martyn in early-nineteenth-century India was condemned by Europeans for associating with the natives and starting schools. "Some thought it simply crazy; others saw it as pernicious; a converted Indian would be harder to keep under." As Martyn recorded in his diary, the Europeans "seem to hate to see me associating at all with the natives, and one gave me a hint a few days ago about taking my exercise on foot."[39] Colonial settlers wanted land, not conversions:

> The missionaries [to New Guinea] from the start found themselves in bitter opposition to the white traders and exploiters, whose attitude was expressed by one of them to John G. Paton in the words "our watchword is 'Sweep these creatures away, and let white men occupy the soil,' " and who, in pursuance of their aim, placed men sick of the measles on various islands in order to destroy the population through disease.[40]

Missionaries had good reasons to oppose trading and colonial oppression, for it was not only contrary to the content of the gospel but also inhibited its spread. Settlers and traders had little interest in missions. It is simply not true that "the Spanish conquistadors arrived in South America with two ambitions: to search for gold and precious minerals, and to convert the local people to Christianity."[41] Few conquistadors wished to convert the native people, for this would have involved accepting that they were the equal of any European and should be treated as sisters and brothers in Christ. When a cleric urged Pizarro, the conqueror of Peru, to stop the destruction of the Indians and to help them instead to understand the gospel, he replied: "I have not come for any such reasons; I have come to take away from them their gold."[42]

In fact, the missionaries frequently had more in common with the native peoples than either had with the colonizing white men. Indeed, the behavior of the colonists was often a serious problem for missions. Neill comments that the "principal obstacle to the evangelisation of the western peoples [of the Americas] was the cruelty with which they were treated by the Spanish colonists."[43] Las Casas reported that the Indians called the white "Christian" colonists "demons"; understandably, when the missionaries arrived, the Indians wanted nothing to do with the gospel. The behavior of colonists had "given reason for the name of Christ to be loathed and abominated by countless people."[44]

The situation was scarcely better farther north. Mid-eighteenth century native Americans told Brainerd that "white people lie, defraud, steal, and drink worse" than the natives who, as a result, were "more wicked and miserable than when you Christian white men came among us." Nor was this restricted to the Americas. In early-nineteenth-century India, Henry Martyn recorded, "Here every native I meet is an enemy to me because I am an Englishman. [Here I am] viewed as an unjust intruder."[45] And on early-nineteenth-century Tanna in the New Hebrides, John Paton lamented, "Sorer and more hopeless [than the behavior of the natives] was the wicked and contaminating influence of, alas, my fellow countrymen," who encouraged war in order to sell weapons, murdered the natives for their resources and deliberately spread measles among the natives, killing a third of the population.[46]

Alliances between missionary and native peoples. Faced with such cruelty and exploitation, many missionaries forged alliances with native people. In seventeenth- and eighteenth-century North America, John Eliot and David Brainerd were both appalled at the oppression of the native people by whites, who wanted their land, traded unfairly and wished to expand the market for alcohol. Eliot petitioned the colonial government, and Brainerd defended the native people against whites who tried to drive them off their land by intimidation.

In nineteenth-century Australia, Lancelot Threlkeld argued for the equality of Aborigines before the law, and a later generation of missionaries repeatedly protested against Australian government policy toward aboriginal peoples. In New Zealand missionaries consistently opposed the European settlement from the early nineteenth century, although without success.

Stereotypes of Native and Missionary

The orthodox story of missionary oppression suggests that native people are passive and "readily abandon their own religious traditions in favour of the doctrines taught by the priests."[47] The evidence for this picture is weak, and the story is demeaning to both native culture and religion.

The stereotype of the native is drawn partly from Darwin's belief that "weaker" races would become extinct rather than evolve and partly from the "noble savage" of the Romantic tradition. This has produced a composite image of vulnerable nobility and earth-friendly lifestyle. Ironically, this sidelines real native peoples and suppresses their struggle, their resistance and their survival.[48] James Miller, an aboriginal author, is rightly scathing of this stereotype:

> [Missionaries] were no more successful in converting Kooris to Christianity than the churches were in converting the white community. If it is said that Christianity destroyed Koori culture, then it can be said that Koori culture was not a strong culture and that Koori society in general was inferior. Such thinking depicts the Kooris to be the helpless victims of brain-washing who abandoned everything that they ever believed in as soon as someone stood up and preached from an open Bible. This was not the case and such thinking degrades Koori society. Kooris were not helpless and Koori culture was not destroyed[49]

Miller's opinion is repeatedly supported in missionary diaries. Take, for example, that of John Eliot, who on October 26, 1646, became the first European to preach in Algonquin. The stereotype is of native people being "brain washed," readily abandoning their traditions and adopting new beliefs for reasons of material self-interest or cultural subservience. Eliot's account tells of a seventy-five minute sermon, after which the Algonquin closely and perceptively questioned him for a further hour and a quarter. When Eliot left, there were many who wished to put more questions to their guest. This is not a picture of a "primitive," passive people overwhelmed by European culture. Indeed, in comparison with the modern custom of a twenty-minute sermon, desultorily received and immediately forgotten, the Algonquin come out of it rather well. What contemporary suburban congregation would be capable of so much?

The orthodox story also stereotypes missionaries, who are cast in the dominant role and stripped of vulnerability or sensitivity before the story begins. Thus we would be unlikely to read of John Paton on Tanna burying his wife and baby son in a grave dug with his own hands, nor of his anguished cry that but for Jesus he would have "gone mad and died beside that lonely grave."[50] The Christian beliefs of the missionaries are, the

orthodox story tells us, austere, repressed and puritanical. The more orthodox the belief, the more flint-faced and joyless. Indeed, Norman Lewis calls
Christian mission an "apparatus for the repression of joy"[51] in the naturally
harmonious and joyful life of the native. This stereotype of the austere missionary was already familiar to Darwin who himself rejected it after staying
with missionaries during his voyages aboard *The Beagle*. Indeed, any famil-
iarity with the literature of biblical Christianity shows that this is a carica-
ture.[52]

The settings. The story of missionary oppression describes native peoples
living harmoniously with nature in a "free world without time and without
fear" until their culture is destroyed by European advance.[53] These images
of pastoral innocence have the same Romantic origins as the stereotype of
the noble savage and are just as misleading. Native societies have not
always been joyful, peaceable or just, and missionaries have often been
involved in humanitarian reform. Moreover, the orthodox story also suppresses the part played by modern ideologies in the story of oppression.

The reality of native cultures is diverse and complex. Sometimes native
practices give a respect and wisdom to the elderly that is unknown in most
of western Europe. Hospitality and generosity toward guests is well documented, and some North American and Australian peoples have an understanding of the land as being held in trust, which is closer to the scriptural
view than Western ideas of absolute possession.[54] But traditional societies,
no less than Western ones, have also developed their own patterns of cruelty. The anthropologist Marvin Harris notes that

> the majority of village communities [along the banks of the Amazon and the
> Mississippi] collected enemy heads as trophies, roasted their prisoners of war
> alive, and consumed human flesh in ritual feasts.[55]

In fact, human sacrifice was common in many societies from Brazil to the
Great Plains and was usually followed by cannibalism. The possession and
ritual killing of slaves has also been widespread throughout the world and
long pre-dated the arrival of the white colonists. Recent research has taught
us to be cautious about Western interpretations of such practices. The image
of the savage cannibal seems to have held a fascination for some nineteenth
century commentators, and it is a stereotype we are well rid of.[56] But the
fact remains that native cultures were not always as peaceable or as just as
is often portrayed.

However, to point out that the orthodox story romanticizes native cultures is not to endorse Western oppression, nor to idealize Western "civilization." The Christian gospel gives all people of all civilizations an equal chance to know the truth about themselves and God's creation. No culture comes out of this unscathed. In eighteenth-century Europe, trading in slaves was commonplace, and judicial punishment included amputations, burning and death by torture. In nineteenth-century England, children regularly died through neglect in factories and mines and were exploited in child prostitution. The deaths of some eighty million people through warfare in the twentieth century and the widespread environmental damage caused by industrialization are hardly marks of civilized behavior. European and native cultures alike fall short of biblical shalom.

The interaction of cultures. The story of peaceable native cultures existing in harmony with nature needs to be treated with caution. But so does the story of missionaries indiscriminately imposing an essentially Western culture on native people. Common examples include the use of missionary musical styles or hymnody, the imposition of Western dress or language and the exposure of native people to Western consumer culture. According to Norman Lewis, missionaries deliberately destroy native culture and morale in their hunt for people to capture and convert. Native people and their culture "fall prey" to missionaries who "like weasels . . . go straight for the jugular vein," knowing that demoralized people are easier to convert.[57]

Missionaries inevitably take their home culture with them, but it is an oversimplification to claim that they indiscriminately impose it on others. Rather, missionaries interact with local cultures in complex ways, often over long periods. The sixteenth-century Jesuits in Peru anticipated that the two cultures would continue to interact for years, possibly centuries, before a stable cultural form emerged. In Brazil the early missionaries "did not attempt to impose a change from an aboriginal tribal culture to the Western culture of the time," although *mutual* cultural change did result.[58] The "mission Indian" was not a "simple primitive" manipulated by missionaries but was actively shaping Western traditions to local culture, enriching both.[59] If we abandon the picture of missionaries wreaking havoc on passive native people, a more complex story emerges.

Take the alleged destruction of native art and the imposition of Western iconography and musical traditions by missionaries. Norman Lewis, pursuing his belief that Christianity is joyless, is typical in his claim that "most missionaries" outlaw "musical instruments and jollifications of any kind in

missionary compounds."[60] Recent scholarship has undermined such gener-
alizations. For example, music thrived in early colonial Latin America, and
its art was a complex interaction between indigenous and European traditions. Amerindian artisans drew upon preconquest iconographies in their
paintings for the Catholic Church, producing a new synthesis of traditions.[61]

Another commonly cited example of cultural oppression is that native
people are forced to wear European dress or hairstyle on their conversion,
or to adopt other Western customs.

> The African's clothing, or rather lack of it, concerned the missionaries to an
> obsessive degree. . . . The battle to clothe Africa was highly symbolic [of the
> attempt to civilize it].[62]

There are, indeed, well-documented cases of such cultural insensitivity.
For example, in 1647 Native American converts around Concord (Massachusetts) were required to "wear their hair comely as the English do."[63] But
if this sometimes occurred, so also did the adoption by missionaries of
native customs. Many missionaries chose to identify with native culture
rather than their own. Sixteenth-century Jesuit missionaries to China and
Japan wore local dress and followed local customs. In the 1850s both Hudson Taylor and William Burns did likewise. Such acculturation was not
restricted to the customs of the native ruling classes. José de Anchieta, the
influential mid-sixteenth-century Jesuit missionary to Brazil, recommended
adopting Indian customs such as sleeping in nets, as well as the Indian diet.
Some grew so accustomed to the native style that it was Western tradition
that seemed strange. Charles Darwin noticed that some missionaries were
so familiar with tattooed faces that "a plain [i.e., untatooed] face looked
mean, and not like that of a New Zealand gentleman."[64]

Missionaries are also alleged to have imposed their native tongue on
indigenous people. Bonilla cynically observes of the Franciscans in mid-sixteenth-century Amazonia that "their pious work was marked, among other
things, by giving Spanish names to everything."[65] Colonists often used
European names, but the majority of early missionaries realized that if they
were to communicate with the native people, they had to learn the people's
language. The first written forms of many languages were the result of missionary attempts to translate the Bible. Although not their specific intention,
this work helped codify and preserve languages. The anthropologist Mary
Haas estimates that "ninety per cent of the material [currently] available on

American Indian languages" is missionary in origin.[66]

Sometimes these familiar allegations of missionary cultural oppression have a hidden agenda. Sam Padilla, a native member of the Ecuadorian Auca people but with a Western background, explained to a visiting academic that the "worst enemy [the Auca] have are the missionaries," who "had forced the Aucas to wear clothes . . . [and] read the Bible, and [had] sown confusion in their simple, pure minds."[67] Padilla wished to preserve Auca culture and was supported in this by his partnership with a United States tourism company promoting the "untouched, unexplored, undiscovered" Amazon. As the tour material explained, the Auca live in the very womb of Dame Nature:

> The Aucas live in rain forests where rushing rivers and high mountains form a natural barrier, isolating them from the outside world. The Indians literally live off the bountiful land. . . . The tribesmen wear little more than G-strings. They have no monetary system. All food and materials are shared equally.[68]

The language of Western romanticism has here been appropriated for the rhetorical purposes of advertising copy. The tourist literature would be drained of local color by the sight of the tribesmen wearing more than G-strings and leaning against trees reading their Bibles.

Missionaries and reform. In all societies it is the powerless who are most vulnerable to abuse, whether widows, slaves, children or the elderly. As might be anticipated from the gospel's concern for the poor, missionaries have been especially active in opposing the oppression of vulnerable members of society. Charles Darwin observed at first hand that "human sacrifices . . . infanticide . . . bloody wars, where the conquerors spared neither women nor children—all these have been abolished . . . by the introduction of Christianity."[69] Missionaries (and in Europe, Christian reformers) have often been in the vanguard of humanistic reforms. This is not to claim that they were alone. Reform often involved complex alliances between many interests. For example, while missionaries since William Carey have opposed the custom of *sati*,[70] its abolition involved their alliance with Hindu reformers and colonial administrators. Are missionaries always wrong to oppose such aspects of native culture?

In early-twentieth-century Kenya, missionaries were vocal opponents of clitoredectomy, especially medical missionaries who published accounts of its consequences in medical journals from the 1920s. Missionaries encouraged converts to renounce the practice, despite native protest. They forged alliances with humanitarian and feminist groups in England who raised the issue in Parliament. Were they mistaken? Their dilemma has its contemporary equivalent in the Western debate about female genital mutilation. Many, like the missionaries, oppose it out of humanitarian concern, but others reject this opposition as a racist prejudice that can see only "primitive" and "barbaric" practices. The standards by which we assess a culture foreign to our own are inevitably complex. But authentic engagement with other cultures entails making judgments, and a postmodern refusal to do so can amount to indifference and bad faith.

Beyond doubt, many native peoples have been dispossessed and their native culture undermined. Yet this is more likely to have been, and continues to be, the result of straightforward violence than of native people tricked by new beliefs that easily overwhelmed their own fragile customs. The historian and theologian Stephen Neill concludes that the "weight of evidence tells heavily against" the accusation that missionaries have been responsible for the destruction of native cultures.[71]

Hidden Ideologies
The story of missionary oppression has its roots in the soil of eighteenth-century Enlightenment anticlericalism, but it grew along with the nineteenth-century expansion of mission. The Russian explorer Otto von Kotzebue was one of the first to voice the now familiar allegations. He argued that missionaries had destroyed native cultures and covertly supported colonial powers under the guise of Christian civilization. He was opposed by the unlikely figure of Charles Darwin, who drew on his personal observations during the voyages of *The Beagle* in the 1830s. Darwin also gave one of the earliest explanations for the persistence of the myths about missionaries. He argued that missionary reform was opposed by whites who wished to exploit native women:

> I believe that, disappointed in not finding the field of licentiousness quite so open as formerly, they will not give credit to a morality which they do not wish to practise or to a religion which they undervalue, if not despise.[72]

This explanation may not be as far-fetched as it at first appears. The nineteenth-century imagination pictured Africa as a place of exotic sexual experiences, populated by black women of uninhibited natural passion and promiscuity.[73] This belief served as an alibi for the sexual abuse of women by the might of colonial power. Such myths die hard.

Norman Lewis records visiting a recently evangelized village in Vietnam. Lewis was accompanied by a colleague whose humanistic credentials were unimpeachable—as he was "much attracted to the teaching of Jean-Paul Sartre." They noticed that the women wore blouses and, believing that missionaries had persuaded them to do this, took offense. Lewis records his traveling companion's plea to the native chief, "'At least tell the women to take their missionary blouses off while we're here.' The chief rapped out a word of command and the women began to strip to the waist." Evidently this response met with Lewis's approval, for he enthuses that "in a few seconds the reception parade was ready and we made our way to the chief's house between two score or so of freely and splendidly displayed torsos."[74] This misogynist "parade" of native women to the gaze of visiting Westerners does not appear to trouble Lewis and represents for him the freeing of native women from cultural oppression by missionaries.

Whatever truth there may have been in Darwin's suspicions in the nineteenth century, his explanation for the stereotyping of missionaries is too limited for the dawn of the twenty-first century. As we have seen, the story of missionary oppression has had several effects. It has stereotyped native people and their cultures, it has hidden the historical conflicts between missionaries and Western colonial interests, and it has suppressed the role of Enlightenment and evolutionary ideologies in exploitation and oppression. As a result, the orthodox story has had an important role in promoting the grand story of modernity as deserving of our loyalty, for it blames all the ills of colonial exploitation on the church and on Christian beliefs. The modern mind gains an alibi for its part in the oppression of native people and covers up its complicity in wide-scale human misery. Enlightenment and Darwinian ideologies evade responsibility for their part in oppression, and the modern mind retains its trust in its own rationality and enlightened tolerance. The missionary is painted as the bigoted and superstitious antagonist of the enlightened rationalist, but this is an antagonist that the modern mind needs to sustain its own self-image.

5

THE HUMAN BODY
A Story of Repression

I N THE LAST CHAPTER WE SAW NORMAN LEWIS OFFENDED AT THE SIGHT
of native women wearing blouses, which he believed missionary
prudery had forced on them. In the next chapter we will hear of
witches as independent, assertive women oppressed by a patriarchal
church's fear of female sexuality. These are just two examples of a widely
believed story that tells us how the church has denied the body and is
afraid of sexuality. At best, Christianity is said to sideline the physical body;
at worst, to hate it. The female body is supposed to be particularly despised
as impure and a source of temptation. Sexuality, we are told, is repressed by
Christians, finding its outlet in censoriousness, prudery or sadomasochistic
pleasure in pain and punishment. Christianity, so the story goes, is a religion oriented to the next world, with its ethereal spirit beings, and it deni-
grates all aspects of this one.

The Myth of Sinful Flesh
In the book accompanying his popular British television series *The Body in
Question*, Jonathan Miller described Christianity as more concerned for the
"metaphysical fate of mankind" than the "physical order of nature." The
Pompeian murals of the second century A.D. present bodies as solid and
delightful, a world in which "man was obviously pleased to linger." Blind
to the different historical contexts, Miller contrasts these with medieval
European art, which he regards as symptomatic in its portrayal of bodies as
unreal and lacking sensual depth: "little more than hieroglyphs," images

for a society impatient for the next world.[1] According to Miller, Christianity gives the metaphysical, spiritual soul more importance than the merely material body.

For the pioneering French feminist Simone de Beauvoir this reflects an internal battle:

> The Christian is divided within himself; the separation of body and soul, of life and spirit, is complete; original sin makes of the body the enemy of the soul; all ties of the flesh seem evil.[2]

This "story of sinful flesh" has four central plot features.

1. *All flesh is evil.* De Beauvoir repeatedly tells us that Christianity is opposed to the body. The warfare of good and evil corresponds to the conflict of the spirit with the body. According to Christianity, she claims, "evil is an absolute reality; and the flesh is sin."[3]

2. *Body hating.* As a direct result of this warfare between the spiritual good and the bodily evil, Christians learn to hate the body just as we love the good. Christianity, says de Beauvoir, is "a religion that holds the flesh accursed"; it bears unremitting "hatred for the flesh."[4]

3. *Sex-denying.* Such hatred for the flesh is sex-denying, for sex is fleshly and therefore sinful: "With Christianity . . . came the idea that sex was sinful, that Adam and Eve were expelled from Eden because of sexual sin."[5]

4. *Virgin or whore.* The repression of sexuality has particularly serious consequences for women. Christians are said to believe that women, represented by Eve, were the cause of the Fall, embody a lurking demonic power, are carnal and lustful, and entrap men. Women are either sexually innocent virgins or sexually promiscuous whores. As one recent author puts it: "Official Church doctrine . . . preached that woman was the source of all evil (since Eve trafficked with the Serpent) . . . and that sex and the body were dirty and vile."[6]

The body and sex. The church, we are told, "did everything it could to decry and degrade [sex]."[7] Elizabeth Rouse of the London College of Fashion claims:

> It is quite commonly believed that we wear clothes because certain parts of our bodies are shameful and need to be covered. Attitudes of this kind have their origins in the religious mythology of Judaeo-Christian tradition, in particular in the story of Adam and Eve.[8]

Christianity's supposed repression of sex is linked to masochistic and unhealthy attitudes. Books such as George Orwell's *A Clergyman's Daughter* or Jeanette Winterson's *Oranges Are Not the Only Fruit* describe young women emerging into liberty from emotionally and sexually repressive Christian backgrounds. Orwell's heroine, Dorothy, hated cold baths and "for that very reason made it a rule to take all her baths cold." This body-hating masochism is especially inclined to punish the flesh for spiritual shortcomings: "She made it a rule, whenever she caught herself not attending to her prayers, to prick her arm hard enough to make blood come."[9] Bertrand Russell concludes that Christian attitudes toward sex are "morbid and unnatural."[10] "In the Middle Ages," we are told, "whole villages were . . . given to whipping themselves to drive out wicked thoughts—but what sinful bliss the pain of the whip could excite."[11]

It is no coincidence that Winterson's and Orwell's novels concern young women, for it is women who are said to have suffered most from Christianity's supposed repression of sex. Rosemary Radford Ruether cites a fourteenth-century Dominican preacher John Broomyard, who described "woman" as "a painted tombstone that conceals a rotting corpse." She considers this belief to be characteristic of both the medieval mind and of Puritanism.[12] The supposed link between women, sexuality and sin results in both the Christian persecution of the witch and the veneration of the virgin: "Christianity respects the consecrated virgin, and the chaste and obedient wife, in spite of its hatred for the flesh."[13]

In the next chapter we will see that the link between women, the body and sinful flesh leads to a new story—that of the witch as an independent, wise and sexually expressive woman. In this story the church, bastion of male power and privilege, attempts to repress female power that is linked to ancient pagan religions, accounting for the witch-hunts of early-modern Europe.

The sin of anesthesia. There have so far been only general hints that the "story of sinful flesh" carries the myth of the "warfare between science and religion." The story is certainly naturalistic; it breaks the supposed association of the body with sin by rejecting the existence of sin itself. Indeed, it rejects any notion that humans owe a duty to anyone or anything other than themselves. Moreover, it does this in the name of science. After all, it is the modern discoveries by biology, especially evolution, which are thought to have shown us that we are ultimately but flesh, and it is modern medical science that has banished superstitious remedies.

Particularly clear evidence that the myth of the "warfare between science and religion" remains in the driving seat is provided by the story of "Eve's curse." According to this, the church opposed the introduction of scientific anesthesia in childbirth in the nineteenth century.

Anesthesia was first used to relieve the pain of childbirth by James Simpson in 1847, but "preachers argued that God intended birth to be painful."[14]

> The introduction of anesthesia was not [at first] looked on favorably by everyone. Some thought it was unnatural and wrong to alleviate the suffering inflicted on mankind by God as a retribution for his sins.[15]

The reference, of course, is to Genesis 3:16: "To the woman he said, 'I will greatly increase your pangs in childbearing, in pain you shall bring forth children,' " which is here understood as a norm or law that we overrule at our peril.

The James Simpson story seems to have originated in that compendium of misleading tales, Andrew White's *A History of the Warfare of Science with Theology*:

> From pulpit after pulpit Simpson's use of chloroform was denounced as impious and contrary to Holy Writ; texts were cited abundantly, the ordinary declaration being that to use chloroform was "to avoid one part of the primeval curse on women."[16]

This story has been investigated in detail by consulting the medical and religious literature of the period. In fact, religious opposition to Simpson's use of anesthesia in childbirth was "virtually non-existent," although it was opposed on other grounds, including medical, physiological and moral.[17] The story of Eve's curse is, however, absent. The only significant work traced by the science historian A. D. Farr that did deal specifically with the biblical point of view was by an evangelical Anglican, who defended the use of anesthesia in childbirth. Few versions of the story of Eve's curse mention Simpson's own Christian conversion.

Origins of the Myth

Like most modern myths, that of "sinful flesh" marshals and distorts history for its own purposes. However, to reject distorting myths is clearly not an endorsement of the church's treatment of the body over its two-thousand-year history. It is undoubtedly true that some Christians have held misogynist and dualistic opinions, devaluing the body. It is easy to find examples from the Catholic tradition of scourging the body to nineteenth-century Protestant prudery. De Beauvoir repeatedly cites Tertullian, Ambrose and John Chrysostom to illustrate the "savagely anti-feminist Jewish tradition," and she uses "Puritan" as a synonym for repressive attitudes toward the body and sexuality.[18] But the issue is not whether, in a two-thousand-year tradition, it is possible to find instances of the "story of sinful flesh." It would be surprising if we could not. The question is whether these are authentic expressions of, to use de Beauvoir's phrase, the "Jewish tradition," or distortions of it in need of reform. A review of the influence of biblical teaching does not support de Beauvoir's opinion. Where scriptural authors have had most impact, a different history emerges.[19]

If the denigration of the body is more a Christian heresy than Christian orthodoxy, where did this influence on the church come from? It can be traced to the repeated injection of Greek thought into the church body, initially administered by the early fathers but subsequently repeated by Aquinas's synthesis of Aristotle with the Bible in the thirteenth century, and the vogue for Neo-Platonism during the Renaissance.[20]

From a very early period Greek thought drew a sharp division between body and soul, and it came in time to devalue the former in favor of the latter. By the fourth century B.C., this bias was firmly established. So, for Plato, the soul is created first, then embodied. The relationship between it and the body is at best one of tension, at worst one of imprisonment, with the soul chained to the body. Such imprisonment prevents the soul from gaining a true perception of the world: "If we would have true knowledge of anything, we must be quit of the body . . . purification is . . . the release of the soul from the chains of the body."[21] This Greek dualism was constantly read into the Bible, with serious consequences for the Western cultural tradition.

The Authentic Christian Body

What then might a more authentically Christian attitude to the body be like? We can get a clue about this from the biblical teaching about the resurrection—not the freeing of the soul from its bodily imprisonment as in Hellenistic thought, nor the mystical flight of an ethereal spirit, but the resurrection of the physical body to a new life on a restored earth. At the center of the faith is a very material, bodily belief. It was, of course, the scandal of this "bodyliness" that prompted the early Christian heresy of docetism—the misapprehension that Christ's bodily incarnation was only an appearance. The philosopher Stephen Clark notes that it is an oddity of modernist critiques of Christianity that the faith "is abused both for neglecting bodily matters and for insisting on the crude materialism of a physical resurrection. If the body . . . [were not] immortal, neither should it be given much importance."[22] But it is. As William Temple noted:

> Christianity is the most materialistic of all great religions. The others hope to achieve spiritual reality by ignoring matter—calling it illusion (*maya*) or saying that it does not exist. . . . Christianity, based as it is on the Incarnation, regards matter as destined to be the vehicle and instrument of spirit.[23]

This is virtually the opposite of the conclusion reached by Jonathan Miller from his comparison of Pompeian and "medieval" art.

Many authors have noted that the biblical terms translated "soul," "spirit" and "body" do not refer to different parts of a human being in any straightforward sense. Calvin, for example, was fully aware that the apostle Paul used both *flesh* and *spirit* interchangeably with *soul*.[24] But we have become so accustomed to Greek dualism that we tend to read into the Bible conflicts that are not there. For example, it is often claimed that Paul, in particular, contrasts "flesh" and "spirit," suggesting an irreconcilable conflict between the two (Rom 7; 1 Cor 15:44-53 and Gal 5:17 are commonly cited). Body and soul are said to be set against one another, so that those who love their soul must hate their body. Moreover, as the body is especially associated with sexuality, this negative attitude spreads to sex also.

In his discussion of these passages, the philosopher Paul Helm insists that we must be careful to understand how the words *flesh* and *spirit* are being used if we are to understand what the apostle Paul means.[25] Sometimes Paul uses the word *flesh* to mean simply "human beings" (e.g., Gal 1:16) or "physical descent" (e.g., Rom 9:5).

> But when Paul uses the term figuratively it refers, not to the human body as distinct from the soul or spirit, but to the whole of the life of the non-Christian . . . as that life is lived in neglect of God or in opposition to God.[26]

As Calvin says in his commentary on Romans, flesh is "all the endowments of human nature, and everything that is in man, except the sanctification of the Spirit."[27] Thus a "fleshly person" need not be especially sensual or given to bodily excess:

> All parts of the soul were possessed by sin [since the fall] . . . it is foolish and

> unmeaning to confine the corruption . . . to what are called sensual motions.[28]

> The nature of man, in both parts of his soul [is] . . . fully depicted . . . by the words of our Saviour, "that which is born of the flesh is flesh." But it will be said, that the word *flesh* applies only to the sensual, and not to the higher part of the soul. This, however, is completely refuted by the words both of Christ and his apostle.[29]

Similarly, when Paul uses the term *spirit* figuratively and contrasts it with *flesh*, he is referring to the Christian who seeks to live a life in obedience to the will of God, dependent on God's grace. The body and mind are as much involved in this as the "soul."

Misreadings of Paul often occur. For example, 1 Corinthians 15:44-45 is cited to support a dualistic opposition of "body" and "spirit." Speaking of the resurrection of the dead, Paul tells us that the body is "sown a natural body, it is raised a spiritual body" (NIV). This is sometimes understood as teaching a split between the material, natural "body" and the "spirit." But in the original Greek language of the New Testament, "natural" or "physical" body is literally "soulish" body, and it is this that is contrasted with "spiritual" body. Yet "Paul does not teach [that] a future body is made of 'spirit' . . . any more than a present body made out of 'soul.' "[30] Indeed, Paul tells us that if there were no physical resurrection of the dead, we would still be in our sins. The Greek view that in death the spirit breaks free of the chains of the body undermines the Christian doctrine of atonement, for this depends on "physical" resurrection.

Our tendency to understand Paul as teaching a split between body and spirit is something we bring to the Bible rather than something we learn from it. Indeed, for Paul the body is not only central to the gospel but can be the temple of the Holy Spirit (1 Cor 6:19).

In the Bible we see almost the opposite to the teaching of Plato. God made human beings out of dust and in his own image. The body, not the spirit, was created first, and life was breathed into it. But this process is not to be understood as God putting our spirit into a bodily container as Plato believed, for all other creatures have the breath of life too (e.g., Gen 6:17). The uniqueness of Adam lay in his body, not the "life" common to him and animals. He welcomed Eve not as a "kindred spirit" but as "bone of my bones and flesh of my flesh" [31] (see Gen 2:7; Ezek 37). "The body, not the soul, is the characteristic element of Hebrew personality."[32]

So we are like God, but as an image, for we are created finite and dependent on God both in our origin and for our moment-by-moment existence. Moreover, we are created as bodily creatures and as a mutuality: "Male and female he created them" (Gen 1:27). When God created the sun, moon and stars, he did so by the divine fiat, "Let there be," emphasizing his word of power and his sovereign will: "and it was so" (Gen 1:6-7). The use of the phrase "Let *us* make" (Gen 1:26) first occurs with the creation of human beings, highlighting personal relatedness and the community of will within the Trinity, as well as divine power. The moon cannot image God; humans are to do so. God declares his creation "good" even before human beings are created; when he makes people, in all their "bodyliness," he declares creation "very good."

Why, then, has the Christian view of humanness become so closely associated with body hating, misogyny and the denial or repression of sexuality? To understand this, we need to return to the Greek view that has so influenced the church's teaching.

Gender

There is a good principle, which has created order, light, and man; and a bad principle, which has created chaos, darkness and woman. (Pythagoras)[33]

Pythagoras lived and worked in the sixth century B.C., and his views are shared by later Greek authors. For Plato, man is the "superior sex," and his doctrine of reincarnation sets out man's fate if he does not come up to scratch:

> He who lived well during his appointed time was to return and dwell in his native star, and there he would have a blessed and congenial existence. But if he failed in attaining this, at the second birth he would pass into a woman. . . . [If she persists in evil, she would become an animal].[34]

True, Plato taught that women were above slaves and barbarians, and he advocated their education on an equal basis with men, but it went without saying that women's achievements would always be the lesser.[35]

Within this framework, sexual union had a strongly functional purpose. For example, Plato advocated the strict regulation and eugenic control of the breeding of superior men who would be groomed to rule others. There was little place for committed relationships between one man and one woman, or for family life. Among these highest types of men, wives were held in common and children reared not to know their parents.

The situation for women does not improve with Aristotle for, like his master Plato, he regarded women as inferior men, as naturally passive and "subject" to man, the active "ruler": "For the female is, as it were, a mutilated male . . . for there is only one thing they have not in them, the principle of soul."[36] Women symbolized the realm of matter, body and imperfection; "man," however, was associated with spirit, soul and the divine.[37] These are familiar associations, often wrongly attributed to the Bible.

This Greek view of women as inferior infiltrated the early Christian church and has plagued Western culture ever since. It is in sharp contrast to the biblical vision of *gendered humanness.*

When God made human beings in his own image, "male and female he created them." From the beginning, humanness has been a mutual biunity, with no room for the Greek idea of man as "superior" to woman, or more "divine." Both equally are created from the dust of the earth, excluding the Greek association of women with earthly matter. Moreover, our bodily, gendered creativity is affirmed in the first blessing we received from God ("Be fruitful and multiply," Gen 1:28). Sexuality has been integral to "spiritual" human existence, to living in the will of God, from the beginning and has no more to do with sin or the Fall than any other aspect of humanness. The Song of Solomon is a celebration of love and with all its physical passion is often seen as pointing to the relationship between Christ and the church. There is no distance between our identity as imaging God and our existence as bodily, gendered people.

When human beings sinned, all creation suffered, including the relationships between men and women. We no longer worship God but have exchanged his glory for the image of some aspect of creation and his truth for a lie. We worship and serve the creature rather than the creator. N. T. Wright has suggested in a lecture that among the first aspects of God's image to be affected by this idolatry are gender and gender relationships. Certainly the Greeks, who were, as Paul ironically remarked, "in all things very religious," gave sex a leading role in their idolatrous cults. But Wright has in mind more the *patterns* of cultural idolatry, which become so ingrained that they seem normal. For example, by making man the ruler and woman the natural subject, Aristotle made a norm of the curse in Genesis 3. In Romans 1 Paul emphasizes that another *cultural pattern* to be affected by idolatry is that of gender identity and gender orientation.

In the Bible procreation is not only the means by which God's humanity was to fill the earth, but was given particular status as a meeting place between humanity and God in, for example, the experiences of Sarah and Abraham, Elkanah and Hannah, Elizabeth and Zacharias, and Joseph and Mary. The birth of the Christ child at the center of human history made it the means for the redemption of the world. Every parent senses an echo of this special status with the birth of a child. Modern sexuality has narrowed this to a purely human affair and routinized contraception has given us sex without reproduction; now that procreation without sex is possible, the split is complete. Dr. Patrick Steptoe, the British pioneer of in vitro fertilization, spoke for the modern view when he said that to insist on connecting human reproduction with sex is to "debase us to the level of the animals."[38] Such denigration of sexuality as "animal" is Greek, not Christian.

An Unholy Alliance

Christian tradition reflects a complex interaction between its biblical and Greek inheritance. Greek conceptions were prominent in the Gnosticism of the second century, which had absorbed the Neo-Platonic language of the spirit imprisoned in base flesh. For Gnosticism, salvation entails escape from the prison of the body into the realm of the spirit. The resurrection body was held to be ethereal and "spiritual," not material. Views such as these influenced many theologians and were often associated with misogyny. "Man" was linked with reason and spirit; "woman" with the body, nature and sin. The superiority of reason over nature was supposed to mirror the superiority of man over woman. We can readily see the ghost of Neo-Platonism hovering over Tertullian's vividly misogynist image of woman as "a temple built over a sewer." John the Scot believed that gender difference was the result of sin, when man's sensuous, fallen nature was embodied in women. The church has formally rejected these teachings and this has diminished but not removed their influence.

With theologians such as Augustine in the fourth century, we see an attempt to reform Greek conceptions through the insights of biblical authors. Thus he rejected Origen's view that rational souls were imprisoned in bodies as a result of sin.[39] However, his Manichean past, with its dualistic split between matter and spirit, sometimes led him to neglect or disparage both the natural world and the human body. Aquinas is best known for his attempt to synthesize Greek and biblical understandings, but the latter is often a controlling force. Thus he too rejects Origen's view that rational creatures were "bound down to bodies," citing Genesis 1:31, and goes further than Augustine in his insistence that happiness does not entail the separation of the soul from the body.[40]

Medieval bodies. The West amalgamated these Greek and biblical views and, not surprisingly, has had a problem with the body and sexuality ever since. The medieval period is often portrayed as obsessed with the sinfulness of the flesh. From the ascetic ideals of monasticism to the tradition of courtly love, from hair shirts to chastity belts, we view this as a time of hatred for the flesh and of unhealthy sexuality. Medieval and early modern society is pictured as overwhelmingly patriarchal, and most older history books scarcely mention women at all, unless they were being rescued, fought over or bearing children to continue a bloodline. From Hildegard of Bingen to Teresa of Ávila or Marguerite of Angoulême, influential women have been marginalized in historical accounts. Recent scholarship is transforming this view. Areas of female power were, in fact, established in both court and convent. Moreover, even at its height the Greek devaluation of both women and the human body was limited by a continuing holistic biblical vision. As the historian Caroline Bynum argues, "The incarnation [of God in Jesus the Christ] meant that the whole human person was capable of redemption," and this sustained a positive image of the body, especially in the experience of women.[41] As we have seen, even Thomistic Catholicism contained an antidualistic theme that placed limits on the Greek identification of man with the "rational soul" to the exclusion of women and "bodyliness." The fourteenth-century poet Dante, while thoroughly immersed in his Greek heritage, was aware too of this other, more truly biblical story. In *The Divine Comedy* he attributes to no less an authority than Solomon a vision of the resurrection body:

> And when we put completeness on afresh,
> All the more gracious shall our person be,
> Reclothèd in the holy and glorious flesh.[42]

The Reformers in Context

As we move toward the modern era, this pattern grows ever more complex. While the Renaissance brought a fresh injection of Greek ideas, the Reformation strengthened the biblical vision. Moreover, social changes transformed human experience and brought new perceptions of what is appropriate for each sex. The incompatible Greek and biblical accounts of the body vied within this changing social context with very different consequences for men and for women.

From the sixteenth century the waning influence of the secluded life throughout Europe greatly restricted one route to power for women. Moreover, the subsequent growth of towns disrupted family and community life more generally, isolating women from their traditional patterns of mutual support. During the industrial revolution in England, the separation of the spheres of work and home further narrowed and defined women's roles to childcare and domestic duties, although from the late eighteenth century this happened fastest among the emerging middle class. The rationalization of society and the separation of private life from the public arena further restricted routes to power. Women were progressively excluded as the spheres of politics, science, art and commerce grew.

In addition to changes arising from social factors, the resurgence of Greek dualism during the Renaissance associated men with science, activity and power, and women with nature, passivity and subjection. As we saw in chapter one, the association of women with nature was to find expression in the seventeenth century as Dame Nature, whose secrets had to be taken forcibly by (male) science.

If the Renaissance strengthened the Greek view of gender relationships, the sixteenth-century Reformation turned attention back to the Bible. The most obvious consequence was the rejection of celibacy as the highest ideal, contributing to the undermining of the secluded life. In this respect it is true that the Reformation narrowed some life choices available to women by speeding the closure of religious houses and the dissolution of the cult of saints. But it also opened up other avenues, redefining the status of women and social dimensions of gender.

Some Reformers, such as Philip Melanchthon, stayed loyal to their Renaissance humanist teachers and took a conservative view of gender. Considering the curse of Genesis 3 it is not surprising that they reflected the opinions of their day and sought to "rule" women linguistically as well as socially. But more radical figures such as John Calvin had their old understanding turned upside down as they rejected tradition in favor of Scripture. In so far as their views were reformed from biblical insight, their divergence from contemporary attitudes was striking.

The affirmation of "bodyliness." Calvin affirmed what Stephen Clark calls "the crude materialism of a physical resurrection" and denied the split between "spiritual" and "physical" that de Beauvoir saw as central to the story of sinful flesh.[43] We have already seen the apostle Paul's discussion of the nature of the body before and after the resurrection in 1 Corinthians 15. Speaking of this passage, Calvin asserts that

> the substance of the body is the same. . . . This is the simple and genuine meaning of the Apostle; and no one may, by philosophising farther, indulge in airy speculations, as those do, who suppose that the substance of the body will be spiritual, while there is no mention here of substance, and no change will be made upon it.[44]

The Reformers asserted the biblical materiality of the body and rediscovered the psalmist's song of wonder that we are "fearfully and wonderfully made." King David was not referring to an ethereal soul but to his body knit together in his mother's womb (Ps 139:13-14). Richard Sibbes was typical of the Reformers and later Puritans when he described the redeemed body as perfect, beautiful, glorious, immortal, powerful and vigorous.[45] Whatever we may think of his choice of words, this is not the language of disembodied spirits. Similarly Matthew Henry comments: "There is a glory reserved for the bodies of the saints, which they will be instated in at the resurrection."[46] Despite the separation in time and place, such language celebrates with Dante "holy and glorious flesh."

If the denigration of the body were native to Christianity as the story of sinful flesh insists, then the return to the Bible should reaffirm it. However, the very opposite was the case during the Reformation, which encouraged an increasingly rich vision of the place of the body within creation. We find an example of this in the art of the period. As we have seen, Jonathan Miller regarded medieval art as encapsulating Christian disdain for the body, with its portrayal of ethereal bodies lacking sensual depth. If this were the expression of an authentic Christian vision, then the Reformation should have further emaciated the portrayal of flesh. But it has often been noted that Dutch seventeenth-century painting, deeply influenced by the Reformation worldview, discovered a renewed respect for realist bodily representation and everyday people doing everyday tasks. We find not insubstantial figures engaged in "spiritual" matters but everyday life in the home, the tavern and the street. People pour milk, play music and marry. All of life belongs to God, who created the world, sustains it and remains concerned about everyday as well as "religious" events.[47] The rich Reformation image of the body as real and substantial also paved the way for the development of anatomy and medicine within a holistic vision of what it is to be human.[48] In Protestant countries anatomy lessons became both a search for knowledge and a demonstration of the mortality of life.

"To give each other delight." The Reformers were not so much antisex as matter of fact about it. Luther's remark that "marriage does not only consist of sleeping with a woman—anybody can do that—but of keeping house and bringing up children" is frank and down to earth and, incidentally, does not stereotype gender roles.[49] Calvin, meanwhile, has often been portrayed as a dour killjoy, advocating sexual repression or the performance of a perfunctory and passionless duty. But he was not opposed to pleasure and did not believe in bare functional necessity:

> Now then, if we consider for what end [God] created food, we shall find that he consulted not only for our necessity, but also for our enjoyment and delight. . . . In herbs, fruits and trees, besides the various uses, [he created] gracefulness of appearance and sweetness of smell. . . . Shall it be unlawful to enjoy that beauty and this odour? In short, has he not given many things a value without having only necessary use?[50]

Calvin rejected the devaluation of the body and sexuality, and the association of "flesh" and original sin with women. Human sexuality, he taught, had been part of the original perfection of Adam and Eve and "conjugal intercourse is . . . pure, honourable and holy, because it is a pure institution of God" allowing "husband and wife to give each other delight."[51] This emphasis on mutuality, remarkable for the sixteenth century, is also applied by Calvin to divorce since, regarding "the marriage bed, the wife has an equal right."[52] In fact, the equal rights of wives in divorce cases were legally enforced in Geneva from the mid-1540s.

For Calvin, as for Luther, marriage affirms a "new joyous appreciation for sexual relations" and is the "context for creating a new awareness of human community with all its pains and joys."[53]

> And hence is refuted the error of some, who think that the woman was formed only for the sake of propagation, and who restrict the word "good" . . . to the production of offspring. . . . [Rather] marriage extends to all parts and usages of life.[54]

However, this celebration of sexuality was not isolated from a recognition that we are sinners and will corrupt even the greatest gift. Few Reformers of the sixteenth century were tolerant of adultery, and they gave men no greater leeway than women. They also opposed prostitution, and here too their attitude was affected by the recovery of a more biblical vision. Aquinas's sanction of prostitution "by analogy to a cesspit for a palace" had been used to defend public brothels as an outlet for uncontrolled male sexuality, but Luther and later Reformers rejected this misogynist rationalization and demanded faithfulness from men as well as from women. This is sometimes portrayed as moralistic, but the historian Carter Lindberg argues that it was "rather an attack on their culture's gender presupposition concerning males." "Luther and those who followed him attempted to redefine their culture's understanding of male gender from uncontrollable impulse to social responsibility."[55] The current debate over sexual abuse and domestic violence raises just this issue, as men seek to disclaim responsibility for their crimes by appealing to supposedly irresistible urges.

Shifts in the cultural understanding of gender had a widespread impact. If the Reformation's rejection of the secluded life and the ascetic ideal narrowed some life choices for women, it broadened and transformed their options in other areas. The Reformers are sometimes castigated for reducing women's roles to those of wife and mother, but this is to oversimplify and to see the Reformation in the light of the later bourgeois domestication of marriage. It is widely accepted by historians that the Reformation's "advocacy of the partnership of marriage as central to the Christian life eventually served to increase the status of women."[56]

These insights influenced the early Puritans in, for example, their affirmation of the right to choose a marriage partner, which, as the historian Christopher Hill observes, "proved so liberating for women" from the late sixteenth century.[57] And they have remained influential ever since, though always entangled with Greek beliefs and, from the late seventeenth century, increasingly affected by the changing social and economic climate. From the late eighteenth century the worldview inherited from the Reformation in northern Europe progressively succumbed to the demands placed on family life by the shifting social pattern of early capitalism. Similarly, in North America the Puritan single standard for both men and women in matters of conduct became progressively difficult to enforce. A double standard was increasingly condoned in which men were allowed license but women's sexual behavior was still regulated. The historian Ava Chamberlain argues that this shift was reflected in the increasingly strained relationship between the latter-day New England Puritan Jonathan Edwards and his Northampton parishioners. While Edwards tried to resist this double standard, he met opposition from some of the more "considerable families" of Northampton who felt that their sons' use of a popular medical text to taunt and ridicule local women was not a matter for church discipline. "For Edwards, understanding the workings of the female body was a means to promote God's sovereignty; for several of his young male parishioners, it was a means to harass girls."[58]

The privatizing and spiritualizing of the Reformation faith produced a loss of radical impetus, although some pockets still existed. For example, in the mid-nineteenth century, women in North America used the Genesis creation account to argue against the subordination of women.[59] By and large, however, Reformation insights were transformed in their changed social context and produced the characteristically modern understanding of the body, with its narrow, physiological focus. This ultimately resulted in the reduction of the richness of human life and experience to the biology of cells and molecules. For the Nobel prize winner Francis Crick

> "You," your joys and your sorrows, your memories and ambitions, your sense of personal identity and free will, are in fact no more than the behaviour of a vast assembly of nerve cells and their associated molecules.[60]

Postmodern commentators have rejected this naturalistic conception of the body, pointing out that not only is human experience irreducibly social, but the body itself carries cultural meanings beyond the biology of cells and molecules. From dieting to working out, from body piercing to cosmetic surgery, from healthy eating to embryo evaluation, the body is subjected to assessment and modification inside and out, and makes strong public statements about who we are. In postmodern times the idea of the body as a natural inheritance seems almost as quaint as the notion that it is God's gift.[61]

Conclusion

As Paul traveled round the ancient world founding churches, he believed that he was establishing centers of the new humanity, restored in Christ. We see from his letters that this included a radical rejection of the Greek and Roman understandings of the body and of gender. Neither is simply an individual issue (although they are that); both involve communal responses to God's law for humanity. Bodily existence is as much a communal issue for the church as "spiritual" renewal.

If we collectively do what our Lord commands, we regain our true humanity, including our gendered bodily humanity, in a community not conformed to the pattern of the culture around us. We neither find truth by acquiescing in stereotypes of sexual identity inherited from the nineteenth century nor by joining the postmodern bandwagon of self-constructed identities and cosmetically customized bodies. Rather, we find it in the recognition of God's love for us as made in his image. It is by continuing in the truth that we are made free (Jn 8:31-32; Rom 12:2).

This call to freedom is to the church, as the people of God, as well as to individuals. It is a call to exhibit the diversity and communal unity that are part of the image of the triune God. Nowhere is this going to be more important than in issues of gendered humanness where we must live out an alternative to prevailing cultural patterns from within a community of faith.

The church has a long history of assumptions about sexuality and stereotypes of gender that it has taken from surrounding cultures. All too often it has seemed to ignore such issues, hoping they will go away, only to capitulate to the terms of the secular debate. This leads us to succumb further to whichever pattern of cultural idolatry is prevalent at the time, rather than working the issues through in a Christian context. Far from resisting debate about gender and sexuality, the Christian community needs to reaffirm why these are important aspects of human experience without elevating them to the only arena within which identity and meaning are defined.

Reform of gender presuppositions is part of the impact of the gospel on a culture and should not be seen in isolation. Neither should the power of the gospel to transform such cultural patterns be underestimated. David Stoll, no advocate of the gospel, has observed that in some parts of Latin America a common effect of conversion is "to put households on a more stable basis, by overcoming male addiction to alcohol, reining in male sexual license, and establishing church authorities as a sort of appellate court for aggrieved women."[62] There is also some evidence that evangelicals have been more effective in reforming destructive patterns of machismo in Colombia than secular feminists. Not that this is a cause for complacency. Some of the reforms in that country have also been associated with the displacement of patterns of male control from family life into the church itself.[63] Only a lack of imagination limits the possibilities open to the church. When as a community we recover true, gendered human experience, we will be better able to image God to the world.

6

WITCHES
A Story of Persecution

AN IMPORTANT SUBPLOT OF THE STORY OF SINFUL FLESH INVOLVES THE oppression of women. This is nowhere clearer than in the story of the witch hunts[1] of the sixteenth and seventeenth centuries. This relates that many millions of women throughout Europe, mainly the elderly, poor and isolated, were tortured by the church into confessing nonexistent crimes before being burnt to death.

> If you're accused of witchcraft, you're a witch. Torture is an unfailing means to demonstrate the validity of the accusations. There are no rights of the defendant . . . [with] the Pope's encouragement guaranteed, Inquisitors began springing up all over Europe.[2]

Like the stories we have seen already, this presents itself as a history of intolerance, of "a Christian conspiracy" by a powerful church to oppress the weak: "The history of Christianity is the history of persecution."[3] However, unlike the stories of Galileo and Darwin, the victims of prejudice and superstition are no longer lone heroes but women in their millions. The villain, though, is familiar:

> [The Inquisitors] could not be mistaken. The confessions of witchcraft could not be based on hallucinations, say, or attempts to satisfy the Inquisitors and stop the torture. . . . Those who raise such possibilities are thus attacking the Church and *ipso facto* committing a mortal sin. Critics of witch-burning were punished and, in some cases, themselves burnt. The Inquisitors and torturers were doing God's work. They were saving souls.[4]

Some have seen this as a consequence of the Christian doctrine of original sin. Since we are all guilty already, there is no need to bother with justice or inquiry. Religious judges simply condemned women out of hand.[5]

Witchcraze

Rationalist historians have explained the witch craze as a product of religious fanaticism. It was "created by scholastic theologians and papal inquisitors and reflected the religious superstition and intolerance of a pre-scientific age." Consequently it disappeared in the Age of Reason, "when Europe became enlightened and the authorities stopped using legal force to impose their beliefs on the populace."[6] More romantic accounts envisage witchcraft as an ancient religion of the people, rooted in the "strong and bright and vigorous religions" of Greek paganism, and see it as a dim expression of the democratic spirit that came of age in the eighteenth-century Enlightenment.[7]

In Catholic countries, confessions are presented as the product of torture by the Inquisition. In Protestant, especially Puritan, areas such as Salem, Massachusetts, the physical convulsions experienced by the "bewitched" are explained as hysteria brought on by repressive patterns of Puritan child-care or as convulsive ergotism.[8] Whatever the cause, the stories of the witch craze are unanimous that the prejudices of the church transformed these natural phenomena into nonexistent crimes that it persecuted cruelly.

Many authors draw particular attention to the fact that the victims were overwhelmingly women. If there were ever any doubt about the church's misogyny, this removes it. Misogyny also provides an alternative explanation for the growth of witchcraft. According to this view the witch craze was an attempt by the rising male medical profession to gain control of the regulation of women's bodies by persecuting the female midwives and healers who had traditionally helped women. The church connived in this, accounting for the ecclesiastical hostility to midwives in "witch manuals" such as the fifteenth-century *Malleus Maleficarum (The Hammer of Evildoers).*[9]

The Plot Thickens

In recent years these various explanations of the witch craze have appeared increasingly doubtful as scholars have studied witchcraft more carefully. The picture that emerges is not the one we have been led to expect. As long ago as 1928 Montague Summers called the belief that witches went to the stake in England "a popular and fast-grounded, if erroneous, opinion" of the "ignorant," better suited to the "romanticist and story book" than the "scholar and historian."[10] The fact is that the number of witchcraft prosecutions has often been greatly exaggerated, and we now know that the Inquisition tended to moderate rather than incite them.

It has gradually been recognized that there is no all-encompassing picture of persecution, not least because there is no single entity that we can identify as witchcraft.[11] Women described themselves as witches or were so described for many different reasons. At one extreme there may have been a systematic attempt at demon worship, while at the other there was a vague and general sense of wonder at the natural world. Many witchcraft accusations involved vindictive petty squabbles or attempts to control the uncertainties of life. Other historians have suggested that witchcraft provided a route to power for women who were otherwise powerless, or a means of expressing feelings of envy or hatred that are otherwise unacceptable.

Sometimes witchcraft was just a convenient way of explaining otherwise unaccountable behavior. For example, in Shakespeare's *Othello*, Desdemona's father, a respectable Venetian senator, accuses Othello of bewitching or drugging her. For a pillar of Venetian society this is the only way that he can account for Desdemona's agreeing to marry a Moor. The reference to drugs parallels our modern usage when we say, "She must be on drugs," in order to explain otherwise bizarre actions. The accusation is not necessarily meant literally, nor is it intended to comment on the effectiveness or otherwise of drugs (or witchcraft) in compelling people to act against their nature.

This diversity suggests that accusations of witchcraft could have various meanings. They might be terms of abuse, attempts to explain strange behavior or allegations of causing serious harm. People in the sixteenth and seventeenth centuries were quite able to distinguish between these, just as casual allegations of "being on drugs" do not nowadays necessarily result in a prosecution. Indeed, it is not surprising that disparate phenomena have all been described by the term *witchcraft* when we consider that the literature covers the whole of Europe and North America over a period of nearly three hundred years. There were correspondingly many responses to this diversity, including a range of reactions by the church.

It has also been increasingly questioned whether witchcraft did greatly increase after 1450 or decrease after 1700, as had been almost universally assumed until recently. Witchcraft may have been just as common before the fifteenth century, but trials were often at a local village level, were summary and commonly by "ordeal." Because the records of such proceedings have not survived, it is difficult to assess how frequent they were. Similarly, the popular beatings and lynchings of women for witchcraft continued into the nineteenth century, but again because this was not sanctioned by judicial or church authority, it does not count as part of the witch craze.[12] From this perspective the rise and decline of witchcraft trials are to be understood in the context of the increased regulation and rationalization of power during the early modern period, leading to the centralization and formalization of legal proceedings. It is not necessarily a mark of Enlightenment overcoming superstition.

If the witch craze is to some extent a product of the documents available and of selective definition, it is also deeply marked by the presuppositions of rationalist, mainly male, historians. The persecution of witches has been seen as a religious superstition that came to an end with the growth of science in the seventeenth century. But this supposes a sharp distinction between "superstitious" beliefs and scientific reason, which did not exist until a much later period. The belief that the witch craze was stopped by the Enlightenment is now widely regarded as a "rationalist interpretation."[13]

Witch Reality?

There is, then, a good deal of uncertainty about what counts as witchcraft and whether it suddenly grew or declined. However, almost all versions of the story of witch-hunting agree that "supernatural" witches did not exist in reality. This skepticism is a very recent and specifically Western interpretation of witchcraft. Most people of the world throughout most of its history have taken supernatural witchcraft to be real. This does not necessarily mean that they have been gullible and superstitious. The Inquisitors of the sixteenth century believed that supernatural witches existed, but they were also well aware that some of those accused of witchcraft were simply ill or confused. Many people today believe that witches exist; for example, the promise of protection against witches is a live issue for many African Independent Churches. Witch beliefs are also growing more common in the West. Treating such experience as illusory is characteristic of modern Eurocentrism, and it presents a special problem for Western scholars:

> Who among those who study witchcraft and magic has not been faced by the inevitable question "Do you think witches actually existed?" To answer "no" is to be condescending towards the subject; to answer "yes" is to be labelled a crackpot.[14]

As with the orthodox story about missionaries, a denial of the supernatural reality is a denial of the experience of all those directly involved, whether witches, villagers or the church. The prejudices of the modern mind hollow out the very center of witchcraft, the supernatural, and discounts the experience of thousands of women.[15]

Contemporary scholars increasingly view the routine denigration of supernatural experience as the prejudice of "indignant rationalists," "more concerned to castigate the witch-baiters for their credulity and cruelty than to understand what the phenomenon was all about."[16]

Once we abandon these rationalist prejudices, it is possible to set witch-hunting within its social and political context, and to avoid at least the more patronizing attitudes of earlier historians. For example, a community is not necessarily acting irrationally if it acts against witches who are trying to harm others by magic, since a belief in magic or the use of poisons may indeed result in actual injury.[17]

Witchcraft, village and court. Contrary to the orthodox story, witchcraft was not principally a church matter, nor was the Inquisition the prime mover in the prosecution of witches. In fact, the majority of prosecutions concerned not abstruse heretical opinions about the devil but the run-of-the-mill suspicions and tensions of village life when property was lost or stolen, the beer failed to ferment or the bread to rise. People commonly appealed to magic and witchcraft to explain tragedies and misfortunes, or more generally to gain power over neighbors. The story of witch-hunting ignores the experience of those involved in such domestic matters and reduces the women involved to anonymous ciphers who appear only to illustrate the cruelty of the persecutors; the more women who are persecuted, the crueler the church.

At the opposite extreme to these local village affairs were an important minority of cases that linked witchcraft to political intrigue and the power of the state. For example, in 1578 Elizabeth I suspected that an attempt had been made to kill her by witchcraft, and the statute of 1581 made it an offense to try to prophesy the queen's future "by witchcraft, conjurations, or other like unlawful means." Witchcraft could have political consequences.[18]

Nor was Elizabeth alone in her suspicions. Earlier monarchs had also treated it as a serious threat, and James I blamed it for causing a tempest at sea that had nearly drowned him.

The story of witch-hunting has neglected the context of village and court, and has focused instead on exceptional and sensational cases, highlighting the cruelty of the witch-hunter or the hysteria of the witches. Thus witch-hunts are associated with particularly notorious individuals: Krämer and Sprenger in Germany, Matthew Hopkins in Essex, England, and Cotton Mather in Salem, Massachusetts.

The witches: stereotypes and misogyny. The characters in the story of witch-hunting are well known. There are the witches: old, ugly or lonely women who lived on the margins of society. Perhaps widowed, perhaps insane, they did not fit into village life and naturally came under suspicion whenever misfortune befell. These are the accused. They are persecuted by powerful men who scoured the countryside looking for victims to torture and burn.[19]

These stereotypes are misleading. One study of witchcraft in late-sixteenth-century Venice found that witches were equally represented in all age groups, with nearly as many under twenty-five as over forty-six years of age. Moreover, the idea of the witch as ugly is not common in testimonies of the time, and most of those bringing witchcraft charges were women, not men.[20] Scholz Williams has even argued that as formal court trials of witches replaced village trials by ordeal, the juridical status of women was elevated by establishing codes of evidence and adjudication.[21] For Reginald Scot, the late-sixteenth-century Puritan writer on witchcraft, the physical stereotyping of the witch was a sign of the accuser's prejudice and hence of the accused's innocence.

The picture of witch-hunting as straightforward misogyny is simplistic, and the stereotypes of women are features of the modern mind that devised the witch-hunting story, rather than of the sixteenth or seventeenth centuries.[22] As with the stereotype of the "passive native," such images of women result in the anonymity of individuals and the disparagement of their experience. They become anonymous and appear in their millions, to be tortured and burned en masse throughout Europe. Moreover, by ridiculing supernatural witchcraft, the modern mind has denied the women concerned cultural and social power.

The Question of Numbers

The number of witches executed is usually placed in the millions, sometimes over ten million.[23] The estimate that the number executed in Paris alone was "almost infinite" must hold the record, although Michelet comes a close second with his assertion that if the state had not restrained the "worthy bishops, [they] would have burned all their subjects."[24] Several authors refer to this as a "holocaust" or, alluding to genocide, as "gynocide."[25] Lecky gives several examples of towns or provinces where he claims that hundreds of people were executed, suggesting that this was commonplace throughout Europe:

> And these are only a few of the more salient events in that long series of persecutions which extended over almost every country, and continued for centuries with unabated fury.[26]

It is obvious that if such slaughter did indeed take place, continuing with "unabated fury" over a period of three hundred years, it would have significantly depleted the population of Europe. And yet exaggerations of this kind still regularly appear in the story of witch-hunting. Accurate estimation is often hard, but the case of the notorious Matthew Hopkins, commonly known as "Witchfinder General," is well documented. He sentenced about two hundred people to death from 1645 to 1647. But Hopkins has become notorious precisely because this was not typical. The feminist witchcraft scholar Diane Purkiss refers to the orthodox story as the "myth of the Burning Times."

Recent attempts to estimate the numbers involved have produced a very different picture. First, contrary to Lecky's confident assertion that his examples are typical of "almost every country" extending over centuries, the rates vary enormously between countries and over time. Many people were executed in Scotland, Germany, Switzerland and France but few in England. More surprising, the death rate in Italy and Spain was low, especially where the Inquisition was involved. Moreover, the rates varied within a single country. In Essex there were some eighty executions in the one hundred years up to 1645 for an average population of about one hundred thousand people; this was high for England.[27] Robin Briggs observes that "the substantial majority of towns and villages did not experience a single trial, successful or otherwise, over the whole period."[28]

Most recent estimates put the number of executions at about 150 to 300 people per year throughout all of Europe and North America, three quarters of whom were women. Over a period of about three hundred years this amounts to between forty thousand and one hundred thousand people.[29] This is an appalling enough catalog of human suffering, but to refer to it as "gynocide" or a "holocaust" is both misleading and offensive to those groups who have suffered actual genocidal assaults in recent generations. It is a centerpiece of the story of witch-hunting that religious persecution is particularly cruel and that the number and ferocity of executions far exceed anything that occurred once religious superstition was displaced by science and reason. But, as Trevor-Roper pointed out three decades ago, if we are to believe this, we have to ignore the fact that genocide is an invention of the modern world.[30] For it was the twentieth century that taught us about slaughter on a mass scale, not the sixteenth.

Even taking into account the different populations, three hundred people per year does not even begin to compare with the standards set by the modern world. One million people were killed during the five months of the Battle of the Somme in 1916, twenty-five thousand on the first day. Six million people died in the extermination camps of Europe in six years, and fifteen to twenty million people died in Soviet forced labor camps.[31] If we include fatalities of war during the "peace" since 1945, some eighty million people have been killed this century, with a high proportion of women and children. It takes modern science, organization and an iron will to achieve this—mere superstition is not enough. But we need not look to warfare or the twentieth century. The human race has repeatedly behaved with indescribable cruelty throughout recorded history. We have regularly killed large numbers of people in the course of everyday life, through superstition, neglect and indifference as well as through the scientific rigor of modern times. The anthropologist Marvin Harris estimates that the pre-Columbian Aztecs sacrificed about fifteen thousand people each year from a far smaller population base than that of Europe.[32] They would have exceeded the total number of witchcraft executions in less than a decade. The terror that followed the Enlightenment-inspired revolution in France resulted in some fifty thousand deaths in two years; witchcraft trials took hundreds of years to reach a comparable total.

The fact is that somewhere between 90 percent and 99 percent of the cruel deaths reported by the story of witch-hunting are fictional. Exaggeration on this scale requires explanation. What can have possessed so wide a range of authors to imagine the torture and execution of millions of women? No doubt there are many social and psychological factors involved here, but by inventing so many deaths and attributing them to the church, the modern mind evades its own responsibilities and gains an alibi for the unprecedented slaughter of the twentieth century. Recognizing this, postmodern authors regard all claims to possess the one-and-only truth as equally oppressive, whether that truth is religious or the modern truth of science and history. This is another story that I take up in the next chapter.

The Villain: The Church and Religion

If the witches are the tragic heroines of the story of witch-hunting, the villain of the piece is the church, often appearing in the guise of the Inquisition. We are told that throughout Europe priests and Puritans alike sought out women to torture and execute. "The church of Rome . . . strained every nerve to stimulate the persecutions," and "the zeal of the ecclesiastics . . . was unflagging."[33] In fact, recent research has shown that far from "stimulating the persecutions," the church, whether Catholic or Protestant, often had a moderating effect. If we recall the social context of prosecutions, this becomes less surprising than it appears at first sight.

Witches did not usually face the bizarre accusations beloved of the orthodox story. Rather than congress with demons, naked dancing or broomstick flying, the charges were more likely to concern ordinary village life: the failure of crops, missing clothes and commonplace jealousies. As a result, most prosecutions were lay, not religious, initiated not by "ecclesiastics" concerned with esoteric issues of theology but by women worried about their families.

The Roman Catholic Church and the Inquisition. Carl Sagan's picture of the Inquisition going from village to village in its hunt for elderly women has become less popular among scholars as the role of native villagers and lay authorities has been uncovered and as "it became apparent that neither scholasticism nor the Inquisition was as hostile to Witchcraft as earlier believed."[34]

In fact, detailed studies have shown that the Inquisition, far from "stimulating the prosecutions," acted as a brake on lay courts and popular zeal. As the historian William Monter notes, "The mildness of Inquisitorial judgements on witchcraft contrasts strikingly with the severity of secular judges throughout northern Europe"; "most secular European legal systems punished their prisoners more severely than the Inquisition."[35] In Southern Europe the execution rate was low, especially in Italy and Spain—precisely where the Inquisition was involved—because of the higher standards of proof that it demanded.[36] Even a writer as hostile to the Inquisition as Jean Plaidy admits that the Spanish Inquisition prosecuted witches rarely in comparison with lay authorities. She points out that the Inquisition demanded evidence, investigated the truth of charges and was suspicious of fantastical confessions. Contrary to Carl Sagan's belief that the Inquisitors disregarded motives of jealousy or revenge in those who made accusations, they were in fact required to investigate such matters carefully. Thus a twenty-eight-year-old woman, Anastasia Soriana, presented herself before the tribunal at Murcia in 1584 and declared that she had had a carnal relationship with a devil. She was told to go home because she was suffering from delusions. She presented herself again at the tribunal at Toledo with the same story. Again she was sent home. Far from encouraging prosecutions the Supreme Council of the Inquisition protected women against charges of witchcraft.[37] The distinguished historian Hugh Trevor-Roper concludes, "In general the established church was opposed to the persecution" of witches.[38]

Puritans and the Protestant church. If the Inquisition has been misrepresented in the story of witch-hunting, the Protestant churches have scarcely fared any better. The late-seventeenth-century witchcraft trials in Salem, Massachusetts, are often cited to illustrate the spread of witchcraft prosecutions with Protestantism into the new world.[39] The tale is notorious and has been portrayed in books, plays and film. It contains everything the orthodox story might wish: bigoted Puritans, bizarre and extravagant manifestations, executions, poor women condemned and a North American Indian connection. No less a person than the Puritan leader Cotton Mather is implicated, and he is portrayed as a wild-eyed fanatic who instigated the whole affair from a mixture of misogyny and bigotry. The only things missing are torture and burning at the stake.

The events in Salem have been studied in great detail, and there are any number of theories about what happened. Rather than add another, I will focus upon Cotton Mather and his role in the trials.

Cotton Mather was a third-generation Puritan minister who had already published a book on witchcraft in 1689, which treated accusations with balanced skepticism. The irrational Puritan bigot of legend was, in fact, a Fellow of the Royal Society and a careful observer.[40] In 1692 he was invited by Governor Phips to advise on the Salem trials. Phips had become concerned at the number of people who had been accused of witchcraft and was at a loss as to what to do about the acute sufferings of those involved. The result was *The Wonders of the Invisible World*, which Mather published late in 1692. Although he insisted on the need for evidence and gave guidelines for the conduct of the trials, the book was a partisan defense of his friends who sat as judges at Salem. Despite his doubts about "spectral evidence" and his opposition to some of the judges' methods, he did little to bring the trials to an end.[41] The result was that twenty people were executed before a halt was called. Mather appears to have quickly regretted his part in this, for in a diary entry of 1694 we find him wondering whether the witness statements were "delusions." In 1696 he wrote that he doubted that anyone would be able to understand the Salem events, and by 1697 he had concluded that the court was in error and wished that he had stopped the proceedings. This did not assist those who died, but equally it is not the picture of the fanatical bigot we have been led to expect.

Although Mather could have acted more decisively, he certainly did nothing to stimulate the prosecutions. Nor, in fact, did any of the other ministers involved. The historian Chadwick Hansen has concluded that "the clergy were, from beginning to end, the chief opponents to the events at Salem." Cotton Mather, he says, "was anything but the wild-eyed fanatic of tradition," and he rather generously refers to him as "a model of restraint and caution."[42]

The Salem events have become notorious not because they were typical of their times but because they were exceptional. Far from witchcraft trials being rife among Puritan communities in North America, the Salem trials more or less sum up the extent of witch prosecutions in New England during the seventeenth century. The picture of a persecution fomented by Puritan preachers is simply false.

The Reformer John Calvin is often identified as a zealous witch-hunter, and the resurgence of witchcraft trials in England during Elizabeth I's reign has been blamed on the Marian exiles returning with rigid Calvinist theologies and influencing public policy. Puritan ministers in England and North America are pictured as whipping up popular superstition through their terrifying sermons and producing hysteria in unfortunate women through their repression of healthy sexuality.

In fact, Calvin was not especially interested in witchcraft at all. He regarded it as a delusion for which the cure was the gospel, not execution.[43] He argued that there is no evidence in the Bible for the exotic manifestations of witchcraft and that witches are unable to cause direct harm. His focus was on God rather than witches or demons. These views influenced the skeptical writers of the sixteenth century, who ridiculed the more exotic manifestations of witchcraft and regarded most witches as ill or credulous. As the historian Keith Thomas observes, "The leading sceptical writers . . . all urged that the 'continental' conception of witchcraft as devil-worship was unacceptable because it had no Biblical justification."[44]

This does not fit the picture of fanatic Calvinism, however, so sixteenth-century skeptics have generally been regarded as Enlightenment men out of their time who anticipated modern psychiatry in their belief that many witches were ill. Thus Reginald Scot, who wrote *Discoverie of Witchcraft* in 1584, is said to have "anticipated learned opinion of the next century," and his religious beliefs are downplayed.[45] But Scot argues from providence, not progress, citing Calvin approvingly. He is skeptical about the spirits said to appear to witches, not because they have been banished by reason and science but because they are not consonant with the Word of God. Similarly, the Essex vicar George Gifford drew his arguments from orthodox Calvinism. Like Scot, he criticized the prosecution of witches, which he regarded as a deception by the devil to encourage superstitious remedies and divert attention from the need for repentance and faith. The remedy for outbreaks of witchcraft was not the prosecution of witches but the gospel, putting on the "whole armour of God."[46] By attributing witchcraft to the devil, we denigrate the providence and grace of God. James Hitchcocke argues that Gifford's views are closer to the spirit of Calvinism than were those of the Puritan William Perkins, who uncritically repeated many contemporary prejudices.[47]

In fact, the Protestant churches were no more enthusiastic about witch-hunting than the Inquisition. Contrary to Carl Sagan's belief they were aware that the accused might be ill or afraid and required independent judicial assessment of accusations with properly tested evidence. The Reformed (Calvinist) Church in the Netherlands encouraged restraint by lay courts in prosecuting witches and recommended cautioning, exclusion from communion or apology to the aggrieved. Interventions by churches to bring about reconciliation between the accused and the accuser were common.[48]

Calvinistic skepticism about witches and their exotic activities was inspired by a return to the Bible, but it was not new. The church had long rejected folk beliefs about witchcraft:

> [The] Church of the Dark Ages did its best to disperse these relics of paganism [i.e. witch beliefs]. . . . In general, the Church, as the civiliser of nations, disdained these old wives' tales. They were the fragmentary rubbish of paganism which the light of the Gospel had dispelled.[49]

The rejection of exotic beliefs about conjuring up bad weather or flying was the rule rather than the exception, and St. Boniface and Charlemagne were typical in their condemnation of burning supposed witches.[50] The famous sixteenth-century skeptics extended and developed these well-established arguments rather than creating them ex nihilo in a burst of rational anticipation. Perkins and Mather, whatever their faults, drew on the same tradition and likewise tried to distinguish between genuine witchcraft, illness and malicious accusation. Even the notorious Matthew Hopkins banned "rusticall people" from abusing those accused of witchcraft, rejected evidence obtained under duress and dismissed accusations involving "any improbability [or] impossibility" such as flying or broomstick riding.[51] The "skeptics" of the sixteenth century are part of a tradition, not isolated rationalists ahead of their time.

> In the German Southwest [of the sixteenth and seventeenth centuries] much of this opposition or moderation in matters of witchcraft came from [Catholic and Protestant] preachers. They were not forerunners of Enlightenment scepticism but pious men . . . who insisted that man's proper response to hardship was repentance and reform of life, not the pursuit of witches.[52]

Settings: The Dark Ages and the Enlightenment

The story of witch-hunting has two settings: a dark, medieval world ignorant of science and under the sway of religion and superstition, and a later enlightened period when reason banished superstition and men were freed from the fear of witches. We might loosely call these periods the "Dark Ages" and the "Enlightenment" respectively.

The idea of the Dark Ages, with its flat earth and excommunicated comets, however, is mythical and reinforces the modern mind's conviction of its own tolerance and rationality. The belief that the church uncritically accepted bizarre and sensational tales about witches is equally ill-founded. The story of witch-hunting, however, relies on these stereotypes of the Dark

Ages and the Enlightenment. Thus, for Lecky, witchcraft was due to a "general credulity" that declined only when "prevailing modes of religious thought" gave way to reason.[53] However, it is not in general possible to draw the sharp distinctions between "modes of religious thought" and early science, which Lecky blithely assumes. Indeed, early modern science, far from universally rejecting witchcraft, sometimes assisted in its investigation. In England, midwives and physicians medically examined suspects for "witch marks"—the physical signs said to be associated with witchcraft. In the Lancashire witch trials of 1633, Sir William Harvey, who had discovered the circulation of blood in 1628, led a team of doctors and midwives to provide such expert medical evidence.

Historians have long recognized that there is something wrong with the thesis that witchcraft ended with the Renaissance and Enlightenment. As long ago as 1969 Hugh Trevor-Roper asked why, if this view is correct, the witch craze grew in particular in the two centuries that followed the Renaissance recovery of Greek ideas of reason rather than in the Dark Ages of the medieval period.[54]

Lecky's confidence that science would bring enlightenment and progress is viewed more critically now than it was in the nineteenth century. The violence and persecution of the modern world is on a scale that far outweighs the cruelties visited on women accused of witchcraft. The Enlightenment faith in reason no longer seems plausible. Instead, witchcraft is seen as a sign of the way people understood the world they lived in. This puts it in a more complex and concrete context of social, economic and political history: the status of women and the routes to power open to them, the conflicts and tensions of village life and the specific anxieties of poor people over the health of animals or the growth of crops. Within this setting, witchcraft is a rational, though superstitious, response to illness and catastrophe.

Props. Like our other stories, that of witch-hunting has its conventions and props. Probably the best known is the broomstick, used by witches to fly by night to their "sabbaths." This prop is almost universal in modern portrayals and together with a pointed hat is essential garb for the well-dressed witch.

The ancient belief that witches can fly was dismissed by canon law as a folktale. Indeed, papal rulings, canon law and Inquisitorial Directories tended to reject the exotic manifestations of witchcraft as pagan superstition until Heinrich Krämer and Jakob Sprenger published their *Malleus Malefi-*

carum in about 1486.[55] This book repeatedly appears in the story of witch-hunting on account of its bizarre and sensational content, which fits well with the stereotype of medieval religion.

Heinrich Krämer and Jacob Sprenger, Dominican Inquisitors, believed that they had a special mission to prosecute witches. However, the local priests and the German church authorities did not agree with them and opposed their activities. They appealed directly to the new pope, Innocent VIII, who supported them by issuing a bull, *Summis Desiderantes*, against witchcraft in 1484. He also commissioned Krämer and Sprenger to write a guide for witch prosecutors. And so the *Malleus Maleficarum* was born.

The orthodox story regards Krämer and Sprenger's notorious book as typical of the bigotry and cruelty of the medieval church throughout Europe. Carl Sagan describes it as a "technical manual for torturers" and implies that it was widely used by the Inquisition in "God's work" of torture and burning.[56] Even distinguished historians refer to it as "the guide and beaconstar of the . . . Inquisition," "a handbook used at witch trials" that "codified the belief in witches for the sixteenth century, a century which witnessed their burning in every part of Europe."[57]

This reputation as the standard manual of the church is wholly undeserved. The *Malleus Maleficarum* was in fact treated with suspicion by the Inquisition and was not extensively used in witch trials. From Venice to Germany and the Netherlands, studies have shown little or no reliance on it: "Its influence and authority have been vastly exaggerated by most scholars." Moreover, its language made it "accessible only to scholars and not to many lawyers or even to the average judge."[58]

Torture and justice. The second prop in the story of witch-hunting is the torture chamber. The popular picture of the Inquisition, from Monty Python's famous "Spanish Inquisition" sketch to films like *The Name of the Rose*, is of the fanatical and routine use of torture to force victims to confess: "The most horrendous tortures were routinely applied to every defendant, young or old, after the instruments of torture were first blessed by the priest."[59]

It is undoubtedly true that torture was widely used in many judicial proceedings from the fifteenth century onward, and many sickening accounts of the horrors endured by astonishingly courageous women and men survive. But when Carl Sagan writes that torture routinely proved the validity of witchcraft accusations, he is drawing on the widespread and uncritical acceptance of the story that the church, especially the Inquisition, mercilessly and indiscriminately used torture in witchcraft trials.

Recent historical scholarship has recognized that the Inquisition compared favorably with contemporary standards of secular justice.

> In contrast to the secular courts, the Inquisition was a model of moderation and due process. The Holy Office was sceptical about the validity of confession obtained by torture, and did not employ torture as a matter of course.[60]

In Protestant countries, torture was used in witchcraft trials in both Scotland and Northern Europe, although the worst excesses occurred when political intrigue was suspected. However, there "seems not to have been one single occasion where torture of a woman for suspected witchcraft was licensed" in England, despite the fact that women were commonly whipped to obtain evidence in criminal cases and torture was used for milder felonies, including burglary and assault.[61]

The background for the use of torture in witchcraft trials was its use in criminal proceedings generally. Some historians have argued that the use of torture grew as formal tribunals displaced trial by ordeal or combat. As courts increasingly used new standards of proof, obtaining and sifting evidence became more important. Whereas the survival, or otherwise, of a suspect subjected to trial by ordeal itself demonstrated either guilt or innocence, the newer courts required other means of testing the truth. In this context, torture became a means of rational investigation, replacing the "trial by swimming" that a suspect might face in summary village justice. Inquisitorial skepticism about the results of torture was often associated with the better organization of church proceedings and the better standard of education of its officers. For example, the moderation of the Venetian Inquisition resulted from its local strength, close accountability to Rome and the high standards of training and discipline. The lay courts often lacked these qualities and treated their suspects more severely. "Given . . . a strong Inquisition which followed the guidelines laid down for it by the Church, witchcraft prosecution was unlikely to result in mass hysteria and persecution."[62]

The Postmodern Story of Witchcraft

So far I have discussed the story of witch-hunting as it was developed by rationalist historians in the late eighteenth and nineteenth centuries. This dominated discussion during most of the twentieth century and carries the modern myth that reason brings enlightenment and toleration. However, for those whose Enlightenment faith is waning, an important variant of the orthodox story is emerging that carries a different, postmodern myth.[63]

G. K. Chesterton is said to have remarked that "if people stop believing in religion, they don't then believe in nothing, they believe in everything."[64] Much the same applies when people lose their faith in modernity. Science and reason no longer appear as the unambiguous good that once they seemed; nor are they able, in Goethe's phrase, to explain away the "sprites" of religious or mystical experience. Mysticism, magic and mumbo jumbo, once equally banished by the light of reason, return and reoccupy the land tenfold. A quick check in your local bookshop will show that the "Religion" shelf is fully stocked, although it has often been renamed "Religion, mysticism and magic" or even "New Age." There are, however, relatively few recognizably Christian books. The "demise of the spirit of rationalism in Europe," to (mis)quote Lecky, has left the door open to a revival of religion, but of the "old" or "alternative" religion, not necessarily of Christianity. In this context, the story of witch-hunting has been transformed into a postmodern variant.

The postmodern version of the witch story is well told by the feminist witchcraft scholar Diane Purkiss:

> Once upon a time, there was a woman who lived . . . alone, in her house surrounded by her garden, in which she grew all manner of herbs and other healing plants. . . . The woman was a healer and a midwife; she had . . . mystical knowledge derived from her closeness to nature, or from a half-submerged pagan religion. She helped women give birth, and she had healing hands. . . . However, . . . even though this woman was harmless, she posed a threat to the fearful. Her medical knowledge threatened the [male] doctor. Her simple, true spiritual values threatened the superstitious nonsense of the Catholic church, as did her affirmation of the sensuous body. Her independence and freedom threatened men. So the Inquisition descended on her, and cruelly tortured her into confessing to lies about the devil. She was burned alive by men who hated women, along with millions of others just like her.[65]

Clearly this story has many similarities to the earlier, modern version. But it also has important differences. Now it is the figure of the witch herself who is foregrounded, and her female power, knowledge and authority are emphasized. Science, in the person of the male doctor, is as much persecutor as liberator, and while the superstitious Catholic Church is castigated, religion is not necessarily contrasted adversely with reason and science.

Indeed, the less rational forms of religion such as mysticism and paganism, previously seen as the very embodiment of superstition, now appear in a positive light as paths to "knowledge." However, as Purkiss observes, the postmodern story of witch-hunting is no better founded than the modern one was:

> Do you believe this story? Thousands of women do. It is still being retold . . . by women who are academics . . . popular historians, theologians and dramatists. It is compelling, even horrifying. However, in all essentials it is not true, or only partly true, as a history of what happened to the women called witches in the early modern period.[66]

Purkiss goes on to say that there is no evidence that the majority of witches were either healers or midwives, nor that they were sexually liberated, nor that men primarily prosecuted them. The links with pagan nature religions are tenuous and the existence of "mystical knowledge" is a product of the romantic imagination. The Inquisition was generally more lenient than lay courts and did not torture or burn millions of women. "All this," says Purkiss, "has been known for some time."[67]

A more human story. As can be seen from Purkiss's account, the postmodern witchcraft story has some important differences from the modern one. In many ways it does not claim the same historical authority for its key features, nor give the same status to science. Indeed, the very language used to tell the story has changed. Phrases such as "mystical knowledge," "closeness to nature" and "healing hands" evidently belong to a different vocabulary from the more familiar dismissal of women as victims of "hysteria" or ergot poisoning. Religion is no longer the sole villain, nor science and reason unambiguously the heroes. Christianity may not get much of a look, but the "old (pagan) religion" and "true spiritual values" are clearly prized above the male doctors who are trying to regulate and control women's bodies through the impersonal regimes of early modern science. These reversals of the plot and characterization of the modern story of witch-hunting are mixed in with the more familiar historical references. The Catholic Church and the Inquisition make a prominent appearance, cast as usual as cruel torturers who burned women alive by the million. But, even here, there is a subtle difference. The church behaved like this not because it was religious but because it was superstitious; men burned women not because they were priests or Puritans but because they were "men who hated women" and were "threatened" by female "independence and freedom."

The domestic and "spiritual" experience of women now receive more attention than in the oversimplified tale of the "victory" of reason over religion. In many ways the postmodern story of witchcraft occupies a bigger, richer and more human world than the modern orthodox one.

These changes in the language and form of the story result in corresponding changes in the "history" and "science" that appear in the postmodern story. We have seen that the modern story of witch-hunting paints women as passive, emotional creatures, given to hysterical interludes and needing the penetrating light of masculine reason to sort out their troubles. The postmodern story rejects this picture as a male fantasy and substitutes its own history of women's discovery of true spirituality through the old religion of paganism. This is combined with a language of mysticism and healing that sits uneasily with modern rationalism.

Clearly the postmodern story of witchcraft carries a different myth from the simple "warfare of science and religion." We now see a complex picture of competing knowledges and beliefs, each deployed by a specific group of people in order to challenge or maintain their grip on power. Thus the postmodern story of witchcraft tells us that male doctors used their newfound "scientific" knowledge and power to exclude women midwives and healers. This was done by turning women's beliefs and knowledge back against them. The male, "scientific" doctors redefined women's "medical knowledge," obtained through their closeness to nature, as pagan and superstitious. They allied with the male priests to define women's "practical" and "mystical" knowledge as harmful and demonic, the work of witches. Thus witchcraft executions were to "break down and destroy strong women, to dismember and kill the Goddess, the divine spark of being in women."[68] Medical ideas are used to disempower women and to increase the authority and prestige of science itself. If we believe this story, it comes as no surprise to learn that the eminent physician William Harvey, the discoverer of the circulation of the blood, was in league with the church in the search for "witchmarks" during the Lancashire trials of 1633. This postmodern story of competing social groups, of different forms of knowledge each challenging the other to define social reality, is a new development that I will discuss further in the next and last chapter.

The witch and the old religion. The modern story of witch-hunting has its origins in Enlightenment anticlericalism and is written in the language of reason and science, of facts and of natural causes. The postmodern story of witchcraft draws on different roots and appeals to the Romantic themes of spirituality rather than reason, to nature rather than natural causation. The same Romanticism that gave us the picture of the noble savage living in harmony with nature also gives us the wise woman healer with her medicinal plants and closeness to nature. The harmony of her body in its natural balance with the earth enabled her to mix medicines unknown to the doctor isolated from nature in his laboratory.

Just as Rousseau imagined his "noble savage" living a pure life untainted by industrialization, so the postmodern story of witchcraft imagines science and rationalism in league with the industrial world, which has polluted field and stream, and has expelled the spirits of the water and the wild wood. Postmodern witchcraft restores the sisterhood that industrialization had destroyed. "You are a witch by being female, untamed, angry, joyous and immortal."[69] The rational and the scientific, once the very stuff of enlightenment, are now prized less than the primitive and the natural. Just as T. H. Huxley and John Tyndall used the language of pantheism to escape the sterility of Darwinism, so the postmodern story of witchcraft looks to the old religion of paganism to save us from the soulless modern world that is indifferent to human hopes and passions.

We can trace the family history of this tale at the margins of the modern story of witch-hunting. We see it foreshadowed in Jules Michelet's Romantic picture of witchcraft as a democratic protest of the people against the church and his picture of a "strong and bright and vigorous" paganism.[70] Similar beliefs later developed in Germany, with witchcraft as the ancient religion of the Germanic peoples that was suppressed by Christianity. James Frazer incorporated these Romantic themes in his monumental work *The Golden Bough*, and Margaret Murray developed them into the theory that witchcraft is a survival of pagan beliefs suppressed by Christianity. Despite the absence of evidence for such claims, they remain influential in contemporary neopaganism, and the postmodern story of witchcraft draws heavily on them.

Bits and pieces. The postmodern story, then, is put together from bits and pieces appropriated from the past and present without discrimination between historical fact and recent fabrication.

It combines elements of the orthodox story with Romantic themes and is indifferent to the criticism that there is little evidence to support it. It is, in some ways, a richer view of the world than the orthodox story, which rejects the reality of "spiritual" witchcraft out of hand, and it is often more sensitive to the experience of the women and communities involved. In place of the myth of the warfare between science and religion, it substitutes a myth of feminine oppression by male authority. This fits well the contemporary social and cultural context that is skeptical of the grand claims of modernity. However, it is ultimately an unauthentic project as it constructs its own history and self-image out of the fragments lying around in the junkyard of contemporary culture. If the postmodern story draws extensively on the Romantic tradition for its *beliefs*, its *practices* are largely inventions of the twentieth century. As Purkiss remarks, "The Old Religion is no older than the [post-war British] National Health Service."[71]

The dark side. The Romantic image of witchcraft as the survival of the old religion has its dark side. The nineteenth-century literature, especially the picture of an ancient Germanic religion displaced by Christianity, foreshadowed the work of the turn-of-the-century occult scholars who put pagan myths into the service of racism. Because of the early conversion of the region, little is known of pre-Christian Germanic religion, so the imagination has free play. Norse gods such as Odin and Freya provided a refuge from industrialization and an imagined return to a golden age of rural simplicity, of *Volk*, kinship, racial purity and rigid gender roles. This nostalgic vision provided a language and iconography for Nazism in the 1930s. The postmodern story of witchcraft has sanitized its Nordic predecessor to rid it of its "dark side." It is an "old religion" transformed into the Muse by Romantic poets and pre-Raphaelites rather than the less palatable pantheism of the Third Reich.

Modern and Postmodern Stories

Like the stories of Galileo and Darwin, the story of witches, in both its modern and postmodern forms, is a carrier of beliefs. The modern version reinforces the image of the church as bigoted and oppressive. However, the postmodern form focuses more on the issue of tolerance and on Christianity as hostile to genuine forms of "spirituality," especially female spirituality. For Diane Purkiss, this postmodern witch story "legitimates [the] identification of oppression with powerful institutions, and above all with Christianity. . . . [It] explains the origins and nature of good and evil. It is a religious myth, and the religion it defines is radical feminism."[72] In the conclusion that follows, I will argue that the postmodern myth that it defines is broader than simply "radical feminism."

CONCLUSION
Modern Myths in a Postmodern World

MANY PEOPLE IN THE WEST STILL TAKE IT FOR GRANTED THAT OUR society, with its scientific achievements and democratic politics, is the fruit of Enlightenment reason and humanism.[1] Most continue to applaud its technical "know-how" and progress, although a growing minority have more doubts, pointing to the environmental destruction that technology brings in its wake and the subversion of national democracies by global market forces. But whether praised or derided, the modern mind confidently still asserts that it is reason and facts that sustain its self-confidence and underpin its hope for the future.

I have argued throughout this book that this is a myth. When we look at the way that the modern mind sustains and passes on its faith in itself, we find not facts and reasoning but stories. From popular encyclopedias to books by philosophers such as Bertrand Russell, narrative, not analysis, is given a central place in explaining our world to us. The self-confidence of the modern world is associated with its achievements, but it is perpetuated by the myths carried in stories about Galileo or witch-hunts.

Myths are taken seriously, including that of the warfare between science and religion. The otherwise urbanely tolerant man, philosopher Daniel Dennett, talks of putting religions "in a cage" when they offend against his canons of scientific truth. He offers, as candidates for caging, those Baptist parents who are "deliberately misinforming . . . children about the natural world"—by telling them that there are alternatives to neo-Darwinism.

"Misinforming a child," he tells us, "is a terrible offence."[2] Indeed, Andrew Brown reports that one distinguished conference speaker regarded it as child abuse, fully equivalent to physical assault:

> Children have a right not to have their minds addled by nonsense. And we as a society have a duty to protect them from it. So we should no more allow parents to teach their children to believe in the literal truth of the Bible, or that the planets rule their lives, than we should allow parents to knock their children's teeth out or lock them in a dungeon.[3]

The means Western societies have adopted to prevent parents from knocking their children's teeth out is to remove those children from their families and to prosecute the parents as criminals. Disciples of this kind of fundamentalist rationalism insist that theirs is the only truth, and they wish to prevent anyone from passing on alternative views, which they regard as irrational and obnoxious. It is not only Christians and astrologers who come under the ban. Any departure from the orthodox story is likely to meet with hostility. Rupert Sheldrake, a Cambridge biochemist, is a well-known advocate of a holism in nature that cuts across more orthodox views. His book *A New Science of Life* attracted an editorial in the prestigious scientific journal *Nature* under the title "A Book for Burning?" The reviewer underlined his liberal credentials by asserting that "even bad books should not be burned," but he was so incensed by Sheldrake's unorthodoxy that he could not resist calling Sheldrake's "infuriating tract" "the best candidate for burning there has been for many years."[4] This immoderate outburst drew a wave of criticism, not least from the editor of *New Scientist*, who referred to it as "a trial by editorial" and asked if *Nature* had "abandoned the scientific method."[5] Fortunately, this kind of doctrinaire rationalism, while still a force in some areas, has largely had its day and is unlikely to spread far in any of the major Western democracies in the foreseeable future.

The Role of "Religion"

Of course, it is not surprising that modernity makes use of stories. All societies have used narrative to pass on their core beliefs. What is more surprising is that religion continues to feature so prominently, and that to maintain religion as an adversary the stories distort both history and science, the very "facts" and "reason" that the stories claim to defend. At first blush it might seem that the achievements of technology and liberal humanism could speak for themselves. Why is the modern mind not self-sustaining in the generation of scientific knowledge and technological success? Why are the stories so focused on a supposed warfare with religion rather than telling, say, of the heroes of medicine such as Alexander Fleming? As we have seen, even the story of Simpson's groundbreaking discoveries in anesthesia high-lighted a supposed religious opposition.

I have already suggested that one function of the persistence of these myths is to repress another story, one less congenial to the modern mind: the role of characteristically modern ideals—such as civilization, freedom and progress—in the oppression of the powerless and in the despoliation of the natural world. Modern myths constantly reinvent a superstitious image of religion in order to brush it aside and with it the story of modernity's role in oppression. But there is another aspect to this: doctrinaire rationalism seems less plausible than it once did.

In the 1960s science seemed to promise progress, and in Britain the wel-fare state looked able to provide answers to the inequalities and injustices that have plagued less civilized times. Beggars on the streets were part of the local color of the hippie pilgrimage to India and were inconceivable on the streets of Swinging London or Times Square in New York. This is now a lost world. Cardboard cities appeared in the prosperous 1980s, and we see young women with small children begging for food in the new millennium. In the 1960s the then British prime minister Harold Wilson spoke of the "white heat of technology" leading us into a better future of cheap nuclear power. Nowadays, the promise is tainted by the recollection of the 1986 Chernobyl disaster in the Ukraine, which left ten thousand square kilome-ters uninhabitable and caused an unknown number of cancers and birth defects. Modernity's utopian dream invites skepticism as much as faith.

Actual catastrophes such as Chernobyl, as well as those waiting in the wings such as global warming, are forcing the unreconstructed modern mind on to the defensive. Not only has the modern hope of an ever better world patently run into the sand, but modern science and humanist ration-ality are creating a world of despoliation and human suffering. Life in the Aral Sea has been decimated by severe pollution from the Russian cotton industry. Over two thousand people died, and an unknown number have long-term illnesses as a result of the chemical leak in Bhopal in 1984. Disas-ters of this kind force modern forms of rationality to justify their existence.[6]

In this changed context the role of the modern myths of humanism and progress is more ambiguous than it was. Among unreconstructed modernists such as Richard Dawkins or Daniel Dennett, the stories are repeated ever more stridently, with calls for "caging" Baptists and astrologers. The need for a scapegoat becomes ever more urgent as the ills wrought by the modern vision become more apparent. For Dawkins, "the world appears as bright islands of scientific enlightenment surrounded by a ravening darkness of ignorance and religion."[7] Although unlikely to gain widespread assent, this reaction is important, and its continuing force should not be underestimated. However, a more common response is the tactical use of modern myths in a much broader debate.

Tactics, Not Strategy

The modern mind is convinced that it has found the one and only truth, and that this truth is liberating and will lead to a better, purer world. For such a faith, modern myths are strategically important in passing on this belief to the next generation and in popularizing it among the general public. But many nowadays have lost faith in science as the harbinger of progress pure and unalloyed. All the old idols have collapsed, whether scientific utopias, Marxism or laissez-faire capitalism. Indeed, many postmodern writers argue that the modern story has been deeply implicated in oppression and doubt whether any globally liberating truth exists.[8] However, the modern stories have not in consequence disappeared. Postmodernism has found a place for them but a more tactical one.

Modern stories are dominated by the alleged superiority of reason and Enlightenment humanism over religion, which is pictured as superstitious and oppressive. Modern truth is, as Carl Sagan imagines it, a candle in the darkness of religious bigotry. Postmodern commentators are skeptical of claims to possess the only way to the truth and distance themselves from this aspect of modern myths. Such claims, they feel, inevitably lead to oppression, as in Dennett's desire to cage views he does not share. As a result, modern stories are used selectively in support of local arguments and disputes. This more tactical use of modern myths leads to some strange bedfellows. For example, the same person who argues from the story of Galileo that superstitious beliefs hold up scientific progress might, in the next breath, ask about your astrology sign or turn out to be adept in the power of crystals. The old opposition between science (= good, enlightenment, reason) and religion (= bad, superstition, faith) is breaking down, and more complex alignments have become possible.

Modern Stories in a Postmodern Setting

Postmodernity's tactical use of modern myths is congenial to its eclectic spirit and its delight in narrative. Unlike the modern mind it does not reject out of hand either tradition or religion but incorporates them into its kaleidoscope of stories without concerning itself with how the varied components might fit together in a greater whole. Indeed, postmodern commentators are deeply skeptical of whether any such "greater whole" exists.

Stories therefore find a natural home in postmodernity, but their tactical use leads to some variations on a theme. For example, the orthodox story portrays Galileo too much as the rational man of modernity for him to be wholly satisfactory as a postmodern hero. Fortunately there is an alternative at hand: Giordano Bruno, who appeals more to postmodern sensibilities. Bruno combines Copernicanism with the cabala and with a supposedly ancient Egyptian form of magic. Moreover, he was executed by the church in 1600, allegedly for teaching Copernicanism, so he makes a good substitute for Galileo. This story of Bruno, the martyr to science, combines science with mysticism and is becoming increasingly popular. In fact, Bruno is even less the martyr than Galileo was.[9]

Similar variations are found in other modern stories. Thus the postmodern version of the story of missionary oppression highlights not that faith is a delusion but that all attempts to convert others to a one-and-only truth, whether religious or scientific, are oppressive. This would apply as much to Daniel Dennett as to David Livingstone.

A Richer Vision?

We saw in the last chapter that the story of witch-hunting has a postmodern variation that abandons the idea that witchcraft is an empty superstition, or that witch-hunting is a straightforward example of the bigotry and cruelty of religion relieved only by Enlightenment reason and toleration. For many postmodern authors the persecution of witches illustrates the oppression of female spirituality by male reason. Religion, albeit the old religion of pagan animism and nature worship, appears in a positive light, and Enlightenment rationality is allied with the enemy. It is the "supernatural" or "spiritual" aspects of the story, despised and suppressed by the modern mind, which come center stage.

In these postmodern variations on the modern stories, the simple opposition between priest and scientist is replaced by complex interactions between different groups with different fields of knowledge, each competing for social and political power: institutional religion versus Bruno's ancient Egyptian mysticism, Western missionaries versus native spiritualities, male doctors versus wise women. They include new themes of mysticism and the spiritual search, which would be excluded from the modern orthodox versions. The keynote is both-and rather than either-or. This inclusiveness makes it difficult to identify distinctive postmodern myths, although pluralist beliefs are common, and the New Age visionary George Trevelyan has advocated James Lovelock's *Gaia hypothesis*, with its quasi mystical ideas of harmony and interconnectedness, as a myth for our postindustrial society.[10] These ideas are clearly more open to questions of religion and belief than the modern myths, but there is a price to pay.

The modern mind celebrates reason and truth as the royal road to freedom and justice. Postmodern skepticism toward this can appear to be an openness to "spirituality," to human experiences of joy and love and to a sense of irrational mystery in nature. This certainly avoids the modern tunnel vision that rejects all forms of religion as superstition, and it escapes the intolerance that seeks to cage views it does not share. But it can also undercut the very Enlightenment faith that has driven Western thought for the past two centuries without clearly replacing it with anything else.

Those who have committed their lives to humanist inquiry in the spirit of the Enlightenment are inclined to feel that postmodern stories breed "an atmosphere of permissiveness towards questioning the meaning of historical events" and encourage "a relativistic approach to the truth": "much of history seems to be up for grabs and attacks on the Western rationalist tradition have become commonplace." Some even implicate it in the denial of the Holocaust.[11] While we need not agree with such views, it seems unlikely that postmodern myths will be able to sustain the concepts of truth and justice that persisted in the Enlightenment tradition and that had their roots in the biblical vision.[12]

The Bible Narrative

We experience our lives through time, and it is therefore not surprising that we respond positively to narrative accounts. Indeed, many theologians have emphasized in recent years that the Bible is a narrative. This is not, in fact, a new insight. Arabella Hankey expressed much the same thought when she wrote "tell me the old, old story . . . of Jesus and his glory, of Jesus and his love." Few until relatively recently have supposed that thinking of the gospel as story invalidates it, as either historical or theological truth.

Narratives are not just gripping accounts. They may also have profound cultural power. I have described six stories that pass on powerful modern myths and distort history and truth in the process. Forceful narratives need not equate with fiction, however. Reliable narratives may be just as influential as those that misrepresent what they portray.

The biblical narrative has deeply marked the development of Western societies. For example, the creation motif implies that the world can be experienced and known by us because we have been created to live in it. We expect to find a harmony and coherence that reflect the character of the triune Creator and that can be grasped by our reasoning, to be specified as laws—the very expectation that nurtured the growth of early modern science. Similarly, the Reformation's recovery of biblical motifs of providence, calling and dominion have all had significant cultural and historical impacts.

The modern mind inherited these motifs from the Reformation, and secularized God's faithfulness into autonomous natural laws, his providence into progress and dominion into domination.[13] As it did so, it transformed the Reformation vision into a fundamentally different worldview. It denied that creation is the Lord's and that human beings are sinners in need of redemption, and it produced its own myths and impoverished the truth.

Many postmodern authors recognize that there is something wrong with the modern story. They reject the clinical detachment that was the condition for modern objective knowledge and doubt the doctrine of progress whose social, environmental and political consequences can no longer be ignored. This has not resulted in a turn toward the full biblical narrative, but it has highlighted some biblical motifs that had found sanctuary from rationalism in the Romantic movement and were preserved there, albeit in a distorted form. Yet postmodernity's appropriation of these motifs has transformed them, just as modernity's did. Thus Luther's emphatic "God for us" was secularized into the sovereign, expressive individual of the Romantic movement; in postmodernity, an identity built around "expressivity" is replacing the austere humanism of modernity. Ironically, this threatens to undermine any understanding of "humanness" at all; in Michel Foucault's colorful phrase, humanity will "be erased, like a face drawn in sand at the edge of the sea."[14] Similarly, postmodernity has taken "nature" from the Romantic vocabulary and has recovered a sense of empathy with creation. This has replaced modern ideas of exploitation and progress, although in the process, "creation" has been impoverished and secularized into the "environment." Other aspects of the Romantic tradition have been raided to yield a renewed emphasis on commitment, tolerance and community. These biblical motifs, recovered but distorted, have joined forces in the postmodern mosaic with a variety of other traditions, sometimes including alternative spiritualities and religious texts.

The postmodern critique recognizes the inadequacy of the modern stories and is recovering many biblical motifs hidden by the darkness of rationalism. But it also transforms them, just as modernity did. Moreover, in its rejection of Enlightenment reason it also risks losing that sense of order and pattern within the natural world that gave rise to the expectation that rationality was worth pursuing. At worst, it so obscures providence in its rejection of progress that it sees nothing left but to entertain us.

The power of the story tempts us to suspend our disbelief, and both modern and postmodern stories get carried away with their myths. Secularized and distorted versions of biblical motifs are taken up as though there were nothing better. Modernity and postmodernity, however, exhibit different responses to narrative. The modern story claims to rely on facts and reason but sacrifices them to the myths it carries in order to establish the plausibility of the modern worldview. Nevertheless, modern stories retain a sense of truth and justice from their biblical heritage, and in this arena Enlightenment and Christian worldviews can make common cause. However, as the nineteenth-century influence of rationalism on Christianity shows, such alliances must tread carefully.[15]

Postmodern stories are skeptical of whether any all-embracing truth exists, and they entertain us with a kaleidoscope of multifaceted accounts. Yet we can also share the postmodern insights that truth is not exhausted by the forms of reason that have enabled modern humankind to penetrate the mechanisms of nature. Christians can make common cause with postmodern insights into the environment, community and tolerance. However, we must not forget that these are only distorted versions of the biblical motifs, vaguely shadowing the full scriptural truth.

Only the biblical narrative uniquely tells the truth that it reveals to us and that other stories feed on and distort. So while we can welcome aspects of both modern and postmodern stories, we must not align ourselves with either of them. The Bible recounts a truthful narrative and provides a basis for this in the Author's revelation of himself and his actions in history. This revelation imbues our own story and that of the world we know with an eternal significance. This story, which is great with promise and warning, does not merely inform, in the Enlightenment mode, nor entertain, in post-modern style, but demands that we engage with it, and ultimately that we engage with its Author in all our humanity.

Notes

Introduction: Stories & Myths

[1]This is a broad summary of four centuries of Greek usage of the term *mythos*. It had, of course, a wide range of meanings, from Plato's sense of events beyond reason to later contrasts with *logos*. The English word *myth* is similarly used in many ways, some quite ill-defined, making it a slippery term to tie down. Were it not that it is so common, it might be better to avoid it altogether.

[2]N. T. Wright, *The New Testament and the People of God* (London: SPCK, 1992), pp. 424-27.

[3]Compare 1 Timothy 1:4; 4:7; 2 Timothy 4:4; Titus 3:14.

[4]Stephen Neill, ed., "Jesus and History," in *The Truth of God Incarnate* (London: Hodder & Stoughton, 1977), p. 71.

[5]Lawrence Stone, "History and Postmoderism III," *Past and Present* 135 (1992): 193.

[6]Roger Scruton, *Modern Philosophy: An Introduction and Survey* (London: Hodder & Stoughton, 1996), p. 6.

[7]C. S. Lewis, *The Pilgrim's Regress: An Allegorical Apology for Christianity, Reason and Romanticism* (London: Bles, 1933), pp. 35-36, his emphasis.

[8]It is almost always *man*. This use of *man* for humankind is characteristic of modernity, and I will use *man* and its cognates where I am speaking of the modern vision.

[9]The reader interested in this discussion should see the classic text of Barthes, *Mythologies* (London: Vintage, 1993), to which some of these paragraphs are indebted. Barthes, however, draws an inadequate distinction between language and broader worldview issues. I hope to discuss this in detail elsewhere.

[10]J. B. Russell, *Inventing the Flat Earth* (New York: Praeger, 1991), p. 3.

[11]Carl Sagan and A. Druyan, *Comet* (London: Michael Joseph, 1985), p. 25.

[12]Russell, *Inventing the Flat Earth*, pp. 5-6, emphasis in the original.

[13]Arild Holt-Jensen, *Geography: Its History and Concepts* (London: Harper & Row, 1981), p. 11.

[14]John W. Draper, *History of the Conflict Between Religion and Science* (London: Kegan Paul, 1890), pp. 160, 163.

[15]Andrew D. White, *A History of the Warfare of Science with Theology in Christendom*, (London: Macmillan, 1896), 1:97, 108.

[16]Sagan and Druyan, *Comet*, pp. 26-27.

[17]Patrick Moore, *Guide to Comets* (London: Lutterworth, 1977), pp. 61-62, cf. p. 22.

[18]Draper, *History of the Conflict*, pp. 269, 320.

[19]Sagan and Druyan, *Comet*, p. 26.

[20]Ibid., p. 28.

[21]The use of the term *scientist* is, of course, an anachronism. It was coined by William Whewell in 1834 and only subsequently came into general usage.

[22]Bede *A History of the English Church and People* 5 (c. 731; reprint, Harmondsworth: Penguin, 1968), chap. 23.

[23]See William E. H. Leckey, *History of the Rise and Influence of the Spirit of Rationalism in Europe*, 2 vols. (London: Longmans, 1890).

[24]J. P. Moreland, *Christianity and the Nature of Science: A Philosophical Investigation* (Grand Rapids, Mich.: Baker, 1989), p. 101, quoted in Arthur Jones, *Science in Faith* (Romford: Christian Schools Trust, 1998), p. 9. For a discussion of the "warfare" thesis see John Hedley Brooke, *Science and Religion* (Cambridge: Cambridge University Press, 1991); and David C. Lindberg and Ronald L. Numbers, *God and Nature* (Berkeley: University of California Press, 1986), pp. 1-18.

[25]Colin A. Russell, "The Conflict Metaphor and its Social Origins," *Science and Christian Belief* 1, no. 1 (1989): 7.

[26]Bertrand Russell, "Has Religion Made Useful Contributions to Civilisation?" in *Why I Am Not a Christian* (London: Unwin, 1930), pp. 28-44.

[27]Bob Goudswaard, *Capitalism and Progress* (Toronto: Wedge, 1979).

[28]Owen Chadwick, *The Secularisation of the European Mind in the Nineteenth Century* (Cambridge: Cambridge University Press, 1975), pp. 162-63.

[29]Arthur R. Peacocke, *Theology for a Scientific Age* (London: SCM Press, 1993), p. 1, emphasis mine.

[30]For an assessment, see David Lyon, *The Steeple's Shadow* (London: SPCK, 1985).

[31]Andrew Brown, *The Darwin Wars* (London: Simon & Schuster, 1999), p. 25.

[32]John Gillot and Manjit Kumar, *Science and the Retreat from Reason* (London: Merlin, 1995), p. 147.

[33]Christopher H. Dawson, *Progress and Religion* (London: Sheed & Ward, 1929), p. 19.

[34]Francis Darwin, ed., *The Life and Letters of Charles Darwin,* (London: Murray, 1887), 1:316.

[35]Scruton, *Modern Philosophy*, p. 2.

[36]H. G. Wells, *Men Like Gods* (London: Odhams, 1921), p. 369.

[37]Brian J. Walsh and J. Richard Middleton, *The Transforming Vision* (Downers Grove, Ill.: InterVarsity Press, 1984), chap. 2.

[38]Bertrand Russell, *Sceptical Essays* (London: Allen & Unwin, 1960), p. 101.

[39]For a discussion of the role of social institutions, see Craig Gay, *The Way of the (Modern) World* (Grand Rapids, Mich.: Eerdmans, 1998).

Chapter 1: Galileo
[1]This will be the subject of chapter four. See Marion Morrison, *Indians of the Andes* (Hove, U.K.: Wayland, 1986), p. 16.

[2]Bertrand Russell, *History of Western Philosophy* (London: Allen & Unwin, 1947), p. 556.

[3]George Bernard Shaw, *Saint Joan* (Harmondsworth: Penguin, 1946), p. 17.

[4]William E. H. Lecky, *History of the Rise and Influence of the Spirit of Rationalism in Europe* (London: Longmans, 1890), 1:274-75.

[5]Patrick Moore, *A Beginner's Guide to Astronomy* (London: PRC Publishing, 1997), p. 12.

[6]P. Whitaker, review of Richard Dawkins's *River Out of Eden* in *New Internationalist* 282 (1996): 33.

[7]Carl Sagan, *Pale Blue Dot* (London: Hodder Headline, 1995), p. 46.

[8]Bertolt Brecht, *Life of Galileo*, trans. J. Willet (London: Methuen, 1980), pp. 29, 87.

[9]Catherine Headlam, ed., *The Kingfisher Encyclopedia* (London: Kingfisher, 1991), p. 277.

[10]Stephen Hawking considers that the church adopted this picture of the universe as being "in accordance with Scripture, for it had the great advantage that it left lots of

room outside the sphere of fixed stars for heaven and hell" (*A Brief History of Time* [London: Bantam, 1988], p. 4). This is not very likely. While, for example, the fourteenth-century Florentine poet Dante Alighieri places the Empyrean (roughly, "heaven") beyond the sphere of the stars, this is more the exploitation of contemporary cosmology than a reason to embrace it. Hawking's suggestion that hell was also seen as beyond the fixed stars is nonsensical, as that is the place of perfection and harmony. It is no surprise, therefore, that Dante's inferno is in the depths of the earth, at the center of the universe where all gross matter descends. Dante does not appear concerned one way or the other over the volume of space which hell would occupy, but the idea that it is at the center of the earth obviously places limits on its extent if we take these images literally. C. S. Lewis, in his celebrated allegory *The Pilgrim's Regress* (London: Bles, 1933), pictures hell as occupying an infinitessimally small space.

[11]Russell, *History of Western Philosophy*, p. 559. Compare Francis Crick, *The Astonishing Hypothesis: The Scientific Search for the Soul* (London: Touchstone, 1994), pp. 4-5. See also Edwin A. Burtt, *The Metaphysical Foundations of Modern Physical Science* (London: Kegan Paul, 1925), pp. 4, 6; and John W. Draper, *History of the Conflict Between Religion and Science* (1874; reprint, London: Kegan Paul, 1890), pp. 168–69.

[12]Lecky, *History of the Rise*, 1:viii.

[13]James R. Newman, *Science and Sensibility* (New York: Simon & Schuster, 1961), 1:54, 56.

[14]Dante Alighieri, *The Divine Comedy*, trans. D. L. Sayers and B. Reynolds (Harmondsworth: Penguin, 1962), 3:22.

[15]Galileo Galilei, *Dialogue Concerning the Two Chief World Systems*, trans. S. Drake (1632; reprint, Berkeley: University of California Press, 1967), p. 37, cf. p. 268.

[16]Draper, *History of the Conflict*, p. 175.

[17]An important exception is Galileo's near contemporary Blaise Pascal, who was troubled by the size of the universe: "The eternal silence of these infinite spaces filled me with dread" (*Pensée* 95, no. 201 [Harmondsworth: Penguin, 1966]). However, it is unclear whether this sense of angst was occasioned by a specifically Copernican universe; Ptolemy's model would have been more than large enough to evoke such thoughts from a soul such as Pascal's. Robert White notes that the only "centrism" which interested Calvin was "theocentrism" (see Robert White, "Calvin and Copernicus: The Problem Reconsidered," *Calvin Theological Journal* 15, no. 2 [1980]: 243).

[18]Charles Darwin, *The Descent of Man* (1871; reprint, London: Murray, 1894), p. 619, emphasis mine.

[19]Fred Hoyle and N. C. Wickramasinghe, *Evolution from Space* (London: Dent, 1981), p. 2.

[20]Bertrand Russell, *A Free Man's Worship*, in *The Basic Writings of Bertrand Russell*, ed. R. E. Egner and L. E. Denonn, (1903; reprint, London: Allen & Unwin, 1961), p. 72.

[21]Burtt, *Metaphysical Foundations*, p. 25, cf. p. 23ff.

[22]Thomas S. Kuhn, *The Structure of Scientific Revolutions* (Chicago: University of Chicago Press, 1970), pp. 75-76.

[23]Draper, *History of the Conflict*, pp. 167-68.

[24]Jerome J. Langford, *Galileo, Science and the Church* (Ann Arbor: University of Michigan Press, 1971), p. 35.

[25]Draper, *History of the Conflict*, pp. 167-68.

[26]Georgio de Santillana, *The Crime of Galileo* (London: Heinemann, 1958), p. xii.

[27]*Universal Knowledge A to Z* (London: Odhams Press, 1938), p. 476; cf. S. Kauffman, *At Home in the Universe: The Search for Laws of Complexity* (Harmondsworth: Penguin, 1995), p. 16.

[28]Sagan, *Pale Blue Dot*, p. 44.

[29]Langford, *Galileo, Science and the Church*, p. 134.

[30]*Universal Knowledge*, p. 476; cf. Draper, *History of the Conflict*, p. 172.

[31]A. N. Whitehead, *Science and the Modern World* (Cambridge: Cambridge University Press, 1946), p. 2.

[32]Russell, *History of Western Philosophy*, p. 556.

[33]Clive Morphet, *Galileo and Copernican Astronomy* (London: Butterworth, 1977), p. 4; cf. M. Sharratt, *Galileo: Decisive Innovator* (Cambridge: Cambridge University Press, 1996), p. 221.

[34]Maurice A. Finocchiaro, *Galileo and the Art of Reasoning* (London: Reide, 1980), p. xvi.

[35]William R. Shea, "Galileo and the Church" in *God and Nature*, ed. David C. Lindberg and Ronald L. Numbers (Berkeley: University of California Press, 1986), p. 132.

[36]See Finocchiaro, *Galileo and the Art of Reasoning*; Pietro Redondi, *Galileo: Heretic* (Harmondsworth: Penguin, 1987); Mario Biagioli, *Galileo Courtier* (Chicago: University of Chicago Press, 1993); and Rivka Feldhay, *Galileo and the Church* (Cambridge: Cambridge University Press, 1995).

[37]Richard J. Blackwell, *Galileo, Bellarmine, and the Bible* (Notre Dame, Ind.: University of Notre Dame Press, 1991), p. 120ff.

[38]Galileo Galilei, *Discoveries and Opinions of Galileo*, trans. S. Drake (New York: Anchor, 1957), p. 181.

[39]Russell, *History of Western Philosophy*, p. 550.

[40]Kuhn gives Andrew D. White, *A History of the Warfare of Science with Theology in Christendom* (London: Macmillan, 1896), 1:127, as his source (Kuhn, *The Copernican Revolution* [Cambridge, Mass.: Harvard University Press, 1957], p. 192).

[41]Edward Rosen, "Calvin's Attitude Towards Copernicus," *Journal of the History of Ideas* 21, no. 3 (1960): 431-41.

[42]See Reijer Hooykaas, *Religion and the Rise of Modern Science* (Edinburgh: Scottish Academic Press, 1972); Rosen, "Calvin's Attitude"; and Robert White, "Calvin and Copernicus: the Problem Reconsidered," *Calvin Theological Journal* 15, no. 2 (1980): 233-43 for a discussion of this and of similar quotations. For an opposing view to Rosen's, see J. Ratner, "Some Comments on Rosen's 'Calvin's Attitude Towards Copernicus,' " *Journal of the History of Ideas* 22 (1961): 382-85; and White, "Calvin and Copernicus" for the subsequent debate.

[43]John Calvin, *Commentary on Genesis* (Edinburgh: Banner of Truth, 1965), pp. 80, 85-86.

[44]H. W. Turnbull, ed., *The Correspondence of Isaac Newton* (Cambridge: Cambridge University Press, 1960), 2:331.

[45]Quoted in Langford, *Galileo, Science and the Church*, pp. 65-66; see also Thomas S. Kuhn, *The Copernican Revolution* (Cambridge, Mass.: Harvard University Press, 1957), p. 197.

[46]This does not imply that Calvin was a Copernican. He was not. However, he rarely comments on cosmology. In the *Genesis* commentary he remarks: "We indeed are not ignorant . . . that the earth . . . is placed in the centre [of the heavens]" (Calvin, *Commentary on Genesis*, p. 61), which was the recognized opinion among astronomers in 1554. Calvin's most caustic comments on heliocentrism appear to have been

in a sermon on Corinthians, but it is debatable whether he is referring to Copernicus (White, *Calvin and Copernicus*, p. 236).

[47]Turnbull, ed., *Correspondence of Isaac Newton*, 3:233, language modernized.

[48]Roger Cotes, preface to *Sir Isaac Newton's Mathematical Principles of Natural Philosophy and His System of the World*, ed. F. Cajori (1785; reprint, Berkeley: University of California Press, 1966), 1:xxxii-xxxiii.

[49]The relationship between religion and science is complex, and many images other than conflict have been suggested, including independence, dialogue, integration, consonance and assimilation. See Ian G. Barbour, *Religion and Science* (San Francisco: Harper, 1990); John Polkinghorne, *Science and Theology* (London: SPCK, 1998); and Colin A. Russell, *Cross-Currents: Interactions Between Science and Faith* (Leicester, U.K.: Inter-Varsity Press, 1985).

[50]Robert Boyle, "From the Publisher to the Reader," in *Experiments and Considerations Touching Colours* (London: Henry Herringham, 1664).

[51]Thomas Sprat, *The History of the Royal Society of London*, ed. J. I. Cope and H. W. Jones (1667; reprint, London: Routledge, 1959), p. 327.

[52]Peter Gay, *The Enlightenment* (London: Wildwood, 1973), 1:132.

[53]Calvin, *Commentary on Genesis*, p. 62.

[54]John Calvin, *Institutes of the Christian Religion*, ed. J. T. McNeill, trans. Ford Lewis Battles (1559; reprint, London: SCM Press, 1961), 1:5.1.

[55]Galileo, *Discoveries and Opinions*, p. 29.

[56]Stanley L. Jaki, *Science and Creation* (Edinburgh: Scottish Academic Press, 1986).

[57]Tycho Brahe, quoted in John D. Barrow, *The World Within the World* (Oxford: Clarendon, 1988), p. 59.

[58]Richard S. Westfall, *Science and Religion in Seventeenth Century England* (Ann Arbor: University of Michigan Press, 1973), p. 197.

[59]Hooykaas, *Religion and the Rise*, p. 26.

[60]Richard Dawkins, *River Out of Eden* (London: Weidenfeld and Nicolson, 1995), p. 33.

Chapter 2: Darwin

[1]Richard Hofstadter, *Social Darwin in American Thought* (New York: Braziller, 1959), p. 3.

[2]Andrew Brown, dust jacket to *The Darwin Wars* (London: Simon & Schuster, 1999).

[3]Mary Midgley, "The Religion of Evolution," in *Darwinism and Divinity*, ed. John Durant (Oxford: Blackwell, 1985), p. 154. See also Mary Midgley, *Evolution as Religion* (London: Methuen, 1985). Of course, neither she nor the present chapter comments directly on the scientific merits of evolution.

[4]Richard Dawkins, *The Selfish Gene* (Oxford: Oxford University Press, 1989), p. 1.

[5]Aristotle *Physics* 2.8.198b.29f, trans. P. H. Wicksteed and F. M. Cornford (London: Heinemann, 1960).

[6]I am discussing the story that transmits Darwinism for the modern mind. Its scientific merit is not dealt with here.

[7]Linda Gamlin, *Evolution* (London: Dorling Kindersley, 1993), pp. 36, 58.

[8]Henry B. D. Kettlewell, *The Evolution of Melanism* (Oxford: Clarendon, 1973), p. 315.

[9]Theodore D. Sargent, Craig D. Millar and David M. Lambert, "The 'Classical' Explanation of Industrial Melanism: Assessing the Evidence," *Evolutionary Biology* 30 (1998): 302. See also Kettlewell, *Evolution of Melanism*, pp. 3, 40, where he writes with

more caution. Other distinguished scholars make the same claim, for example, Richard E. Leakey, *The Illustrated Origin of Species* (London: Book Club Associates, 1979), p. 30.

[10]Richard Dawkins, *Climbing Mount Improbable* (London: Viking, 1996), p. 78.

[11]For a fair review of recent research, see Jerry A. Coyne, "Not Black and White," *Nature* 396, no. 6712 (1999): 35–36.

[12]Sargent, Millar and Lambert, " 'Classical' Explanation," p. 300.

[13]Charles Darwin, *The Origin of Species* (1859; reprint, Harmondworth: Penguin, 1968), pp. 171-72, 454-55, 459-60, emphasis mine.

[14]Perhaps I should say "sciences," for there are many competing species: from neo-Darwinism to Stephen Gould's punctuated-equilibrium theory, from Margulis's cooperationalism to the Panspermia theories of Hoyle, Wickramasinghe and Crick. It is not yet clear which species will survive in the competitive scientific environment. Nothing contained in this chapter is intended as comment on this issue.

[15]Charles C. Gillespie, *Dictionary of Scientific Biography* (New York: Scribner, 1971), 3:574. See also the cover note in the Penguin edition of *The Origin of Species*.

[16]Magnus Pyke and Patrick Moore, *Everyman's Scientific Facts and Feats* (London: Dent, 1981), p. 198.

[17]Isaac Asimov, *Asimov's Chronology of Science and Discovery* (London: Collins, 1990), p. 333.

[18]Steve Parker, *Charles Darwin and Evolution* (London: Belitha, 1992), p. 18.

[19]Colin A. Russell, *Cross-Currents: Interactions Between Science and Faith* (Leicester, U.K.: Inter-Varsity Press, 1985), p. 158.

[20]James R. Newman, *Science and Sensibility* (New York: Simon & Schuster, 1961), 1:56.

[21]Stuart Kauffman, *At Home in the Universe: The Search for Laws of Complexity* (Harmondsworth: Penguin, 1995), p. 10.

[22]Darwin, *Origin of Species*, pp. 458-59.

[23]Fred Hoyle and N. C. Wickramasinghe, *Evolution from Space* (London: Dent, 1981), p. 2.

[24]René Taton, ed., *Science in the Nineteenth Century* (London: Thames and Hudson, 1967), pp. 477-78.

[25]Gillespie, *Dictionary of Scientific Biography*, 3:574.

[26]Francis Darwin, ed., *The Life and Letters of Charles Darwin* (London: Murray, 1887), 2:324-25.

[27]Francis Darwin, ed., *More Letters of Charles Darwin* (London: Murray, 1903), 1:157.

[28]John R. Lucas, "Wilberforce and Huxley: A Legendary Encounter," *Historical Journal* 22, no. 2 (1979): 313-20.

[29]Edward J. Larson, *Summer for the Gods* (New York: BasicBooks, 1997), p. 241.

[30]Ibid., p. 241; Jerome Lawrence and Robert E. Lee, *Inherit the Wind* (London: Four Square Books, 1960), pp. 86, 122.

[31]Lawrence and Lee, *Inherit the Wind*, pp. 64, 40.

[32]William Jennings Bryan, "God and Evolution," in *Evolution and Religion*, ed. G. Kennedy (Boston: D. C. Health, 1957), p. 24.

[33]Larson, *Summer for the Gods*, p. 241.

[34]Bryan, "God and Evolution," p. 23.

[35]Larson, *Summer for the Gods*, p. 39.

[36]Bryan, "God and Evolution," p. 25.

[37]George W. Hunter, *A Civic Biology* (New York: American Book, 1914), p. 261.

[38]Ibid., p. 263.

[39]Ibid., p. 196.

[40]Larson, *Summer for the Gods*, pp. 38-40, 27; cf. pp. 28, 115, 271 n. 64.

[41]Barbara Reynolds, introduction to *The Divine Comedy*, by Dante, vol. 3, *Paradise*, (Harmondsworth: Penguin, 1962), p. 24.

[42]Kauffman, *At Home in the Universe*, p. 6.

[43]See David N. Livingstone, *Darwin's Forgotten Defenders* (Grand Rapids, Mich.: Eerdmans, 1987); and James R. Moore, *Post Darwinian Controversies* (Cambridge: Cambridge University Press, 1979).

[44]Walter F. Cannon, "The Bases of Darwin's Achievement: A Revaluation," *Victorian Studies*, December 5, 1961, pp. 109-32.

[45]Owen Chadwick, *The Secularisation of the European Mind in the Nineteenth Century* (Cambridge: Cambridge University Press, 1975), p. 174, cf. 183-88.

[46]Taton, *Science in the Nineteenth Century*, p. 477.

[47]Parker, *Charles Darwin and Evolution*, p. 18.

[48]Darwin, *Origin of Species*, p. 452.

[49]Letter to J. Jenyns, in *The Life and Letters of Charles Darwin*, ed. Francis Darwin (London: Murray, 1887), 2:34.

[50]Niles Eldredge, *Time Frames* (London: Heinemann, 1986), p. 28, his emphasis.

[51]Twentieth-century physicists revised Kelvin's calculations in the light of the discovery of nuclear processes; contemporary estimates of the earth's age are compatible with Darwinism.

[52]Darwin, *More Letters*, 1:130. Darwin is here paraphrasing Sedgwick, who wrote: "sides were almost sore" (Darwin, *Life and Letters*, 2:248).

[53]Thomas F. Glick, ed., *The Comparative Reception of Darwinism* (Austin: University of Texas Press, 1972), p. 4.

[54]George J. Mivart, "Darwin's *Descent of Man*," reprinted in D. L. Hull, *Darwin and His Critics* (Cambridge, Mass.: Harvard University Press, 1973), p. 358.

[55]Peter J. Bowler, *Evolution: The History of an Idea* (Berkeley: University of California Press, 1984).

[56]Niles Eldredge, *Reinventing Darwin* (London: Weidenfeld and Nicolson, 1995), p. 95.

[57]Eldredge, *Time Frames*, p. 144.

[58]Gordon Stowell, ed., *The Book of Knowledge* (London: Waverly, 1960), 3:321.

[59]Michael Behe, *Darwin's Black Box* (New York: Free Press, 1996).

[60]Kauffman, *At Home*, p. 8, cf. pp. vii, 13, 150.

[61]Michael Denton, *Evolution: A Theory in Crisis* (London: Burnett, 1985), p. 77.

[62]Fred Hoyle and N. C. Wickramasinghe, *Life Cloud: The Origin of Life in the Universe* (London: Dent, 1978), p. 32; Hoyle and Wickramasinghe, *Evolution from Space*, p. 3; Fred Hoyle and N. C. Wickramasinghe, *Cosmic Life Force* (London: Dent, 1988), p. 135. For a balanced summary of the quantitative questions physicists would like neo-Darwinists to answer, see J. Polkinghorne, *Science and Christian Belief* (London: SPCK, 1994), pp. 16ff.

[63]None of these critics is a creationist, who would, of course, also reject Darwin's views.

[64]Glick, *Comparative Reception*, p. 402.

[65]Parker, *Charles Darwin and Evolution*, p. 18.

[66]Larson, *Summer for the Gods*, p. 20.

[67]Jean Gayon, *Darwinism's Struggle for Survival* (Cambridge: Cambridge University Press, 1998), pp. 397, 8, cf. p. 3.

[68]Adrian Desmond, *Huxley: The Devil's Disciple* (London: Michael Joseph, 1994), p. 362, cf. pp. 270-71; O. Stanley, "T. H. Huxley's Treatment of Nature," *Journal of the History of Ideas* 18 (1957): 120-27.

[69]John Tyndall, "Presidential Address," *Report of the British Association for the Advancement of Science,* London (1874): xcii, xciii n. See also Russell, *Cross-Currents*, pp. 178, 183, and Stanley, "T. H. Huxley's Treatment."

[70]J. B. S. Haldane, *The Inequality of Man and Other Essays* (London: Chatto and Windus, 1932), p. 113.

[71]Julian Huxley, *Evolution in Action* (New York: Mentor, 1953), p. 132; see also Andrew Brown, *The Darwin Wars* (London: Simon & Schuster, 1999), pp. 39ff., 189, 217.

[72]C. Mann, "Lynn Margulis: Science's Unruly Earth Mother," *Science* 252 (1991): 381.

[73]Kauffman, *At Home*, p. 8.

[74]G. G. Simpson, cited in Dawkins, *Selfish Gene*, p. 1.

[75]H. Ellegard, *Darwin and the General Reader: The Reception of Darwin's Theory of Evolution in the British Periodical Press, 1859-1872* (Göteborg: Elanders Boktryckeri Aktiebolag, 1958), p. 43.

[76]For a survey of the origins of Darwin's views, see D. R. Oldroyd, "How Did Darwin Arrive at His Theory?" *History of Science* 22 (1984): 325-74.

[77]Karl Marx and Friedrich Engels, letter of June 18, 1862, in *Selected Correspondence* (Moscow: Foreign Languages, 1956), pp. 156-57.

[78]Richard C. Lewontin, *The Doctrine of DNA* (Oxford: Blackwell, 1996), pp. 9-10.

[79]Stephen J. Gould and Niles Eldredge, "Punctuated Equilibria," *Paleobiology* 3 (1977): 145.

[80]Richard Dawkins, *River Out of Eden* (London: Weidenfeld and Nicolson, 1995), p. xi.

[81]Bertrand Russell, *Human Knowledge: Its Scope and Limits* (London: Allen & Unwin, 1948), p. 48.

[82]James R. Moore, "Socializing Darwinism" in *Science as Politics,* ed. L. Levidow (London: Free Association Press, 1986).

[83]Herbert Spencer, *Social Statics* (1851; reprint, New York: Kelly, 1969), 1.2.4 (p. 65). Spencer, of course, was writing of evolution generally; he did not adopt Darwinian ideas until the 1860s.

[84]This should not be overstated. The phrase "social Darwinism" was a late arrival and only gained currency from the 1890s. Moreover, there is some evidence that Darwinian accounts were more common in later social theory than among contemporary capitalists. Ideas of social evolution long predated Darwin but were refreshed by Darwinism.

[85]A "meme," by analogy with "gene," is a cultural unit, such as Darwinism, which is replicated in a population.

[86]Matt Cartmill, *A View to a Death in the Morning: Hunting and Nature Through History* (Cambridge, Mass.: Harvard University Press, 1993), p. 270.

[87]John Hedley Brooke, *Science and Religion* (Cambridge: Cambridge University Press, 1991), p. 292.

[88]Ernst Haeckel, quoted in Peter Medawar, *The Threat and the Glory* (Oxford: Oxford University Press, 1991), p. 104.

[89]H. W. Koch, ed., *The Origins of the First World War* (Basingstoke: Macmillan, 1977), pp. 330-31; W. Baumgart, *Imperialism* (Oxford: Oxford University Press, 1982), pp.

83ff.; M. Hawkins, *Social Darwinism in European and American Thought 1860-1945* (Cambridge: Cambridge University Press, 1997), chap. 8. Crook's dissent (P. Crook, "Historical Monkey Business," *History* 84, no. 276 [1999]: 633-57) from the majority view is unconvincing, as not even Darwin would satisfy his criterion for "serious Darwinian speculation."

[90]Alfred R. Wallace, "The Origin of Human Races and the Antiquity of Man Deduced from the Theory of 'Natural Selection,' " *Journal of the Anthrolopolgical Society of London* (1864): clxiv-clxv, his emphasis.

[91]Thomas H. Huxley, *Lay Sermons, Addresses and Reviews* (New York: Macmillan, 1899), p. 17.

[92]Ibid., p. 22.

[93]Charles Darwin, *The Descent of Man* (1871; reprint, London: Murray, 1894), p. 597.

[94]Evelleen Richards, "Huxley and Women's Place in Science," in *History, Community and Evolution*, ed. James R. Moore (Cambridge: Cambridge University Press, 1989), p. 281, cf. pp. 260-61, 256.

[95]C. S. Lewis, *That Hideous Strength* (London: Pan, 1955), p. 243.

[96]Darwin, *Descent of Man*, p. 618.

[97]Haldane, *The Inequality of Man*, p. 24.

[98]Michael Freeden, "Eugenics and Progressive Thought: A Study in Ideological Affinity," *Historical Journal* 22, no. 3 (1979); and Greta Jones, *Social Darwinism and English Thought* (Brighton: Harvester, 1980).

[99]Marie Stopes, quoted in J. Grier, "Eugenics and Birth Control: Contraceptive Provision in North Wales 1918-1939," *Social History of Medicine* 11, no. 3 (1998): 445.

[100]Marie Stopes, quoted in Richard A. Soloway, *Demography and Degeneration* (London: Chapel Hill, 1990), pp. 34, 80.

[101]Adolf Hitler, *Mein Kampf* (London: Hurst and Blackett, 1925), p. 239.

[102]Daniel Gasman, *The Scientific Origins of National Socialism* (London: MacDonald, 1971), p. xxii.

[103]Daniel C. Dennett, *Darwin's Dangerous Idea* (Harmondsworth: Penguin, 1995), p. 464.

[104]Asimov, *Asimov's Chronology*, p. 380. For contrasting discussions of Spencer's role, see Hawkins, *Social Darwinism*, chap. 4; and J. D. Y. Peel, *Herbert Spencer: The Evolution of a Sociologist* (London: Heinemann, 1971), p. 141ff.

[105]James R. Moore, "Socialising Darwinism," in L. Levidow, ed., *Science as Politics* (London: Free Association Press, 1986).

[106]Adrian Desmond and James Moore, *Darwin* (London: Michael Joseph, 1991), p. xxi.

[107]Darwin, *Descent of Man*, p. 133, cf. p. 138.

[108]A. N. Whitehead, *Science and the Modern World* (Cambridge: Cambridge University Press, 1946), p. 256.

Chapter 3: The Environment

[1]P. Singer, *Animal Liberation* (Wellingborough, U.K.: Thorsons, 1976), p. 226. This view is watered down on page 206 of the 1990 edition of Singer's book.

[2]Lynn White, "The Historical Roots of Our Ecologic Crisis," *Science* 155, no. 3767 (1967): 1203-7, reprinted in J. R. Berry, ed., *The Care of Creation* (Downers Grove, Ill.: InterVarsity Press, 2000), chap. 1.

[3]Keith V. Thomas, *Man and the Natural World: Changing Attitudes in England 1500-*

1800 (London: Allen Lane, 1983), p. 23. For critical responses to White's article see Lewis W. Moncrief, "The Cultural Basis for Our Environmental Crisis," *Science* 170, no. 3957 (1970): 508-12; Arthur R. Peacocke, *Creation and the World of Science* (Oxford: Oxford University Press, 1979), pp. 274ff.; and Robin Attfield, "Christian Attitudes to Nature," *Journal of the History of Ideas* 44 (1983): 369-86.

[4]Cited in Lawrence Osborn, *Guardians of Creation* (Leicester: Apollos, 1993), p. 24.

[5]Jonathon Porritt, foreword to *God Is Green*, by Ian Bradley (London: Darton, Longman & Todd, 1990), p. v.

[6]Arnold Toynbee, cited in Stephen R. L. Clark, "Is Nature God's Will?" in Andrew Linzey and D. Yamamoto, eds., *Animals on the Agenda* (London: SCM Press, 1998), p. 123. Clark notes that Toynbee's beliefs have often been refuted, and that the historical role of pantheism in Nazi ideology should caution us against embracing it as the "right religion."

[7]White, "Historical Roots," p. 1205.

[8]Ibid., p. 1207.

[9]Ibid., p. 1206.

[10]Aristotle *Politics* 1256b.15f, in Jonathan Barnes, ed., *The Complete Works of Aristotle*, 2 vols. (Princeton, N.J.: Princeton University Press, 1984).

[11]J. Donald Hughes, *Ecology in Ancient Civilisations* (Albuquerque: University of New Mexico Press, 1975), pp. 149, 154; see also John Passmore, *Man's Responsibility for Nature* (London: Duckworth, 1974).

[12]Cameron Wybrow, *The Bible, Baconism, and Mastery over Nature: The Old Testament and Its Modern Misreading* (New York: Peter Lang, 1991).

[13]I will refer to the doctrine of "stewardship" as it was developed by the sixteenth-century Reformers and has been widely employed in this context since. However, I have some sympathy with Hugh Spanner's argument that a doctrine of "kingship" may be more biblical ("Tyrants, Stewards—or Just Kings?" in Linzey and Yamamoto, *Animals on the Agenda*). For a discussion of Christian attitudes toward creation, see Attfield, "Christian Attitudes," who rebuts the views of White and Passmore among others.

[14]See also Psalm 19; 96:11-13; 98; 148:1-4; Is 55:12. The same doctrine is reflected in Christian hymnody. For example, Isaac Watts's hymn "Joy to the World" exhorts "heav'n and nature" to sing, and "fields and floods, rocks, hills and plains" to "repeat the sounding joy" of the church's songs.

[15]Marvin Harris, *Cannibals and Kings: The Origins of Cultures* (New York: Vintage, 1978), pp. 164-65.

[16]P. Cohen, "The Drying of a Continent," *New Scientist* 156, nos. 2113-2114 (1997): 6; see also Peacocke, *Creation and the World*, p. 277.

[17]Moncrief, "Cultural Basis."

[18]Pagan animism certainly inhibited the growth of science for fear of impiety and called on magic to protect against retribution from the spirits of the natural world. But fear of natural forces is not the same as a sense of responsibility toward creation. See R. Hooykaas, *Religion and the Rise of Modern Science* (Edinburgh: Scottish Academic Press, 1972).

[19]Attfield, "Christian Attitudes," p. 376.

[20]White, *Historical Roots*, p. 1206.

[21]Space prevents further discussion of this doctrine, but it should be noted that contrary to common human practice, dominion does not include other human beings.

[22]Thomas, *Man and the Natural*, pp. 155ff.; Wybrow, *Bible, Baconism, and Mastery*.

[23]Cooperative partnership is implicit in Genesis 3:17–19, where it is disrupted by the curse. See Spanner, "Tyrants, Stewards—or Just Kings?"

[24]Andrew Linzey, *Animal Theology* (London, SCM Press, 1994), p. 126, cited in Tony Sargent, *Animal Rights and Wrongs: A Biblical Perspective* (London: Hodder & Stoughton, 1996), p. 73.

[25]Thomas Sprat, *The History of the Royal Society of London*, ed. J. I. Cope and H. W. Jones (1667; reprint, London: Routledge, 1959), pp. 124, 327.

[26]Of course, as Job shows, the truths that creation teaches us are not necessarily the comfortable and sentimental platitudes we might like to hear.

[27]The Jewish Vegetarian Society points out that the scriptural promises associated with the covenants are always the fruit of the vine, garden or field, never the flesh of slain beasts; Sargent, *Animal Rights*, p. 114.

[28]See also Jonah 4:11; Matthew 6:26; 10:29–30; Luke 12:6–7.

[29]Emphasis mine. See also Hosea 2:18; Ezekiel 34:25–28; Isaiah 65:25; Zechariah 14:20.

[30]See Matthew 25:14–28 and Luke 16:1–15 for Jesus' use of just such norms.

[31]Sargent, *Animal Rights*, p. 32.

[32]Josephus *Against Appion* 2:210-15, trans. H. St. J. Thackeray, vol. 1 (London: Heinemann, 1956). Josephus may have had Psalm 84:1–3 in mind when he refers to "suppliants."

[33]Even authors such as Calvin and Primatt show this trait. Primatt, for example, employs the idea of "use," which he explicitly derives from Aristotle and which sits uneasily with his more biblical understanding of dominion and care (Humphrey Primatt, *A Dissertation of the Duty of Mercy and Sin of Cruelty to Brute Animals*, ed. R. D. Ryder [Fontwell, Sussex: Centaur, 1992], p. 19).

[34]Scott Ickert, "Luther and Animals: Subject to Adam's Fall?" in Linzey and Yamamoto, *Animals on the Agenda*, p. 98.

[35]Thomas, *Man and the Natural*, pp. 24ff., 155ff., 166. I will use the term *Puritan* inclusively to incorporate the Presbyterians of the seventeenth century and the Puritan followers of the eighteenth century, such as Cowper and Edwards.

[36]John Ray, *The Wisdom of God Manifested in the Works of Creation* (London, 1701), p. 196, cf. p. 379.

[37]Thomas, *Man and the Natural*, pp. 154, 180. It is worth noting that Thomas regards this as a "paradox" (p. 156), as he follows White in assuming that Christianity is anthropocentric. This leads Thomas to the remarkable assertion that Calvin is "firmly anthropocentric" in his presentation of dominion (p. 154, also p. 157). Now, Calvin has been called many things but rarely "anthropocentric," let alone "firmly" so. In fact, the very passages cited by Thomas reflect Calvin's accustomed God-centeredness. But the word *God* is not part of Thomas's lexicon of the real. For him, reality stops at man, as does the center of the world. As a result he is deaf to any other way of speaking. Uncomprehending "paradox" and implausible descriptions of Calvin are bound to follow. However, Calvin does remain a man of his time and shows a complex interaction of Stoic and biblical sources (e.g., John Calvin, *Commentary on Genesis* [Edinburg: Banner of Truth, 1965], p. 96, and *Institutes of the Christian Religion*, ed. J. T. McNeill, trans. Ford Lewis Battles [1559; reprint, London: SCM Press, 1961], 2.14.22).

[38]Thomas, *Man and the Natural*, p. 180.

[39]Thomas Aquinas *Summa Theologica* 1.96.1-2, trans. Fathers of the English Dominican Province (New York: Benziger).

[40]Priscella Heath Barnum, ed., *Dives and Pauper* (c. 1410; reprint, Oxford: Oxford University Press, 1980), 1.2:35, lines 39ff., language partially modernized.

[41]John Calvin, *Sermons on Deuteronomy* (1583; reprint, Edinburgh: Banner of Truth, 1987), p. 877, spelling modernized and order changed; see also pp. 560-62, 774, 776.

[42]Primatt, *Dissertation of the Duty*, p. 44.

[43]John Flavel, *Husbandry Spiritualised*, in *The Works of John Flavel* (1669; reprint, Edinburgh: Banner of Truth, 1968), 5:186.

[44]Primatt, *Dissertation of the Duty*, p. 16.

[45]Calvin, *Sermons on Deuteronomy*, p. 770, also pp. 780, 877-78. A similar point is made by Primatt, *Dissertation of the Duty*, p. 30.

[46]William Perkins, quoted in Thomas, *Man and the Natural*, p. 157. Compare R. Venning, *The Plague of Plagues* (1669; reprint, London: Banner of Truth, 1965), pp. 138ff., and John Calvin, *The Epistles of Paul to the Romans and to the Thessalonians* (1543 and 1551; reprint, London: Oliver and Boyd, 1912), p. 173.

[47]Venning, *Plague of Plagues*, p. 140.

[48]Phillip Stubbes, *Anatomy of the Abuses in England in Shakespere's Youth*, ed. F. J. Furnivall (1583; reprint, London: Tribune, 1882), p. 181.

[49]William Cowper, *The Task* 6, in *The Poetical Works*: 129-241 (1785; reprint, London: Oxford University Press, 1967), p. 229. This poem by Cowper contains a sustained and deeply moving critique of human cruelty in a characteristically late-Calvinistic framework.

[50]Thomas B. Macaulay, *History of England*, ed. C. H. Firth (1857; reprint, London: Macmillan, 1913-1915), 1:142.

[51]Christopher Hill, *Reformation to Industrial Revolution* (Harmondworth: Penguin, 1971), p. 43.

[52]Samuel R. Gardiner, *History of the Commonwealth and Protectorate* (London: Longmans, 1903), 2:284-85.

[53]Stubbes, *Anatomy of the Abuses*, pp. 178, 182. See also Flavel, *Husbandry Spiritualised*, 5:166; Primatt, *Dissertation of the Duty*, p. 3; W. Haller, *Foxe's Book of Martyrs and the Elect Nation* (London: Cape, 1963), p. 56.

[54]C. H. Firth and R. S. Rait, eds., *Acts and Ordinances of the Interregrum* (London: Stationary Office, 1911), 2:861; and S. R. Gardiner, *History of the Commonwealth and Protectorate* (London: Longmans, 1903), 2:285, 4:32.

[55]Thomas, *Man and the Natural*, p. 180.

[56]Primatt, *Dissertation of the Duty*, p. 87, emphasis his.

[57]Thomas, *Man and the Natural*, p. 154.

[58]David Lyon, *Postmodernity* (Buckingham, U.K.: Open University Press, 1994), pp. 4-6.

[59]René Descartes, *Discourse on Method*, trans. F. E. Sutcliffe (1637; reprint, Harmondsworth, U.K.: Penguin, 1968), pp. 75-76.

[60]Claude Bernard, cited in Klug, "Can We See," p. 208.

[61]Dawkins, *Selfish Gene*, p. 20.

[62]J. Bulwer, introduction to *Anthropometamorphosis* (London: William Hunt, 1653), B6.

[63]William Paley, *Natural Theology* (London: Faulder, 1802).

[64]S. R. L. Clarke, "Is Nature God's Will?" in A. Linzey and D. Yamamoto, eds., *Animals on the Agenda* (London: SCM Press, 1998), pp. 128-29.

[65]Thomas, *Man and the Natural*, p. 278; see also Peacocke, *Creation and the World*, pp. 255-318.

[66]Richard C. Lewontin, *The Doctrine of DNA* (Harmondsworth: Penguin, 1992), p. 12.

[67]C. Mann, "Lynn Margulis: Science's Unruly Earth Mother," *Science* 252 (1991): 378, 381.

[68]Lynn Margulis and Carl Sagan, *Origins of Sex* (New Haven, Conn.: Yale University Press, 1986), p. 7.

[69]Lewontin, *Doctrine of DNA*, pp. 12-13.

[70]See, for example, Margulis and Sagan, *Origins of Sex*.

[71]James E. Lovelock, *Gaia: A New Look at Life on Earth* (Oxford: Oxford University Press, 1979); L. Hunt, "Send in the Clouds," *New Scientist* 158, no. 2136 (1998): 28-33. See also the subsequent correspondence in *New Scientist*, esp. Lovelock, July 11, 1998, p. 57.

[72]Rupert Sheldrake, *The Rebirth of Nature* (London: Random House, 1990).

Chapter 4: The Missionaries

[1]Richard Nile, *Australian Aborigines* (Hove, U.K.: Waveland, 1992), p. 46.

[2]Marion Morrison, *Indians of the Andes* (Hove, U.K.: Waveland, 1986), p. 16

[3]Bertrand Russell, "Has Religion Made Useful Contributions to Civilisation?" in *Why I Am Not a Christian* (London: Unwin, 1930), pp. 35-36.

[4]Pamela Odijk, *The Aborigines* (South Melbourne: Macmillan, 1990), p. 41. This book was written for children.

[5]Norman Lewis, *The Missionaries* (London: Secker and Warburg, 1988), pp. 99, 103.

[6]Ibid., pp. 143-44, 205. D. Stoll, *Is Latin America Turning Protestant?* (Berkeley: University of California Press, 1990), p. 12; Stewart Gill, "Conquerors or Saviours?" *Kategoria* 7 (1997): 9-26.

[7]Philip Goldring, cited in D. N. Collins, "Culture, Christianity and the Northern Peoples of Canada and Siberia," *Religion, State and Society* 25, no. 4 (1997): 381-82.

[8]Lewis, *Missionaries*, p. 102.

[9]Jomo Kenyatta, cited in *New Internationalist* 309 (1999): 10.

[10]Victor D. Bonilla, prefatory note in *Servants of God or Masters of Men?* (Harmondsworth, U.K.: Penguin, 1972).

[11]For example, Augustine (born in modern Tunisia of a Berber mother), Cyprian (Carthage), Athanasius (Alexandria and Egypt) and Origen (Alexandria).

[12]Raymond Williams, *Keywords* (London: Fontana, 1976), pp. 48-49.

[13]Richard Morrison, "Lancelot Edward Threlkeld: A Missionary for the Aborigines," *Kategoria* 10 (1998): 70. Threlkeld, unlike the colonists, had learned Awabakal in order to translate the Bible, and his work has resulted in the preservation of that Aboriginal language in the public domain.

[14]Charles Darwin, *The Voyage of the "Beagle"* (Geneva: Heron, 1845), p. 435.

[15]Ibid., pp. 191-92.

[16]Letter to W. Graham, July 3, 1881, in *The Life and Letters of Charles Darwin*, ed. Francis Darwin (London: Murray, 1887), 1:316.

[17]Stoll, *Is Latin America Turning Protestant?* p. 16.

[18]Anthony Pagden, introduction to Bartolomé de Las Casas, *A Short Account of the Destruction of the Indies*, ed. N. Griffin (1552; reprint, Harmondsworth, U.K.: Penguin, 1992), p. xi.

[19]Richard F. Burton, *A Mission to the Gelele, King of Dahome* (London: Tylston and Edwards, 1893), 2:123.

[20]Alan Moorehead, *Darwin and the Beagle* (London: Hamish Hamilton, 1969), p. 90.

[21]Letter to B. J. Sullivan, June 30, 1870, in *The Life and Letters of Charles Darwin*, 3:127, 128 n.

[22]M. Muller, *Aboriginal Issues: More Facts and Figures* (Geneva: World Council of Churches, 1971).

[23]Gill, "Counquerors or Saviours?" p. 15.

[24]Russell, "Has Religion Made Useful Contributions," p. 29.

[25]Julian Pettifer and Richard Bradley, *The Missionaries* (London: BBC, 1990), p. 133.

[26]This account is taken from several sources, mainly Pagden's introduction to de Las Casas, *Short Account*, p. xxi.

[27]L. Martín, "The Peruvian Indian Through Jesuit Eyes," in *The Jesuit Tradition in Education and Missions*, ed. Christopher Chapple (London: University of Scanton Press, 1993), p. 207.

[28]Ibid., p. 205.

[29]John W. O'Malley, *The First Jesuits* (Cambridge, Mass.: Harvard University Press, 1993), p. 78.

[30]Brian Stanley, *The History of the Baptist Missionary Society* (Edinburgh: T & T Clark, 1992), esp. chap. 3.

[31]Stephen Neill, *A History of Christian Missions* (Harmondsworth, U.K.: Penguin, 1964), pp. 425-30.

[32]Stoll, *Is Latin America Turning Protestant?* pp. 327-28, cf. p. 67. Stoll concedes, however, that this is "not the whole story."

[33]See, for example, the history of slavery in the Congo state from the late fifteenth century (R. Oliver and J. D. Fage, *A Short History of Africa* [Harmondsworth, U.K.: Penguin, 1962], pp. 135, 126ff.).

[34]Stoll, *Is Latin America Turning Protestant?* p. 330.

[35]Charles R. Boxer, *Race Relations in the Portuguese Colonial Empire 1415-1825* (Oxford: Clarendon, 1963), pp. 87-88.

[36]See, for example, Pettifer and Bradley, *Missionaries*, p. 81, and Geoffrey Moorhouse, *The Missionaries* (London: Methuen, 1973), p. 19, although Moorhouse's book is too well researched to present just the orthodox story.

[37]Bartolomé de Las Casas, *A Short Account of the Destruction of the Indies*, ed. N. Griffin (1552; reprint, Harmondsworth, U.K.: Penguin, 1992), p. 126, cf. pp. 75-79.

[38]John Thornbury, "David Brainerd," in *Five Pioneer Missionaries*, ed. S. M. Houghton (Edinburgh: Banner of Truth, 1965), p. 72.

[39]Richard T. France, "Henry Martyn," in *Five Pioneer Missionaries*, ed. S. M. Houghton (Edinburgh: Banner of Truth, 1965), p. 270.

[40]Neill, *History of Christian Missions*, p. 355. The native resistance to measles was low, resulting in a high mortality rate.

[41]Morrison, *Indians of the Andes*, p. 16.

[42]Neill, *History of Christian Missions*, p. 170.

[43]Ibid.

[44]Las Casas, *Short Account*, pp. 82, 28-29; cf. Pagden's introduction, p. xv.

[45]France, "Henry Martyn," p. 271.

[46]John D. Legg, "John G. Paton," in *Five Pioneer Missionaries*, ed. S. M. Houghton (Edinburgh: Banner of Truth, 1965), pp. 313-14.

[47]Bonilla, *Servants of God*, p. 15. Bonilla is speaking of the Sibundoy. Tense has been altered.

[48]Duncan Russell, "Stubborn Indianness: Cultural Persistence, Cultural Change,"

Journal of American Studies 32, no. 3 (1998): 507-12.

[49]Gill, "Conquerors or Saviours?" p. 10.

[50]Legg, "John G. Paton," p. 313.

[51]Lewis, *Missionaries*, p. 101.

[52]Jean Williams, "Puritanism: A Piety of Joy," *Kategoria* 10 (1998): 11-35.

[53]David Stoll, *Fishers of Men or Founders of Empire?* (London: Zed Press, 1982), pp. 312-13.

[54]Brian J. Walsh and J. Richard Middleton, *The Transforming Vision* (Downers Grove, Ill.: InterVarsity Press, 1984), chap. 1.

[55]Marvin Harris, *Cannibals and Kings: The Origins of Cultures* (New York: Vintage, 1978), pp. 3-4, cf. pp. 147ff.

[56]Frank Lestringant, *Cannibals: The Discovery and Representation of the Cannibal from Columbus to Jules Verne* (Colombia: California University Press, 1997).

[57]Lewis, *Missionaries*, pp. 101-102.

[58]Charles Wagley and Marvin Harris, *Minorities in the New World* (New York: Columbia University Press, 1964), pp. 27, 28-29.

[59]David Block, *Mission Culture of the Upper Amazon* (Lincoln: University of Nebraska Press, 1994); see also Chapple, *Jesuit Tradition*, part 2.

[60]Lewis, *Missionaries*, p. 109.

[61]T. F. Kennedy, "An Integrated Perspective," in *The Jesuit Tradition in Education and Missions*, ed. Christopher Chapple (London: University of Scanton Press, 1993).

[62]Pettifer and Bradley, *Missionaries*, p. 89.

[63]Neville B. Cryer, "John Eliot," in *Five Pioneer Missionaries*, ed. S. M. Houghton (Edinburgh: Banner of Truth, 1965), p. 204.

[64]Darwin, *The Voyage of the "Beagle,"* p. 426.

[65]Bonilla, *Servants of God*, p. 14.

[66]Mary Haas, quoted in G. McKevitt, " 'Faith Enters by the Ear': Missionary Linguistics in the Pacific Northwest," in *The Jesuit Tradition in Education and Missions*, ed. Christopher Chapple (London: University of Scanton Press, 1993), p. 250.

[67]Sam Padilla, quoted in Stoll, *Fishers of Men*, pp. 312-13.

[68]Ibid., p. 214.

[69]Darwin, *Voyage of the "Beagle,"* p. 414.

[70]*Sati* is the self-immolation of a widow on the funeral pyre of her husband.

[71]Neill, *History of Christian Missions*, p. 355.

[72]Darwin,*Voyage of the "Beagle,"* pp. 414-15.

[73]Dorothy Hammond and Alta Jablow, *The Africa That Never Was: Four Centuries of British Writing About Africa* (New York: Twayne, 1970).

[74]Lewis, *Missionaries*, pp. 40-41, 185.

Chapter 5: The Human Body

[1]Johnathan Miller, *The Body in Question* (London: BBC, 1978), pp. 191-92.

[2]Simone de Beauvoir, *The Second Sex* (Harmondsworth: Penguin, 1972), p. 199.

[3]Ibid.

[4]Ibid., pp. 129, 112.

[5]Desmond Christy, "Funny Old Place, Paradise," *The Guardian*, November 24, 1998, p. 19.

[6]Laurie Cabot, *Power of the Witch* (Harmondsworth, U.K.: Penguin, 1992), p. 62.

[7]Bertrand Russell, "Has Religion Made Useful Contributions to Civilisation?" in *Why I Am Not a Christian* (London: Unwin, 1930), p. 35.

[8]Elizabeth Rouse, quoted in Mike Starkey, *Fashion and Style* (Crowborough, U.K.: Monarch, 1995), p. 43.

[9]George Orwell, *A Clergyman's Daughter* (Harmondsworth, U.K.: Penguin, 1964), pp. 2, 11.

[10]Russell, "Has Religion Made Useful Contributions," p. 29.

[11]Christy, "Funny Old Place," p. 19.

[12]Rosemary Radford Ruether, *Sexism and Godtalk: Towards a Feminist Theology* (London: SCM Press, 1983), p. 81ff.

[13]De Beauvoir, *Second Sex*, p. 112.

[14]Roderick E. McGrew, *Encyclopaedia of Medical History* (London: Macmillan, 1985), p. 17.

[15]Roy Porter, ed., *The Cambridge Illustrated History of Medicine* (Cambridge: Cambridge University Press, 1996), p. 263.

[16]Andrew D. White, *A History of the Warfare of Science with Theology* (London: Macmillan, 1896), 2:63.

[17]A. Derek Farr, "Religious Opposition to Obstetric Anaesthesia: A Myth," *Annals of Science* 40 (1983): 159-77.

[18]De Beauvoir, *Second Sex*, pp. 128-29, 200. Misogyny does not, however, imply a link with a doctrine of "sinful flesh" as de Beauvoir believes. Chrysostom, for example, rejected any simple equation of "flesh" with "sin." See D. Steinmetz, *Calvin in Context* (Oxford: Oxford University Press, 1995), p. 129. The complex interactions of Greek and biblical discourses in these early authors defy simple classification.

[19]G. C. Berkouwer, *Man: The Image of God* (Grand Rapids, Mich.: Eerdmans, 1962), chap. 6.

[20]Brian J. Walsh and J. Richard Middleton, *The Transforming Vision* (Downers Grove, Ill.: InterVarsity Press, 1984), chap. 7. See also J. H. Kok, *Patterns of the Western Mind* (Sioux Center, Iowa: Dordt College Press, 1998).

[21]Plato *Phaedo*, ed. B. Jowett (Oxford: Clarendon, 1953): 1:417-18.

[22]Stephen R. L. Clark, "Is Nature God's Will?" in *Animals on the Agenda,* ed. Andrew Linzey and D. Yamamoto (London: SCM Press, 1998), p. 135.

[23]William Temple, *Readings in St. John's Gospel* (London: Macmillan, 1945), p. xx.

[24]Steinmetz, *Calvin in Context*, p. 134.

[25]Paul Helm, *The Callings* (Edinburgh: Banner of Truth, 1987), pp. 35ff.

[26]Ibid., p. 36.

[27]Cited in Steinmetz, *Calvin in Context*, p. 134. Even as this holistic language predominates, Steinmetz also gives examples of usages that Calvin inherited from the late medieval context.

[28]John Calvin *Institutes of the Christian Religion* 2.1.9, ed. J. T. McNeill, trans. Ford Lewis Battles (1559; reprint, London: SCM Press, 1961).

[29]Ibid., 2.3.1.

[30]Craig S. Keener, *The IVP Bible Background Commentary: New Testament* (Downers Grove, Ill.: InterVarsity Press, 1993), p. 488.

[31]Hugh Spanner, "Tyrants, Stewards—or Just Kings?" in *Animals on the Agenda,* ed. Andrew Linzey and D. Yamamoto (London: SCM Press, 1998), p. 221.

[32]Henry W. Robinson, *The Christian Doctrine of Man* (Edinburgh: T & T Clark, 1911), p. 12.

[33]Quoted in de Beauvoir, *Second Sex*, p. 112.

[34]Plato *Timaeus*, in *The Dialogues of Plato*, ed. B. Jewett (Oxford: Clarendon, 1953), pp.

3:728, 778.

[35]Plato *Republic*, in *The Dialogues of Plato*, ed. B. Jewett (Oxford: Clarendon, 1953), pp. 425ff.

[36]Aristotle *De Generatione Animalium* 2.3.737a.25-30, 1.2.716a.13-20, in *The Complete Works of Aristotle*, ed. J. Barnes, vol. 1 (Princeton, N.J.: Princeton University Press, 1984).

[37]Ibid., 2.1.732a.5-10. Of course, no simplistic opposition of "Christian" to Greek *authors* can be sustained. Not only were the majority of biblical commentators deeply influenced by classical learning, but some aspects of the Greek inheritance were deployed positively in arguments for female equality. See, for example, the sixteenth-century humanist Agnolo Firenzuola, who drew on Neo-Platonic sources in his *On the Beauty of Women* (see J. Murray, "Agnolo Firenzuola on Female Sexuality and Women's Equality," *Sixteenth Century Journal* 22 [1991]: 199-213.) For a recent defense of Aquinas, see M. Nolan, "Aquinas and the Defective Male," *New Blackfriars* 75, no. 880 (1994): 156-65.

[38]Eileen Manion, "A Ms.-Managed Womb," in *The Body Invaders*, ed. A. Kroker and M. Kroker (London: Macmillan, 1988), p. 183.

[39]Augustine *City of God*, 11.23, 13.23, ed. D. Knowles (Harmondsworth, U.K.: Penguin, 1972).

[40]Thomas Aquinas, *Summa Theologica*, trans. Fathers of the English Dominican Province (New York: Benziger, 1982), 1.47.2, 1-2.4.6.

[41]Caroline W. Bynum, *Fragmentation and Redemption: Essays on Gender and the Human Body in Medieval Religion* (New York: Zone, 1991), p. 150.

[42]Dante Alighieri *The Divine Comedy* 3 14.43-45, trans. D. L. Sayers and B. Reynolds (Harmondsworth, U.K.. Penguin, 1962).

[43]Clark, "Is Nature God's Will?" p. 135.

[44]John Calvin, *Commentary on Corinthians* (1546; reprint, Edinburgh: Calvin Translation Society, 1848), 2:51.

[45]Richard Sibbes, *The Redemption of Bodies*, The Works of Richard Sibbes, ed. A. B. Grosart (Edinburgh: Banner of Truth, 1977), 1:167-68.

[46]Matthew Henry, *Matthew's Henry Commentary: Acts to Revelation*, ed. D. Winter (London: Hodder & Stoughton, 1975), p. 334.

[47]Hans R. Rookmaker, *Modern Art and the Death of a Culture* (1978; reprint, Leicester, U.K.: Apollos, 1994), chap. 1.

[48]Philip J. Sampson, "Die Repräsentation des Körpers," *Kunstforum* 132 (1996): 94-111.

[49]Carter Lindberg, *The European Reformations* (Oxford: Blackwell, 1996), p. 364.

[50]Calvin *Institutes* 3.10.2.

[51]Calvin *Commentary on Corinthians* 1:231, on 1 Corinthians 7:6; on Deuteronomy 24:5, quoted in W. J. Bouwsma, *John Calvin: A Sixteenth Century Portrait* (Oxford: Oxford University Press, 1988), p. 137.

[52]John Calvin, *Commentary on the Gospels* (1555; reprint, Grand Rapids, Mich.: Associated Publishers and Authors, n.d.), pp. 378-79.

[53]Lindberg, *European Reformations*, p. 364.

[54]John Calvin, *Commentary on Genesis* (Edinburgh: Banner of Truth, 1965), p. 131, on Genesis 2:18.

[55]Lindberg, *European Reformations*, pp. 365-66.

[56]H. G. Koenigsberger, George L. Mosse, and G. Q. Bowler, *Europe in the Sixteenth Century* (London: Longmans, 1989), p. 137.

[57]Christopher Hill, *Reformation to Industrial Revolution* (Harmondsworth, U.K.: Pen-

guin, 1971), p. 41.

[58]Ava Chamberlain, "The Immaculate Ovum: Jonathan Edwards and the Construction of the Female Body," *The William and Mary Quarterly* 57, no. 2 (2000), pp. 293, 318ff.

[59]N. Isenberg, "Pillars in the Same Temple and Priests of the Same Worship," *Journal of American History* 85, no. 1 (1998): p. 116; Elaine Storkey, *What's Right with Feminism* (London: SPCK, 1985), pt. 4.

[60]Francis Crick, *The Astonishing Hypothesis: The Scientific Search for the Soul* (London: Touchstone, 1994), p. 3.

[61]I have discussed this further elsewhere: see Sampson, "Die Repräsentation"; Miriam E. Sampson and Philip J. Sampson, "The Identity Charade," *Third Way* 20, no. 7 (1997): 11-14; Miriam E. Sampson and Philip J. Sampson, "Looking the Parts," *Third Way* 20, no. 8 (1997): 21-24.

[62]David Stoll, *Is Latin America Turning Protestant?* (Berkeley: University of California Press, 1990), p. 13.

[63]Elizabeth Brusco, "The Reformation of Machismo: Asceticism and Masculinity Among Colombian Evangelicals," in *Rethinking Protestantism in Latin America*, ed. Virginia Garrard-Burnett and David Stoll (Philadelphia: Temple University Press, 1993), pp. 143-58.

Chapter 6: Witches

[1]There are a number of terms in the literature, all of which are used in a pejorative, rather than descriptive, sense: *witch-hunting, witch-baiting, witch mania* and *witch craze* are the most common.

[2]Carl Sagan, *The Demon-Haunted World: Science as a Candle in the Dark* (London: Hodder Headline, 1996), p. 113.

[3]Laurie Cabot, *Power of the Witch* (Harmondsworth, U.K.: Penguin, 1992), pp. 53, 62.
[4]Sagan, *Demon-Haunted World*, p. 116.

[5]Jules Michelet, *Satanism and Witchcraft* (London: Tandem, 1965), p. 12.

[6]Brian P. Levack, *Witch-Hunting in Early Modern Europe*, vol. 3 of *Anthropological Studies of Witchcraft, Magic and Religion*, ed. Brian P. Levack (New York: Garland, 1992), p. ix. Levack rejects this as a "rationalist interpretation," See also William E. H. Lecky, *History of the Rise and Influence of the Spirit of Rationalism in Europe* (London: Longmans, 1890), chap. 1 of vol. 1.

[7]Michelet, *Satanism and Witchcraft*, p. 9.

[8]E. Caulfield, "Pediatric Aspects of the Salem Witchcraft Tragedy," *American Journal of Diseases of Children* 65 (1943): 788-802. For a critical review of the "hysteria" explanation, see H. C. Erik Midelfort, *Witch Hunting in Southwestern Germany 1562-1684* (Stanford, Calif.: Stanford University Press, 1972), pp. 5–6; Chadwick Hansen, *Witchcraft at Salem* (London: Arrow, 1970), pp. 14–15; L. R. Caporael, "Ergotism: The Satan Loosed in Salem," *Science* 192 (1976): 21-26. Ergot is a fungal disease of grain that produces poisoning and can lead to convulsions. For a critical review see N. P. Spanos and J. Gottlieb, "Ergotism and the Salem Village Witch Trials," *Science* 194 (1976): 1390-94.

[9]Barbara Ehrenreich and Dierdre English, *Witches, Midwives and Nurses: A History of Women Healers* (London: Writers and Readers, 1976), pp. 22-37.

[10]Montague Summers, *The Discovery of Witches: A Study of Master Matthew Hopkins, Commonly Called Witch Finder Generall* (London: Cayme, 1928), p. 11ff.

[11]Robin Briggs, *Witches and Neighbours* (London: HarperCollins, 1996), p. 397.

[12]Diane Purkiss, *The Witch in History* (London: Routledge, 1996), pp. 111, 130.

[13]Levack, *Witch-Hunting*, p. ix.

[14]K. A. Edwards, review of *The Witch in History* by Diane Purkiss, *Sixteenth Century Journal* 28, no. 4 (1997): 1433.

[15]Jeanne Favret-Saada, *Deadly Words: Witchcraft in the Bocage* (Cambridge: Cambridge University Press, 1980), pp. 3ff.

[16]Lawrence Stone, "The Disenchantment of the World," *New York Review of Books*, December 12, 1971, p. 17.

[17]Hansen, *Witchcraft at Salem*, chaps. 5, 14.

[18]Purkiss, *Witch in History*, pp. 185, 19-20. See also Shakespeare's *Macbeth*.

[19]Lecky, *History of the Rise*; Radford R. Reuther, *Sexism and Godtalk: Towards a Feminist Theology* (London: SCM Press, 1983), p. 82; Sagan, *Demon-Haunted World*.

[20]Ruth Martin, *Witchcraft and the Inquisition in Venice 1550-1650* (Oxford: Blackwell, 1989), p. 228. Only 26 percent were over forty-six years; 20 percent were below twenty-five years. See Purkiss, *Witch in History*, pp. 91, 127; Midelfort, *Witch Hunting*, pp. 179–90. However, it is difficult to generalize. Midelfort argues that such stereotypes have been common since the sixteenth century.

[21]Gerhild Scholz Williams, *Defining Dominion: The Discourses of Magic and Witchcraft in Early Modern France and Germany* (Ann Arbor: University of Michigan Press, 1995), pp. 64-75.

[22]Purkiss, *Witch in History*, chap. 1.

[23]Sagan, *Demon-Haunted World*, p. 116; M. Daly, *Gyn/Ecology* (London: Women's Press, 1979), pp. 183, 208; Ehrenreich and English, *Witches, Midwives*, p. 24; Purkiss, *Witch in History*, p. 17; Cabot, *Power of the Witch*, p. 50.

[24]Lecky, *History of the Rise*, 1:4; Michelet, *Satanism and Witchcraft*, p. 11.

[25]Hugh R. Trevor-Roper, *The European Witch-Craze of the Sixteenth and Seventeenth Centuries* (Harmondsworth: Penguin, 1969), p. 19; Daly, *Gyn/Ecology*, pp. 196, 200, 202, 204, 206, 221.

[26]Lecky, *History of the Rise*, 1:6.

[27]Marijke Gijswijt-Hofstra and Willem Frijhoff, eds., *Witchcraft in the Netherlands* (Rotterdam: Universitaire Pers, 1991), p. 30; Alan Macfarlane, *Witchcraft in Tudor and Stuart England: A Regional and Comparative Study* (London: Routledge & Kegan Paul, 1970), pp. 61-63.

[28]Briggs, *Witches and Neighbours*, p. 400.

[29]Levack, *Witch-Hunting*, p. ix; Purkiss, *Witch in History*, p. 28; Briggs, *Witches and Neighbours*, pp. 8, 260.

[30]Trevor-Roper, *European Witch-Craze*, p. 22.

[31]These figures are, of course, estimates. Most are taken from Duncan Townson, *Dictionary of Modern History* (Harmondsworth, U.K.: Penguin, 1994).

[32]Marvin Harris, *Cannibals and Kings: The Origins of Cultures* (New York: Vintage, 1978), p. 165.

[33]Lecky, *History of the Rise*, 1:6, 64.

[34]Levack, *Witch-Hunting*, p. ix.

[35]William Monter, *Ritual, Myth and Magic in Early Modern Europe* (Brighton, U.K.: Harvester, 1983), p. 67; and William Monter, *Frontiers of Heresy: The Spanish Inquisition from the Basque Lands to Sicily* (Cambridge: Cambridge University Press, 1990), p. xiii. Monter notes, however, the Inquisition's cultivation of a *reputation* for severity.

[36]Marijke Gijswijt-Hofstra, "Six Centuries of Witchcraft in the Netherlands: Themes, Outlines and Interpretations," in Gijswijt-Hofstra and Frijhoff, eds., *Witchcraft in the Netherlands*, p. 30; Monter, *Ritual, Myth and Magic*, p. 67; Martin, *Witchcraft and the Inquisition*, pp. 253-54.

[37]Jean Plaidy, *The Spanish Inquisition* (London: Hale, 1978), pp. 335-37. Although Plaidy's opinions should usually be treated with caution, she is here expressing the consensus of recent scholarship.

[38]Trevor-Roper, *European Witch-Craze*, p. 37; cf. Briggs, *Witches and Neighbours*, pp. 200-201.

[39]Lecky, *History of the Rise*, 1:8.

[40]Marc Mappen, ed., *Witches and Historians* (Huntingdon, N.Y.: Krieger, 1980), pp. 47, 45.

[41]Hansen, *Witchcraft at Salem*, pp. 200-201.

[42]Ibid., p. 10; cf. Briggs, *Witches and Neighbours*, pp. 311-12.

[43]P. F. Jensen, "Calvin and Witchcraft," *Reformed Theological Review* 34 (1975): 76-86.

[44]Keith V. Thomas, *Religion and the Decline of Magic* (London: Weidenfeld and Nicholson, 1971), p. 570.

[45]H. G. Koenigsberger, George L. Mosse and G. Q. Bowler, *Europe in the Sixteenth Century*, 2nd ed. (London: Longmans, 1989), p. 138.

[46]George Gifford, *A Discourse of the Subtle Practises of Devilles* (London, 1587), chap. 12.

[47]James Hitchcocke, "George Gifford and Puritan Witch Beliefs," in Levack, *Anthropological Studies*, p. 222.

[48]Gijswijt-Hofstra, "Six Centuries of Witchcraft," p. 23.

[49]Trevor-Roper, *European Witch-Craze*, p. 13.

[50]J. B. Russell, *Witchcraft in the Middle Ages* (Ithaca, N.Y.: Cornell University Press, 1972), appendix and pp. 291ff.

[51]Matthew Hopkins, *The Discovery of Witches* (1647), reprinted in M. Summers, *The Discovery of Witches: A Study of Master Matthew Hopkins, Commonly Called Witch Finder Generall* (London: Cayme, 1928), queries 8, 11.

[52]Midelfort, *Witch Hunting*, p. 193.

[53]Lecky, *History of the Rise*, 1:82.

[54]Trevor-Roper, *European Witch-Craze*, pp. 19-22.

[55]For a discussion of this see Martin, *Witchcraft and the Inquisition*, chap. 2, esp. pp. 38ff., and Trevor-Roper, *European Witch-Craze*, p. 13.

[56]Sagan, *Demon-Haunted World*, p. 113.

[57]Michelet, *Satanism and Witchcraft*, p. 101; Koenigsberger, Mosse and Bowler, *Europe in the Sixteenth Century*, p. 136; Koenigsberger and Mosse, *Europe in the Sixteenth Century*, p. 90.

[58]Midelfort, *Witch Hunting*, pp. 22, 113. See also Martin, *Witchcraft and the Inquisition*, p. 58; N. Cohn, *Europe's Inner Demons: An Enquiry Inspired by the Great Witchhunt* (London: Heinemann, 1975), p. 225; M. Gielis, "The Netherlandic Theologians' View of Witchcraft and the Devil's Pact," in *Witchcraft in the Netherlands*, ed. Marijke Gijswijt-Hofstra and Willem Frijhoff (Rotterdam: Universitaire Pers, 1991), pp. 19–20; Monter, *Ritual, Myth and Magic*, p. 67.

[59]Sagan, *Demon-Haunted World*, p. 114.

[60]Carter Lindberg, *The European Reformations* (Oxford: Blackwell, 1996), p. 344.

[61]Purkiss, *Witch in History*, pp. 234-35. Sleep deprivation was, however, licensed by some magistrates in Essex and Suffolk, but it was, if we believe his own account,

opposed by the unlikely figure of Matthew Hopkins. See Hopkins, *Discovery of Witches*, query 8.

[62]Martin, *Witchcraft and the Inquisition*, p. 225. There appears to be a misprint, which I have corrected substituting "prosecution" for "persecution."

[63]For an introduction to the term *postmodern* see Philip J. Sampson, "The Rise of Post-modernity," in Philip J. Samson, V. Samuel and C. Sugden, *Faith and Modernity* (Oxford: Regnum, 1994).

[64]Elizabeth Knowles, ed., *The Oxford Dictionary of Quotations*, 5th ed. (Oxford: Oxford University Press, 1999), p. 211.22.

[65]Purkiss, *Witch in History*, p. 7.

[66]Ibid.

[67]Ibid., p. 8.

[68]Daly, *Gyn/Ecology*, p. 183; cf. pp. 217ff.

[69]Robin Morgan, quoted in Daly, *Gyn/Ecology*, p. 221.

[70]Michelet, *Satanism and Witchcraft*, p. 9.

[71]Purkiss, *Witch in History*, p. 40, cf. p. 34; cf. Briggs, *Witches and Neighbours*, pp. 5-6, 37-38.

[72]Purkiss, *Witch in History*, p. 8.

Conclusion

[1]For a discussion of the deeper roots of science and liberty in the Reformation, see R. Hooykaas, *Religion and the Rise of Modern Science* (Edinburgh: Scottish Academic Press, 1972), and D. F. Kelly, *The Emergence of Liberty in the Modern World* (Phillipsburg, N.J.: Presbyterian and Reformed, 1992).

[2]Daniel C. Dennett, *Darwin's Dangerous Idea* (London: Allen Lane, 1995), pp. 515-16.

[3]Andrew Brown, *The Darwin Wars* (London: Simon & Schuster, 1999), p. 172.

[4]"A Book for Burning?" editorial in *Nature* 293, no. 5830 (1981): 245.

[5]M. Kenward, "Burning Editorials," *New Scientist* 92, no. 1273 (1981): 61.

[6]Mary Douglas, *Risk and Blame* (London: Routledge, 1992).

[7]Brown, *Darwin Wars*, p. 25.

[8]Jean-François Lyotard, *The Postmodern Condition* (Manchester: Manchester University Press, 1984). For a discussion of this view, see David Lyon, *Postmodernity* (Buckingham, U.K.: Open University Press, 1994).

[9]Kirsten R. Birkett, "Giordano Bruno: Enigmatic Martyr," *Kategoria* 6 (1997): 27-46.

[10]Lawrence Osborn, "The Machine and the Mother Goddess," *Science and Christian Belief* 4, no. 1 (1992): 27.

[11]Deborah E. Lipstadt, *Denying the Holocaust: The Growing Assault on Truth and Memory* (New York: Free Press, 1993), pp. 17-18; Joyce Appleby, Lynn Hunt and Margaret Jacob, *Telling the Truth About History* (New York: W. W. Norton, 1994), pp. 223ff.

[12]Kelly, *Emergence of Liberty*.

[13] David Lyon, *Postmodernity* (Buckingham, U.K.: Open University Press, 1994).

[14]Michel Foucault, *The Order of Things* (London: Tavistock, 1970), p. 387.

[15]I have in mind both the liberal tradition and some aspects of Reformed theology. See Craig M. Gay, *The Way of the (Modern) World* (Grand Rapids, Mich.: Eerdmans, 1998); Mark A. Noll, *The Scandal of the Evangelical Mind* (Grand Rapids, Mich: Eerdmans, 1994).

Bibliography

Alighieri, Dante. *The Divine Comedy*. Translated by D. L. Sayers and B. Reynolds. 3 vols. Harmondsworth, U.K.: Penguin, 1962.

Appleby, Joyce Lynn Hunt, and Margaret Jacob. *Telling the Truth About History*. New York: W. W. Norton, 1994.

Aristotle. *Physics*. Translated by P. H. Wicksteed and F. M. Cornford. London: Heinemann, 1960.

Asimov, Isaac. *Asimov's Chronology of Science and Discovery*. London: Collins, 1990.

Attfield, Robin. "Christian Attitudes to Nature," *Journal of History Ideas* 44 (1983).

Augustine, *City of God*. Edited by David Knowles. Harmondsworth: Penguin, 1972.

Barnes, Jonathan, ed. *The Complete Works of Aristotle*. 2 vols. Princeton, N.J.: Princeton University Press, 1984.

Barnum, Priscella Heath, ed. *Dives and Pauper*. 2 vols. Circa 1410. Reprint, Oxford: Oxford University Press, 1980.

Barbour, Ian G. *Religion and Science*. San Francisco: Harper, 1990.

Barrow, John D. *The World Within the World*. Oxford: Clarendon, 1988.

Barthes, Roland. *Mythologies*. London: Vintage, 1993.

Baumgart, Winfried. *Imperialism*. Oxford: Oxford University Press, 1982.

Bede. *A History of the English Church and People*. Circa 731. Harmondsworth: Penguin, 1968.

Behe, Michael. *Darwin's Black Box*. New York: Free Press, 1996.

Berkouwer, G. C. *Man: The Image of God*. Grand Rapids, Mich.: Eerdmans, 1962.

Biagioli, Mario. *Galileo Courtier*. Chicago: University of Chicago Press, 1993.

Birkett, Kirsten R. "Giordano Bruno: Enigmatic Martyr." *Kategoria* 6 (1997): 27-46.

Blackwell, Richard J. *Galileo, Bellarmine, and the Bible*. Notre Dame, Ind.: University of Notre Dame Press, 1991.

Block, David. *Mission Culture of the Upper Amazon*. Lincoln: University of Nebraska Press, 1994.

Bonilla, Victor D. *Servants of God or Masters of Men?* Harmondsworth, U.K.: Penguin, 1972.

"A Book for Burning?" *Nature* 293, no. 5830 (1981): 245-46.

Bouwsma, William J. *John Calvin: A Sixteenth Century Portrait*. Oxford: Oxford University Press, 1988.

Bowler, Peter J. *Evolution: The History of an Idea*. Berkeley: University of California Press, 1984.

Boxer, Charles R. *Race Relations in the Portuguese Colonial Empire 1415-1825*. Oxford: Clarendon, 1963.

Boyle, Robert. *Experiments and Considerations Touching Colours*. London, 1664.

Bradley, Ian. *God is Green*. London: Darton, Longman & Todd, 1990.

Brecht, Bertolt. *Life of Galileo*. Translated by J. Willett. London: Methuen, 1980.

Briggs, Robin. *Witches and Neighbours*. London: HarperCollins, 1996.

Brooke, John Hedley. *Science and Religion*. Cambridge: Cambridge University Press, 1991.

Brown, Andrew. *The Darwin Wars*. London: Simon & Schuster, 1999.

Brusco, Elizabeth. "The Reformation of Machismo: Asceticism and Masculinity Among Colombian Evangelicals." In *Rethinking Protestantism in Latin America*. Edited by Virginia Garrard-Burnett and David Stoll. Philadelphia: Temple University Press, 1993.

Bryan, William Jennings. "God and Evolution." In *Evolution and Religion*. Edited by G. Kennedy. 1922. Reprint. Boston: D C Heath, 1957.

Bulwer, John. *Anthropometamorphosis*. London: William Hunt, 1653.

Burton, Richard F. *A Mission to the Gelele, King of Dahome*. 2 vols. London: Tylston and Edwards, 1893.

Burtt, Edwin A. *The Metaphysical Foundations of Modern Physical Science*. London: Kegan Paul, 1925.

Bynum, Caroline W. *Fragmentation and Redemption: Essays on Gender and the Human Body in Medieval Religion*. New York: Zone Books, 1991.

Cabot, Laurie. *Power of the Witch*. Harmondsworth, U.K.: Penguin, 1992.

Calvin, John. *Commentary on Corinthians*. 2 vols. 1546. Reprint, Edinburgh: Calvin Translation Society, 1848.

———. *Commentary on Genesis*. Edinburgh: Banner of Truth, 1965.

———. *Commentary on the Gospels*. 1555. Reprint, Grand Rapids, Mich.: Associated Publishers and Authors, n.d.

———. *The Epistles of Paul to the Romans and to the Thessalonians*. 1543 and 1551. Reprint, London: Oliver and Boyd, 1912.

———. *Institutes of the Christian Religion*. Edited by J. T. McNeill. Translated by Ford Lewis Battles. 2 vols. 1559. Reprint, London: SCM Press, 1961.

———. *Sermons on Deuteronomy*. 1583. Reprint, Edinburgh: Banner of Truth, 1987.

Cannon, Walter F. "The Bases of Darwin's Achievement: A Revaluation." *Victorian Studies* 5 (December 1961): 109-32.

Caporael, L. R. "Ergotism: The Satan Loosed in Salem?" *Science* 192 (1976): 21-26.

Cartmill, Matt. *A View to a Death in the Morning: Hunting and Nature Through History*. Cambridge, Mass.: Harvard University Press, 1993.

Caulfield, E. "Pediatric Aspects of the Salem Witchcraft Tragedy." *American Journal of Diseases of Children* 65 (1943): 788-802.

Chadwick, Owen. *The Secularisation of the European Mind in the Nineteenth Century*. Cambridge: Cambridge University Press, 1975.

Chamberlain, Ava. "The Immaculate Ovum: Jonathan Edwards and the Construction of the Female Body." *The William and Mary Quarterly* 57, no. 2 (2000): 289-322.

Chapple, Christopher, ed. *The Jesuit Tradition in Education and Missions*. London: University of Scanton Press, 1993.

Christy, Desmond. "Funny Old Place, Paradise." *The Guardian*, November 24, 1998, p. 19.

Clark, Stephen R. L. "Is Nature God's Will? In *Animals on the Agenda*. Edited by Andrew Linzey and Dorothy Yamamoto. London: SCM Press, 1998.

Cohen, P. "The Drying of a Continent." *New Scientist* 156, no. 2113-2114 (1997): 6.

Cohn, Norman. *Europe's Inner Demons: An Enquiry Inspired by the Great Witchhunt*. London: Heinemann, 1975.

Collins, D. N. "Culture, Christianity and the Northern peoples of Canada and Siberia." *Religion, State and Society* 25, no. 4 (1997): 381-92.

Cotes, Roger. Preface to *Sir Isaac Newton's Mathematical Principles of Natural Philosophy and His System of the World.* Vol. 1. Edited by F. Cajori. 1713. Reprint, Berkeley: University of California Press, 1966.

Cowper, William. *The Task 6.* In *The Poetical Works.* 1785. Reprint, London: Oxford University Press, 1967.

Coyne, Jerry A. "Not Black and White." *Nature* 396, no. 6712 (1999): 35-36.

Crick, Francis. *The Astonishing Hypothesis: The Scientific Search for the Soul.* London: Touchstone, 1994.

Crook, P. "Historical Monkey Business." *History* 84, no. 276 (1999): 633-57.

Cryer, Neville B. "John Eliot." In *Five Pioneer Missionaries.* Edited by S. M. Houghton. Edinburgh: Banner of Truth, 1965.

Daly, Mary. *Gyn/Ecology.* London: Women's Press, 1979.

Darwin, Charles. *The Descent of Man.* 1871. Reprint, London: Murray, 1894.

———. *The Origin of Species.* 1859. Reprint, Harmondsworth, U.K.: Penguin, 1968.

———.*The Voyage of the "Beagle."* Geneva: Heron, 1845.

Darwin, Francis, ed. *The Life and Letters of Charles Darwin.* 3 vols. London: Murray, 1887.

———. ed. *More Letters of Charles Darwin.* 2 vols. London: Murray, 1903.

Dawkins, Richard. *Climbing Mount Improbable.* London: Viking, 1996.

———. *River Out of Eden.* London: Weidenfeld and Nicolson, 1995.

———. *The Selfish Gene.* Oxford: Oxford University Press, 1989.

Dawson, Christopher H. *Progress and Religion.* London: Sheed and Ward, 1929.

de Beauvoir, Simone. *The Second Sex.* Harmondsworth, U.K.: Penguin, 1972.

de Las Casas, Bartolomé. *A Short Account of the Destruction of the Indies.* Edited by N. Griffin. 1552. Reprint, Harmondsworth, U.K.: Penguin, 1992.

de Santillana, Georgio. *The Crime of Galileo.* London: Heinemann, 1958.

Dennett, Daniel C. *Darwin's Dangerous Idea.* Harmondsworth, U.K.: Penguin, 1995.

Denton, Michael. *Evolution: A Theory in Crisis.* London: Burnett, 1985.

Desmond, Adrian. *Huxley: The Devil's Disciple.* London: Michael Joseph, 1994.

Desmond, Adrian, and James Moore. *Darwin.* London: Michael Joseph, 1991.

Descartes, René. *Discourse on Method.* Translated by F. E. Sutcliffe. 1637. Reprint, Harmondsworth, U.K.: Penguin, 1968.

Douglas, Mary. *Risk and Blame.* London: Routledge, 1992.

Draper, John W. *History of the Conflict Between Religion and Science.* 1874. Reprint, London: Kegan Paul, 1890.

Durant, John, ed. *Darwinism and Divinity.* Oxford: Blackwell, 1985.

Edwards, K. A. Review of *The Witch in History* by D. Purkiss. *Sixteenth Century Journal* 28, no. 4 (1997): 1433-34.

Ehrenreich, Barbara and Dierdre English. *Witches, Midwives and Nurses: A History of Women Healers.* London: Writers and Readers Publishing Co-operative, 1976.

Eldredge, Niles. *Time Frames.* London: Heinemann, 1986.

———. *Reinventing Darwin.* London: Weidenfeld and Nicolson, 1995.

Ellegard, Henrik A. *Darwin and the General Reader: The Reception of Darwin's Theory of Evolution in the British Periodical Press 1859-1872.* Göteborg, Sweden: Elanders Boktryckeri Aktiebolag, 1958.

Farr, A. Derek. "Religious Opposition to Obstetric Anaesthesia: A Myth?" *Annals of Science* 40 (1983): 159-77.

Favret-Saada, Jeanne. *Deadly Words: Witchcraft in the Bocage.* Cambridge: Cambridge University Press, 1980.

Feldhay, Rivka. *Galileo and the Church*. Cambridge: Cambridge University Press, 1995.

Finocchiaro, Maurice. A. *Galileo and the Art of Reasoning*. London: Reide, 1980.

Firth, C. H., and R. S. Rait, eds. *Acts and Ordinances of the Interregnum*. 3 vols. London: Stationery Office, 1911.

Flavel, John. *Husbandry Spiritualised*. In *The Works of John Flavel*. 1669. Reprint, Edinburgh: Banner of Truth, 1968.

Foucault, Michel. *The Order of Things*. London: Tavistock, 1970.

France, Richard T. "Henry Martyn." In *Five Pioneer Missionaries*. Edited by S. M. Houghton. Edinburgh: Banner of Truth, 1965.

Freeden, Michael. "Eugenics and Progressive Thought: A Study in Ideological Affinity." *Historical Journal* 22, no. 3 (1979): 645-71.

Galilei, Galileo. *Dialogue Concerning the Two Chief World Systems*. Translated by S. Drake. 1632. Reprint, Berkeley: University of California Press, 1967.

―――. *Discoveries and Opinions of Galileo*. Translated by S. Drake. New York: Anchor, 1957.

Gamlin, Linda. *Evolution*. London: Dorling Kindersley, 1993.

Gardiner, Samuel R. *History of the Commonwealth and Protectorate*. 4 vols. London: Longmans, 1903.

Gasman, Daniel. *The Scientific Origins of National Socialism*. London: MacDonald, 1971.

Gay, Craig M. *The Way of the (Modern) World*. Grand Rapids, Mich.: Eerdmans, 1998.

Gay, Peter. *The Enlightenment*. 2 vols. London: Wildwood, 1973.

Gayon, Jean. *Darwinism's Struggle for Survival*. Cambridge: Cambridge University Press, 1998.

Gielis, Marcel. "The Netherlandic Theologians' View of Witchcraft and the Devil's Pact." In *Witchcraft in the Netherlands*. Edited by M. Gijswijt-Hofstra and W. Frijhoff. Rotterdam: Universitaire Pers, 1991.

Gifford, George. *A Discourse of the Subtle Practises of Devilles*. London, 1587.

Gijswijt-Hofstra, Marijke. "Six Centuries of Witchcraft in the Netherlands: Themes, Outlines and Interpretations." In *Witchcraft in the Netherlands*. Edited by M. Gijswijt-Hofstra and W. Frijhoff. Rotterdam: Universitaire Pers, 1991.

Gijswijt-Hofstra, Marijke, and Willem Frijhoff, eds. *Witchcraft in the Netherlands*. Rotterdam: Universitaire Pers, 1991.

Gill, Stewart. "Conquerors or Saviours?" *Kategoria* 7 (1997): 9-26.

Gillispie, Charles C., ed. *Dictionary of Scientific Biography*. Volume 3. New York: Scribner, 1971.

Gillott, John, and Manjit Kumar. *Science and the Retreat from Reason*. London: Merlin, 1995.

Glick, Thomas F., ed. *The Comparative Reception of Darwinism*. Austin: University of Texas Press, 1972.

Goudswaard, Bob. *Capitalism and Progress*. Toronto: Wedge, 1979.

Gould, Stephen J., and Niles Eldredge. "Punctuated Equilibria." *Paleobiology* 3 (1977): 115-51.

Green, Michael, ed. *The Truth of God Incarnate*. London: Hodder & Stoughton, 1977.

Grier, J. "Eugenics and Birth Control: Contraceptive Provision in North Wales 1918-1939." *Social History of Medicine* 11, no. 3 (1998): 443-58.

Haldane, J. B. S. *The Inequality of Man and Other Essays*. London: Chatto and Windus, 1932.

Haller, William. *Foxe's Book of Martyrs and the Elect Nation*. London: Cape, 1963.

Hammond, Dorothy, and Alta Jablow. *The Africa That Never Was: Four Centuries of British Writing About Africa*. New York: Twayne, 1970.

Hansen, Chadwick. *Witchcraft at Salem*. London: Arrow, 1970.

Harris, Marvin. *Cannibals and Kings: The Origins of Cultures*. New York: Vintage, 1978.

Hawking, Stephen. *A Brief History of Time*. London: Bantam, 1988.

Hawkins, Michael. *Social Darwinism in European and American Thought 1860-1945*. Cambridge: Cambridge University Press, 1997.

Headlam, Catherine, ed. *The Kingfisher Encyclopedia*. London: Kingfisher, 1991.

Helm, Paul. *The Callings*. Edinburgh: Banner of Truth, 1987.

Henry, Matthew. *Matthew Henry's Commentary: Acts to Revelation*. Edited by D. Winter. 1710. Reprint, London: Hodder & Stoughton, 1975.

Hill, Christopher. *Reformation to Industrial Revolution*. Harmondsworth, U.K.: Penguin, 1971.

Hitchcocke, James. "George Gifford and Puritan Witch Beliefs." In *Anthropological Studies of Witchcraft, Magic and Religion*. Edited by B. P. Levack. Volume 4. New York: Garland, 1992.

Hitler, Adolf. *Mein Kampf (My Struggle)*. London: Hurst and Blackett, 1925.

Hofstadter, Richard. *Social Darwinism in American Thought*. New York: Braziller, 1959.

Holt-Jensen, Arild. *Geography: Its History and Concepts*. London: Harper & Row, 1981.

Hooykaas, Reijer. *Religion and the Rise of Modern Science*. Edinburgh: Scottish Academic Press, 1972.

Hopkins, Matthew. *The Discovery of Witches*. 1647. Reprint, in M. Summers. *The Discovery of Witches: A Study of Master Matthew Hopkins, Commonly Called Witch Finder Generall*. London: Cayme, 1928.

Houghton, S. M., ed. *Five Pioneer Missionaries*. Edinburgh: Banner of Truth, 1965.

Hoyle, Fred, and Chandra Wickramasinghe. *Cosmic Life Force*. London: Dent, 1988.

———. *Evolution from Space*. London: Dent, 1981.

———. *Life Cloud: The Origin of Life in the Universe*. London: Dent, 1978.

Hughes, J. Donald. *Ecology in Ancient Civilisations*. Albuquerque: University of New Mexico Press, 1975.

Hull, David L. *Darwin and his Critics*. Cambridge, Mass.: Harvard University Press, 1973.

Hunt, L. "Send in the Clouds." *New Scientist* 158, no. 2136 (1998): 28-33.

Hunter, George W. *A Civic Biology*. New York: American Book, 1914.

Huxley, Julian. *Evolution in Action*. New York: Mentor, 1953.

Huxley, T. H. *Lay Sermons, Addresses and Reviews*. New York: Macmillan, 1899.

Ickert, Scott. "Luther and Animals: Subject to Adam's Fall?" In *Animals on the Agenda*. Edited by Andrew Linzey and Dorothy Yamamoto. London: SCM Press, 1998.

Isenberg, N. "Pillars in the Same Temple and Priests of the Same Worship." *Journal of American History* 85, no. 1 (1998): 98-128.

Jaki, Stanley L. *Science and Creation*. Edinburgh: Scottish Academic Press, 1986.

Jensen, P. F. "Calvin and Witchcraft." *Reformed Theological Review* 34 (1975): 76-86.

Jones, Arthur. *Science in Faith*. Romford: Christian Schools Trust, 1998.

Jones, Greta. *Social Darwinism and English Thought*. Brighton: Harvester, 1980.

Josephus. *Against Appion*. Translated by H. St J. Thackeray. Vol. 1. London: Heinemann, 1956.

Kaiser, Christopher. *Creation and the History of Science*. London: Marshall Pickering,

1991.

Kauffman, Stuart. *At Home in the Universe: The Search for Laws of Complexity*. Harmondsworth, U.K.: Penguin, 1995.

Keener, Craig S. *The IVP Bible Background Commentary: New Testament*. Downers Grove, Ill.: InterVarsity Press, 1993.

Kelly, Douglas F. *The Emergence of Liberty in the Modern World*. Phillipsburg, N.J.: Presbyterian and Reformed, 1992.

Kennedy, T. F. "An Integrated Perspective." In *The Jesuit Tradition in Education and Missions*. Edited by C. Chapple. London: University of Scanton Press, 1993.

Kenward, M. "Burning Editorials." *New Scientist* 92, no. 1273 (1981): 61.

Kettlewell, Henry B. D. *The Evolution of Melanism*. Oxford: Clarendon, 1973.

Klug, Brian. "Can We See a Moral Question About Animals?" In *Animals on the Agenda*. Edited by Andrew Linzey and Dorothy Yamamoto. London: SCM Press, 1998.

Koch, H. W., ed. *The Origins of the First World War*. Basingstoke, U.K.: Macmillan, 1977.

Koenigsberger, H. G., and George L. Mosse. *Europe in the Sixteenth Century*. London: Longmans, 1968.

Koenigsberger, H. G., George L. Mosse and G. Q. Bowler. *Europe in the Sixteenth Century*. London: Longmans, 1989. Second edition of Koenigsberger and Mosse, 1968.

Kok, John H. *Patterns of the Western Mind*. Sioux, Iowa: Dordt College Press, 1998.

Kroker, Arthur, and Marilouise Kroker, eds. *The Body Invaders*. London: Macmillan, 1988.

Kuhn, Thomas S. *The Copernican Revolution*. Cambridge, Mass.: Harvard University Press, 1957.

———. *The Structure of Scientific Revolutions*. Chicago: University of Chicago Press, 1970.

Langford, Jerome J. *Galileo, Science and the Church*. Ann Arbor: University of Michigan Press, 1971.

Larson, Edward J. *Summer for the Gods: The Scopes Trial and America's Continuing Debate over Science and Religion*. New York: BasicBooks, 1997.

Lawrence, Jerome, and Robert E. Lee. *Inherit the Wind*. London: Four Square, 1960.

Leakey, Richard E. *The Illustrated Origin of Species*. London: Book Club Associates, 1979.

Lecky, William E. H. *History of the Rise and Influence of the Spirit of Rationalism in Europe*. 2 vols. London: Longmans, 1890.

Legg, John D. "John G. Paton." In *Five Pioneer Missionaries*. Edited by S. M. Houghton. Edinburgh: Banner of Truth, 1965.

Lestringant, Frank. *Cannibals: The Discovery and Representation of the Cannibal from Colombus to Jules Verne*. Colombia: California University Press, 1997.

Levack, Brian P., ed. *Anthropological Studies of Witchcraft, Magic and Religion*. 12 vols. New York: Garland, 1992.

Levidow, Les, ed. *Science as Politics*. London: Free Association Press, 1986.

Lewis, C. S. *The Pilgrim's Regress: An Allegorical Apology for Christianity, Reason and Romanticism*. London: Bles, 1933.

———. *That Hideous Strength*. London: Pan, 1955.

Lewis, Norman. *The Missionaries*. London: Secker & Warburg, 1988.

Lewontin, Richard C. *The Doctrine of DNA*. Harmondsworth, U.K.: Penguin, 1992.

Lindberg, Carter. *The European Reformations*. Oxford: Blackwell, 1996.

Lindberg, David C., and Ronald L. Numbers. *God and Nature*. Berkeley: University of California Press, 1986.

Linzey, Andrew. *Animal Theology*. London: SCM Press, 1994.

Linzey, Andrew, and Dorothy Yamamoto, eds. *Animals on the Agenda*. London: SCM Press, 1998.

Lipstadt, Deborah E. *Denying the Holocaust: The Growing Assault on Truth and Memory*. New York: Free Press, 1993.

Livingstone, David N. *Darwin's Forgotten Defenders*. Grand Rapids, Mich.: Eerdmans, 1987.

Lovelock, James E. *Gaia: A New Look at Life on Earth*. Oxford: Oxford University Press, 1979.

Lucas, J. R. "Wilberforce and Huxley: A Legendary Encounter." *Historical Journal* 22, no. 2 (1979): 313-20.

Lyon, David. *Postmodernity*. Buckingham, U.K.: Open University Press, 1994.

———. *The Steeple's Shadow*. London: SPCK, 1985.

Lyotard, Jean-François. *The Postmodern Condition*. Manchester, U.K.: Manchester University Press, 1984.

Macaulay, Thomas B. *History of England*. Edited by C. H. Firth. Vol. 1. 1857. Reprint, London: Macmillan, 1913.

Macfarlane, Alan. *Witchcraft in Tudor and Stuart England: A Regional and Comparative Study*. London: Routledge & Kegan Paul, 1970.

McGrew, Roderick E. *Encyclopaedia of Medical History*. London: Macmillan, 1985.

McKevitt, G. " 'Faith Enters by the Ear': Missionary Linguistics in the Pacific Northwest." In *The Jesuit Tradition in Education and Missions*. Edited by C. Chapple. London: University of Scanton Press, 1993.

Manion, Eileen. "A Ms.-Managed Womb." In *The Body Invaders*. Edited by Arthur Kroker and Marilouise Kroker. London: Macmillan, 1988.

Mann, C. "Lynn Margulis: Science's Unruly Earth Mother." *Science* 252 (1991): 378-81.

Mappen, Marc, ed. *Witches and Historians*. Huntingdon, N.Y.: Krieger, 1980.

Margulis, Lynn, and Dorion Sagan. *Origins of Sex*. New Haven, Conn.: Yale University Press, 1986.

Martín, L. The Peruvian Indian Through Jesuit Eyes." In *The Jesuit Tradition in Education and Missions*. Edited by C. Chapple. London: University of Scanton Press, 1993.

Martin, Ruth. *Witchcraft and the Inquisition in Venice 1550-1650*. Oxford: Blackwell, 1989.

Marx, Karl., and Friedrich Engels. *Selected Correspondence*. Moscow: Foreign Languages Publishing, 1956.

Medawar, Peter. *The Threat and the Glory*. Oxford: Oxford University Press, 1991.

Michelet, Jules. *Satanism and Witchcraft*. London: Tandem, 1965.

Midelfort, H. C. Erik. *Witch Hunting in Southwestern Germany 1562-1684*. Stanford, Calif.: Stanford University Press, 1972.

Midgley, Mary. *Evolution as Religion*. London: Methuen, 1985.

———. "The Religion of Evolution." In *Darwinism and Divinity*. Edited by J. Durant. Oxford: Blackwell, 1985.

Miller, Jonathan. *The Body in Question*. London: BBC, 1978.

Mivart, George J. "Darwin's *Descent of Man*." 1871. Reprint, in Hull, D. L. *Darwin and*

His Critics. Cambridge, Mass.: Harvard University Press, 1973.

Moncrief, Lewis W. "The Cultural Basis for Our Environmental Crisis." *Science* 170, no. 3957 (1970): 508-12.

Monter, William. *Frontiers of Heresy: The Spanish Inquisition from the Basque Lands to Sicily.* Cambridge: Cambridge University Press, 1990.

———. *Ritual, Myth and Magic in Early Modern Europe.* Brighton, U.K.: Harvester, 1983.

Moore, James R. *Post Darwinian Controversies.* Cambridge: Cambridge University Press, 1979.

———. "Socialising Darwinism." In *Science as Politics.* Edited by L. Levidow. London: Free Association Press, 1986.

———, ed. *History, Community and Evolution.* Cambridge: Cambridge University Press, 1989.

Moore, Patrick. *A Beginner's Guide to Astronomy.* London: PRC Publishing, 1997.

———. *Guide to Comets.* London: Lutterworth, 1977.

Moorehead, Alan. *Darwin and the Beagle.* London: Hamish Hamilton, 1969.

Moorhouse, Geoffrey. *The Missionaries.* London: Methuen, 1973.

Moreland, J. P. *Christianity and the Nature of Science: A Philosophical Investigation.* Grand Rapids, Mich.: Baker, 1989.

Morphet, Clive. *Galileo and Copernican Astronomy.* London: Butterworth, 1977.

Morrison, Marion. *Indians of the Andes.* Hove, U.K.: Wayland, 1986.

Morrison, Richard. "Lancelot Edward Threlkeld: A Missionary for the Aborigines." *Kategoria* 10 (1998): 67-74.

Muller, M. *Aboriginal Issues: More Facts and Figures.* Geneva: World Council of Churches, 1971.

Murray, J. "Agnolo Firenzuola on Female Sexuality and Women's Equality." *Sixteenth Century Journal* 22 (1991): 199-213.

Neill, Stephen. *A History of Christian Missions.* Harmondsworth, U.K.: Penguin, 1964.

———. "Jesus and History." In *The Truth of God Incarnate.* Edited by M. Green. London: Hodder & Stoughton, 1977.

Newman, James R. *Science and Sensibility.* Vol. 1. New York: Simon & Schuster, 1961.

Nile, Richard. *Australian Aborigines.* Hove, U.K.: Wayland. 1992.

Nolan, M. "Aquinas and the Defective Male." *New Blackfriars* 75, no. 880 (1994): 156-65.

Noll, Mark A. *The Scandal of the Evangelical Mind.* Grand Rapids, Mich.: Eerdmans, 1994.

Odijk, Pamela. *The Aborigines.* South Melbourne: Macmillan, 1990.

Oldroyd, David R. "How Did Darwin Arrive at His Theory?" *History of Science* 22 (1984): 325-74.

Oliver, Roland, and J. D. Fage. *A Short History of Africa.* Harmondsworth, U.K.: Penguin, 1962.

O'Malley, John W. *The First Jesuits.* Cambridge, Mass.: Harvard University Press, 1993.

Orwell, George. *A Clergyman's Daughter.* Harmondsworth, U.K.: Penguin, 1964.

Osborn, Lawrence. *Guardians of Creation.* Leicester, U.K.: Apollos, 1993.

———. "The Machine and the Mother Goddess." *Science and Christian Belief* 4, no. 1 (1992): 27-41.

Paley, William. *Natural Theology.* London: Faulder, 1802.

Parker, Steve. *Charles Darwin and Evolution*. London: Belitha, 1992.

Pascal, Blaise. *Pensées*. Harmondsworth, U.K.: Penguin, 1966.

Passmore, John. *Man's Responsibility for Nature*. London: Duckworth, 1974.

Peacocke, Arthur R. *Creation and the World of Science*. Oxford: Oxford University Press, 1979.

———. *Theology for a Scientific Age*. London: SCM Press, 1993.

Peel, John D. Y. *Herbert Spencer: The Evolution of a Sociologist*. London: Heinemann, 1971.

Pettifer, Julian, and Richard Bradley. *The Missionaries*. London: BBC, 1990.

Plaidy, Jean. *The Spanish Inquisition*. London: Hale, 1978.

Plato. *The Dialogues of Plato*. Edited by B. Jowett. 4 vols. Oxford: Clarendon, 1953.

Polkinghorne, John. *Science and Christian Belief*. London: SPCK, 1994.

———. *Science and Theology*. London: SPCK, 1998.

Porritt, Jonathon. Foreword to *God Is Green,* by Ian Bradley. London: Darton, Longman & Todd, 1990.

Porter, Roy, ed. *The Cambridge Illustrated History of Medicine*. Cambridge: Cambridge University Press, 1996.

Primatt, Humphry. *A Dissertation on the Duty of Mercy and Sin of Cruelty to Brute Animals*. Edited by R. D. Ryder. 1776. Reprint, Fontwell, U.K.: Centaur, 1992.

Purkiss, Diane. *The Witch in History*. London: Routledge, 1996.

Pyke, Magnus, and Patrick Moore. *Everyman's Scientific Facts and Feats*. London: Dent, 1981.

Ratner, J. "Some Comments on Rosen's 'Calvin's Attitude Towards Copernicus.' " *Journal of the History of Ideas* 22 (1961): 382-85.

Ray, John. *The Wisdom of God Manifested in the Works of Creation*. London, 1701.

Redondi, Pietro. *Galileo: Heretic*. Harmondsworth, U.K.: Penguin, 1987.

Reynolds, Barbara. Introduction to *Paradise*. In Dante's *The Divine Comedy*. Vol. 3. Harmonds-worth, U.K.: Penguin, 1962.

Richards, Evelleen. "Huxley and Women's Place in Science." In *History, Community and Evolution*. Edited by James R. Moore. Cambridge: Cambridge University Press, 1989.

Robinson, Henry W. *The Christian Doctrine of Man*. Edinburgh: T & T Clark, 1947.

Rookmaaker, Hans R. *Modern Art and the Death of a Culture*. 1978. Reprint, Leicester, U.K.: Apollos, 1994.

Rosen, Edward. "Calvin's Attitude Towards Copernicus." *Journal of the History of Ideas* 21, no. 3 (1960): 431-41.

Ruether, Ruth R. *Sexism and Godtalk: Towards a Feminist Theology*. London: SCM Press, 1983.

Russell, Bertrand. *A Free Man's Worship*. In *The Basic Writings of Bertrand Russell*. Edited by R. E. Egner and L. E. Denonn. 1903. Reprint, London: Allen & Unwin, 1961.

———. "Has Religion Made Useful Contributions to Civilisation?" In *Why I Am Not a Christian*. London: Unwin, 1930.

———. *History of Western Philosophy*. London: Allen & Unwin, 1947.

———. *Human Knowledge: Its Scope and Limits*. London: Allen & Unwin, 1948.

———. *Sceptical Essays*. London: Allen & Unwin, 1960.

Russell, Colin A. "The Conflict Metaphor and its Social Origins." *Science and Christian Belief* 1, no. 1 (1989): 3-26.

————. *Cross-Currents: Interactions Between Science and Faith*. Leicester, U.K.: Inter-Varsity Press, 1985.

Russell, Duncan. "Stubborn Indianness: Cultural Persistence, Cultural Change." *Journal of American Studies* 32, no. 3 (1998): 507-12.

Russell, Jeffrey B. *Inventing the Flat Earth*. New York: Praeger, 1991.

————. *Witchcraft in the Middle Ages*. Ithaca, N.Y.: Cornell University Press, 1972.

Sagan, Carl. *The Demon-Haunted World: Science as a Candle in the Dark*. London: Hodder Headline, 1996.

————. *Pale Blue Dot*. London: Hodder Headline, 1995.

Sagan, Carl, and Ann Druyan. *Comet*. London: Michael Joseph, 1985.

Sampson, Miriam E., and Philip J. Sampson. "The Identity Charade." *Third Way* 20, no. 7 (1997): 11-14.

————. "Looking the Parts." *Third Way* 20, no. 8 (1997): 21-24.

Sampson, Philip J. "Die Repräsentation des Körpers." *Kunstforum* 132 (1996): 94-111.

————. "The Rise of Postmodernity." In Sampson, Philip J., Vinay Samuel and Chris Sugden. *Faith and Modernity*. Oxford: Regnum, 1994.

Sargent, Theodore D., Craig D. Millar and David M. Lambert, D. M. "The 'Classical' Explanation of Industrial Melanism: Assessing the Evidence." *Evolutionary Biology* 30 (1998): 299-322.

Sargent, Tony. *Animal Rights and Wrongs: A Biblical Perspective*. London: Hodder & Stoughton, 1996.

Scruton, Roger. *Modern Philosophy: An Introduction and Survey*. London: Mandarin, 1996.

Sharratt, Michael. *Galileo: Decisive Innovator*. Cambridge: Cambridge University Press, 1996.

Shaw, George Bernard. *Saint Joan*. 1924. Reprint, Harmondsworth, U.K.: Penguin, 1946.

Sheldrake, Rupert. *The Rebirth of Nature*. London: Random House, 1990.

Sibbes, Richard. *The Redemption of Bodies*. In *The Works of Richard Sibbes*. Edited by A. B. Grosart. Edinburgh: Banner of Truth, 1977.

Singer, Peter. *Animal Liberation*. 1976. Reprint, Wellingborough, U.K.: Thorsons, 1990.

Soloway, Richard A. *Demography and Degeneration*. London: Chapel Hill, 1990.

Spanner, Hugh. "Tyrants, Stewards—or Just Kings?" In *Animals on the Agenda*. Edited by Andrew Linzey and Dorothy Yamamoto. London: SCM Press, 1998.

Spanos, N. P., and J. Gottlieb. "Ergotism and the Salem Village Witch Trials." *Science* 194 (1976): 1390-94.

Spencer, Herbert. *Social Statics*. 1851. Reprint, New York: Kelly, 1969.

Sprat, Thomas. *The History of the Royal Society of London*. Edited by J. I. Cope and H. W. Jones. 1667. Reprint, London: Routledge, 1959.

Stanley, Brian. *The History of the Baptist Missionary Society*. Edinburgh: T & T Clark, 1992.

Stanley, O. "T. H. Huxley's Treatment of 'Nature.' " *Journal of the History of Ideas* 18 (1957): 120-27.

Starkey, Mike. *Fashion and Style*. Crowborough, U.K.: Monarch, 1995.

Steinmetz, David. *Calvin in Context*. Oxford: Oxford University Press, 1995.

Stoll, David. *Fishers of Men or Founders of Empire?* London: Zed Press, 1982.

————. *Is Latin America Turning Protestant?* Berkeley: University of California Press, 1990.

Stone, Lawrence. "The Disenchantment of the World." *New York Review of Books*, December 12, 1971.

———. "History and Postmodernity." *Past and Present* 131 (1991): 217-18.

———. "History and Postmodernity III." *Past and Present* 135 (1992): 189-94.

Storkey, Elaine. *What's Right With Feminism*. London: SPCK, 1985.

Stowell, Gordon, ed. *The Book of Knowledge*. 8 vols. London: Waverley, c. 1960.

Stubbes, Philip. *Anatomy of the Abuses in England in Shakespere's Youth*. Edited by F. J. Furnivall. 1583. Reprint, London: Trubner, 1882.

Summers, Montague. *The Discovery of Witches: A Study of Master Matthew Hopkins, Commonly Called Witch Finder Generall*. London: Cayme, 1928.

Taton, René, ed. *Science in the Nineteenth Century*. London: Thames and Hudson, 1967.

Temple, William. *Readings in St John's Gospel*. London: Macmillan, 1945.

Thomas Aquinas. *Summa Theologica*. 3 vols. Translated by Fathers of the English Dominican Province. New York: Benziger, 1982.

Thomas, Keith V. *Man and the Natural World: Changing Attitudes in England 1500-1800*. London: Allen Lane, 1983.

———. *Religion and the Decline of Magic*. London: Weidenfeld and Nicholson, 1971.

Thornbury, John. "David Brainerd." In *Five Pioneer Missionaries*. Edited by S. M. Houghton. Edinburgh: Banner of Truth, 1965.

Townson, Duncan. *Dictionary of Modern History*. Harmondsworth, U.K.: Penguin, 1994.

Trevor-Roper, Hugh R. *The European Witch-Craze of the Sixteenth and Seventeenth Centuries*. Harmondsworth, U.K.: Penguin, 1969.

Turnbull, H. W., ed. *The Correspondence of Isaac Newton*. Vols. 2 and 3. Cambridge: Cambridge University Press, 1960.

Tyndall, John. "Presidential Address." *Report of the British Association for the Advancement of Science*. London, 1874.

Universal Knowledge A to Z. London: Odhams Press, 1938.

Venning, Ralph. *The Plague of Plagues*. 1669. Reprint, London: Banner of Truth, 1965.

Wagley, Charles, and Marvin Harris. *Minorities in the New World*. New York: Columbia University Press, 1964.

Wallace, Alfred R. "The Origin of Human Races and the Antiquity of Man Deduced from the Theory of 'Natural Selection.' " *Journal of the Anthropological Society of London* (1864): clviii-clxxxviii.

Walsh, Brian J., and J. Richard Middleton. *The Transforming Vision*. Downers Grove, Ill.: InterVarsity Press, 1984.

Wells, H. G. *Men Like Gods*. London: Odhams Press, 1921.

Wells, Jonathan. "Second Thoughts About Peppered Moths." *The Scientist* 13, no. 11 (1999): 10-13.

Westfall, Richard S. *Science and Religion in Seventeenth Century England*. Ann Arbor: University of Michigan Press, 1973.

White, Andrew D. *A History of the Warfare of Science with Theology in Christendom*. 2 vols. London: Macmillan, 1896.

White, Lynn. "The Historical Roots of Our Ecologic Crisis." *Science* 155, no. 3767 (1967): 1203-7. Reprinted in *The Care of Creation*. Edited by R. J. Berry. Leicester, U.K.: Inter-Varsity Press, 2000.

White, Robert. "Calvin and Copernicus: The Problem Reconsidered." *Calvin Theological Journal* 15, no. 2 (1980): 233-43.

Whitehead, A. N. *Science and the Modern World*. Cambridge: Cambridge University Press, 1946.

Whittaker, P. Review of *River Out of Eden*, by Richard Dawkins. *New Internationalist* 282 (1996): 33.

Williams, G. S. *Defining Dominion: The Discourses of Magic and Witchcraft in Early Modern France and Germany*. Ann Arbor: University of Michigan Press, 1995.

Williams, Jean. "Puritanism: A Piety of Joy." *Kategoria* 10 (1998): 11-35.

Williams, R. *Keywords*. London: Fontana, 1976.

Wright, N. T. "Romans in a Week." Presented at Regent College Lectures, Vancouver, available on tape.

Wybrow, Cameron. *The Bible, Baconism, and Mastery over Nature: The Old Testament and Its Modern Misreading*. New York: Peter Lang, 1991.

Index